PERIOD LIVING
& TRADITIONAL HOMES
Escapes

Consultant editor
Andrew Lilwall-Smith

Publication in this form copyright © Jarrold Publishing and EMAP London Lifestyle Limited 2005.

Written by Andrew Lilwall-Smith, Peter Brimacombe, Annie Bullen, Kirsty Burrell, Melanie Deeprose, Susie Hodge and Maggie Stevenson.
The moral right of the authors has been asserted.
Consultant editor Andrew Lilwall-Smith.
Edited by Clare Collinson.
Designed by Simon Borrough.
Picture research by Christine Crawshaw and Jan Kean.
Maps by Tim Noel-Johnson using Maps in Minutes.

A CIP catalogue for this book is available from the British Library.

Published by:
Jarrold Publishing
Healey House, Dene Road, Andover,
Hampshire SP10 2AA
www.britguides.com

Period Living & Traditional Homes
Mappin House, 4 Winsley Street,
London W1W 8HF

Set in Sabon and Trade Gothic.
Printed in Singapore.

ISBN   0-7117-3594-8   1/05

KEY: STYLE ERAS

As it's not always easy to tell from the outside of a property which period style lies within, these symbols, which appear above every entry in the book, provide an easy reference guide to the central period style of the interiors.

Tudor and Jacobean
1485–1649

Restoration and Queen Anne
1660–1714

Georgian and Regency
1714–1830

Victorian
1837–1901

Arts and Crafts
1860–1904

Edwardian
1901–1910

Art Deco and the 20th century
1920–1940

Please note that it is not possible to give exact details of opening hours as these are subject to change. Many properties welcome groups all year by appointment, some are open for guided tours only and in some cases pre-booking is essential. It is advisable to check details with the individual properties before visiting.

CONTENTS

Front cover: Detail from a Motor Show panel poster by A.E. Morley, 1933.

Title page: Exuberant plaster swags on a chimneypiece at Wallington Hall, Northumberland (p 233).

Welcome...

In Britain, with its rich and diverse cultural heritage dating back not just centuries, but millennia, we are fortunate enough to have a thrilling array of places that enable us to escape from the everyday to the wonders of another age. On our very doorsteps are buildings, castles and houses which allow us to travel to what L.P. Hartley, in *The Go-Between*, describes as 'the foreign country of the past'.

Whether your personal passion is for the higgledy-piggledy confusion of Tudor palaces, for the romantic medievalism of Victorian Gothic, or for the symmetry and clean lines of Art Deco, with its uniquely streamlined opulence, our small island has it all.

It is perhaps because Britain is an island that so much from the past

survives intact. While on the Continent some of the greatest houses and palaces were stripped of their contents, in Britain ancestral collections have, more or less, been preserved in their entirety, despite the burdens of death duties. Indeed, because Britain has always been an island, but never insular, we have on occasions even gained from other countries' losses, buying up precious treasures from abroad, be it Italian masters during the age of the Grand Tour, or post-revolutionary spoils from France and Russia.

Today, thanks to organizations such as the National Trust, English Heritage, the National Trust for Scotland, Cadw and many other groups and individuals, there is a wealth of buildings both large and small open to anyone with a love of the past and a passion for our creative legacy.

The opening of houses and their gardens to the public, allowing people the chance to escape from the reality of the present into another, different world, is no new occurrence, but dates

Left: Kelmscott Manor, William Morris's country retreat, representative of the ideals of the Arts and Crafts Movement.

Far left: Harewood House, filled with masterworks by the greatest craftsmen and designers of the Georgian period.

Above: Amongst the largest stately homes in the country, Knole remains almost unchanged more than 500 years after it was first built.

Above right: Chatsworth, considered the most impressive treasure house of the North.

back centuries. As readers of Jane Austen's *Pride and Prejudice* will remember, Elizabeth Bennett has an uncomfortable reunion with Mr Darcy whilst visiting his family home, Pemberley, with her aunt and uncle. In fact many of the grandest rooms in what we now call stately homes were designed specifically to be showpieces to awe and inspire.

The family rooms at such magnificent country houses as Chatsworth (p 138) in Derbyshire, Blenheim Palace (p 49) in Oxfordshire and Knole (p 68) in Kent, while undeniably luxurious, are nothing in comparison to their grand state rooms. These were not rooms for everyday living, but places designed to inspire the viewer and impress the visitor, and centuries after they were first devised they still dazzle and delight.

However, Britain's artistic and architectural past is not only to be found in its great stately homes. Whilst these treasure houses, these jewels of design and decoration, may represent this country's crowning glory, there are far

simpler places to escape to that have just as much to give the visitor, even if their offerings are less gilded and less grand. The work of the craftsmen who created these humbler rooms may not be as instantly overwhelming as that of their more famous kinsmen, blessed with wealthy patrons and displayed in the greatest houses in the land, but they too have left behind a legacy that stops us in our tracks and takes us on a journey to the past.

For every Robert Adam, Thomas Chippendale or John Constable, there are other architects, designers and artists whose influence is equally important. Some of the men and women whose genius inspires us are household names, others are almost unknown to all but historians, whilst yet others are forgotten in the mists of time.

To compare the majesty of Harewood House (p 225) in Yorkshire to the traditional simplicity and homespun charm of Kelmscott Manor (p 101) in Gloucestershire would be all but impossible, yet there is no denying the

profound effect of Kelmscott's creator William Morris, the founder of the Arts and Crafts Movement, on interior design. Likewise, the unique creation of Vanessa Bell, Duncan Grant and their Bloomsbury Group friends at Charleston (p 51) in Sussex may have no equal anywhere in the country, but it is still one of the most inspirational of Britain's houses.

Similarly the names John Seeley and Paul Paget are not well remembered by many today, yet from the first moment you enter the wood-lined, high-domed entrance hall created by them at Eltham Palace (p 27) in South-East London, their work becomes unforgettable. And of course, while the names of the original architects and craftsmen behind such Tudor marvels as Plas Mawr (p 247) in Gwynedd are long forgotten, their creations still have so much to offer the modern visitor.

It was a desire to celebrate this diversity and the wonderful mixture of styles found in Britain that led to *Period Living & Traditional Homes Escapes* – a travel guide, a style file and a regional directory that promises to bring the past and the wonders of Britain's artistic heritage to life. While it has been impossible to include every house in Britain open to the public, those which appear on the following pages are truly representative of a unique creativity unrivalled anywhere else in the world.

No matter where you choose to escape to, no matter where you are in the

Left: A unique survivor of the Bloomsbury Set's style of interior design, Charleston is a wonderfully eclectic mix of pattern and colour.

Half ocean liner, half country house, Eltham Palace is the epitome of Art Deco elegance.

or as modern as 2 Willow Road (Ernö Goldfinger's house) (p 47) in London, has been explored and researched by one of a team of talented writers. Sharing their very personal insight into each property, they have captured the real magic of these places first hand.

Personally, as someone with a lifelong passion for beautiful buildings and their interiors, I have found the chance to work on this very special book an incredibly rewarding experience.

I was thrilled to discover – though knowing the magic of these places I should have already suspected – that every time you visit a country retreat, a stately home or historic building, some previously unseen element appears, suddenly something unnoticed becomes apparent, you experience new pleasures and gain a whole new understanding.

Top: Mr Straw's House, a unique time capsule.

Above: The Homewood shows how Modernism can be both comfortable and homely.

country, you will have a practical travel guide to the best buildings and interiors Britain has to offer. The seven invaluable style features covering the most influential design eras, from the Tudors to the 20th century, put our architectural wonders into their historical context.

Every one of the houses included, whether as palatial as Polesden Lacey (p 77) in Surrey or as simple as Mr Straw's House (p 156) in Nottinghamshire, as ancient as Stokesay Castle (p 167) in Shropshire

So, simply turn the pages of this book and discover some of the architectural wonders Britain has to offer. There is a wealth of history waiting to be enjoyed, centuries worth of talent, beautiful buildings and rare interiors to be discovered. Created by all sorts of people for all sorts of reasons and, luckily for us, preserved, loved and, in some cases, lived in today, they allow us the opportunity to see for ourselves the brilliance and richness of the past and so escape to a truly magical place.

ERAS OF STYLE

THE TUDORS AND JACOBEANS
1485–1649

The establishment of the Tudor monarchy in England in 1485 brought stability, peace and prosperity to the country and with them a desire for more permanent buildings. The construction and interior layout of these buildings marked the beginning of modern architecture. In areas where they were available, durable and long-lasting building materials, such as brick and stone, were used in preference to timber for the homes of merchants and better-off farmers, as well as the nobility. The difficulty of transporting these materials meant that building styles had a strong regional identity, with timber buildings persisting in areas such as the West Midlands that lacked local supplies of stone or clay, brick buildings becoming widespread in East Anglia and the Thames Valley, and stone, in all its variations, elsewhere.

Throughout the period, glass became more widely available, changing the exterior appearance of buildings – and their interior comfort – as windows increased in size and number. Large windows became a status symbol – see, for example, the extravagant use of glass at Hardwick Hall (p 145) in Derbyshire. Windows were mullioned or mullioned and transomed, and those that opened did so by means of a hinged metal casement. Glass could be

Above: A linenfold panel at Sizergh Castle.

Left: Little Moreton Hall.

made only in small panes, so windows were leaded and the panes or 'quarries' were arranged in diamond or rectangular patterns or, in some grand houses, more complex geometric designs. At Little Moreton Hall (p 202) in Cheshire, for example, there are more than 36 different designs in the glass.

Another architectural innovation that transformed 15th- and 16th-century houses was the wall fireplace and chimney. Replacing the old central hearth, which had no

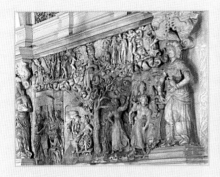

chimney and only a hole in the roof for smoke to escape, the wall fireplace removed smoke efficiently, leaving the interior environment cleaner and allowing full upper storeys to be built. Then, as now, the wall fireplace became the focus of the room and offered enormous scope for decoration, with chimneypieces in important houses displaying elaborate carvings of figures, mythological scenes, strapwork and, later, classical motifs. Fine examples can be seen in many Tudor and Jacobean properties, including Baddesley Clinton (p 131) in Warwickshire, Stokesay Castle (p 167) in Shropshire and Plas Mawr (p 247) in Gwynedd.

Interior walls were plastered or panelled, the panelling covering the whole wall or ending at dado or frieze height. The panelling was usually of oak and consisted of square, linenfold or even more elaborately carved panels set into a grid framework. Tapestry wall hangings covering the walls above the dado panelling provided warmth and colour, and in grand houses, such as Levens Hall (p 201) in Cumbria, fine embossed leather hangings demonstrated the wealth and sophistication of the owner. Where panelling extended to frieze level, the wall above was often filled with highly decorative plasterwork.

Decorative plasterwork is a feature of Tudor and Jacobean ceilings, too, with designs ranging from elegant geometric patterns to complex strapwork and plant tracery.

Although furniture in houses of this period was sparse, consisting of tables, stools, benches or chairs, and beds, it was usually beautifully carved. Textiles – often exquisite needlework produced by the women of the household – added a softer touch. Prized domestic possessions of the wealthy included silverware and glass. *MS*

Above left: Detail of the Elizabethan carved alabaster chimneypiece at Burton Agnes Hall.

Above: Cromwell's Bedroom at Chavenage.

A 16th-century heraldic chimneypiece in the Great Hall at Baddesley Clinton.

FROM THE RESTORATION TO QUEEN ANNE 1660–1714

Ham House, a fascinating Restoration mansion, with atmospheric original interiors.

The Restoration of the monarchy and a flourishing worldwide trade in spices, tea, coffee and other exotic merchandise from the East brought a wealth that spread beyond the nobility to the well-off merchant class. This wealth created a taste for luxury. The exuberant baroque style, brought from Europe when King Charles II returned from exile in 1660, was embraced with enthusiasm by a country freed from the strictures of Puritanism. The style, which combined classical order with flamboyant, curvaceous decoration, continued through the reign of William of Orange and Mary Stuart, encouraged by their own cosmopolitan tastes and nurtured by the skills of immigrant French Huguenot craftsmen, escaping religious persecution in their home country. Daniel Marot, a Huguenot Protestant in the service of William and Mary, helped disseminate the baroque style by producing engravings of his designs for chimneypieces, carved woodwork, metalwork and upholstery. These were widely circulated and his influence can be seen in the interiors of several grand houses of the period.

By the time Queen Anne succeeded to the throne in 1702, Britain was a prosperous place and with the turn of the century came a move to a more

The saloon at Antony.

The Little Dining Room at Petworth House.

Dyrham Park, completed in 1704.

The state bed at Dyrham Park, with upholstery inspired by the work of Daniel Marot.

refined style. Queen Anne interiors were elegant and comfortable, as the extravagant decoration of the Restoration and William and Mary gave way to simpler, shapely lines in furniture. Walls were timber-panelled and painted to mimic more costly timber or marble, and floors were of stone flags or parquet. The blue-and-white delftware and Chinese ceramics loved by Queen Mary remained very fashionable, together with lacquer-ware imported from the East, while collections of classical sculptures and paintings reflected the growing interest in travel.

Architecture of the period is classical in inspiration. Symmetrical with a central pediment, a Queen Anne house typically has a brick façade with stone dressings, a hipped roof and large chimneys. Vertical sliding sash windows, which had recently arrived from the Netherlands, were widely adopted. The arrangement of the windows was regular and orderly, with the largest on the first floor, slightly smaller ones on the ground floor and the smallest on the upper floor. This is most clearly seen in town houses of the period, while country homes such as Antony (p 88) in

Cornwall and Cottesbrooke Hall (p 142) in Northamptonshire demonstrate an even, more repetitive layout. A small round or oval window often punctuated the central pediment, as can be seen at Squerryes Court (p 81) in Kent, and dormer windows in the roof lit the attic rooms. The front door was set centrally in the façade and protected with a rectangular hood.

The interiors of these houses possessed a similar formality, with furniture, when not in use, ranged round the walls. Floors were simply scrubbed or laid with rush matting, but as time went on, the Turkish and Oriental carpets that had previously covered tables were placed on the floor.

The regularity and restraint of Queen Anne architecture had an enduring appeal and a revival of the style in the late 19th century left a lasting mark on the urban landscape of Britain. *MS*

THE GEORGIANS AND THE REGENCY
1714–1830

Spanning more than a century and the reigns of four monarchs, the Georgian and Regency periods had a lasting influence on the architecture and interiors of Britain. Early in the period, classicism emerged as a strong theme, and the sons of noble and wealthy families undertook the Grand Tour, travelling to Italy and other sites of antiquity to immerse themselves in the art, architecture and order of earlier civilizations. In Britain, early Georgian style was informed by the work of 16th-century Italian architect Andrea Palladio, who was a student of Roman architecture and its system of strict mathematical proportion. These principles governed every aspect of Palladian architecture, from the size of rooms to the shapes of doors and windows and the horizontal division of walls into frieze, field and dado, according to classical orders. Grand country houses, such as Houghton Hall (p 185) in Norfolk and Paxton House (p 283) in Berwickshire, were built in the Palladian style, but its classical ideals were adopted at every social level and are evident in the terraces and crescents of Georgian towns throughout the country.

The entrance front at Ickworth, with its pediment and four Ionic columns.

Carving in the State Bedroom at Erddig.

The interiors of many Palladian houses were decorated in the French rococo fashion. Delicate and feminine, rococo style is characterized by asymmetrical shapes composed of C- and S-shaped scrolls, shells, ribbons, leaves and birds painted in pale colours frosted with white and gold embellishments. At the same time, an interest in romantic medievalism emerged that found expression in the Gothic style of pointed arches, stone tracery and other architectural details borrowed from ecclesiastical buildings. A fine example of this is Strawberry Hill (p 45) in Twickenham. As trade with the Orient continued,

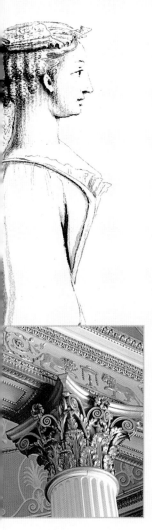

Classical decoration by Robert Adam in the library at Kenwood House.

a taste for chinoiserie grew and Chinese-inspired furniture, wallpaper and ceramics, made no further east than Germany, became fashionable. Decorated with exotic landscapes, dragons, pagodas and Oriental figures, chinoiserie took furniture design to new levels of fantasy.

As the 18th century progressed, these novelty styles gave way to something quieter and more restrained: neoclassicism. Stimulated by the archaeological discoveries of Herculaneum and Pompeii, the style followed classical form, combining elements from ancient Greece and Rome, and was translated by the eminent architect and designer Robert Adam in a light and delicate way that appealed to the English eye. As well as designing buildings, he also created their interiors with plasterwork, furniture, carpets and a colour palette to present a unified scheme. Fine examples of Adam's work can be seen at Kenwood House (p 36), Osterley Park (p 41) and Syon Park (p 47) in London, at Harewood House (p 225) and Newby Hall (p 229) in Yorkshire, and at Kedleston Hall (p 154) in Derbyshire.

Classical and French Empire style dominated the Regency and, following Napoleon's campaign, ancient Egyptian motifs such as sphinxes, lotus flowers and obelisks joined the design repertoire. Though furniture design continued to be light and graceful, the way it was used began to change. Where furniture had previously been lined up along the walls of a room, it was now arranged in smaller conversational groups near the fireplace or around occasional tables, creating a more companionable and much less formal atmosphere. *MS*

The cloister-like Long Gallery at Strawberry Hill.

The saloon at Wallington Hall.

The gallery at Chiswick House.

THE VICTORIANS
1837–1901

The architectural style most often associated with the Victorian period is Gothic revival. Polychromatic brickwork, stone tracery and stained-glass windows, pointed arches, towers and turrets conjure up a picture of a typical Victorian Gothic pile. The style was applied to buildings of diverse status, from gatehouses to grand country houses, such as Tyntesfield (p 119) near Bristol, as well as urban terraces and suburban villas. Solid and conservative, romantic and pious, the Gothic style seemed to match the Victorian mood perfectly and it was a complete change from the classicism that had dictated architectural style for more than a century. The struggle for supremacy between classicism and Gothic revival went on well into the 19th century and was known as the 'battle of the styles'. But while these two were the main contenders, architects explored other design models such as the Italianate style, as seen in Queen Victoria's Isle of Wight home, Osborne House (p 74), and the French style of Waddesdon Manor (p 85) in Buckinghamshire. Speculative builders of ordinary houses were more eclectic in their approach and might incorporate assorted stylistic elements – vernacular, Tudor, classical or Dutch – into a single building.

Eclecticism influenced the design of interiors, too, and now that Britain was a major imperial power and international trading nation, goods from overseas became increasingly available. Aesthetic interiors were strongly influenced by Japanese design and featured blue-and-white china,

ebonized furniture, stylized naturalistic patterns and other Oriental designs. The interior of the artist Linley Sambourne's house (p 38) in London demonstrates this style and shows how smoothly exotic motifs were integrated into a comfortable Victorian home. As well as Japanese design and artefacts, Indian patterns for textiles and wallpapers, Chinese bamboo furniture, Islamic tile designs and wild animal skins all became a familiar part of sophisticated 'artistic' interiors.

The important things in the lives of most middle-class Victorians were

The typically Victorian morning room at Linley Sambourne House.

The Gothic-style staircase at Knebworth House.

status, comfort and prosperity, and their homes were arranged to reflect this. The entrance hall and rooms where visitors might be received were decorated to impress, with marble or cast-iron fireplaces and elaborate plaster cornices and ceiling centres. Many walls were still divided by dado and picture rails into dado, field and frieze and decorated with patterned wallpapers, made more affordable by mechanized printing. Strong, rich colours such as deep red and bottle green were favoured for downstairs rooms and lighter, floral patterned wallpapers for the bedrooms. Upholstery was well stuffed and deeply sprung and windows were dressed with elaborate layered drapes. Perhaps most distinctive aspect of a typical Victorian living room was the quantity of objects displayed on every surface. These were chosen to demonstrate the taste, wealth and cultural refinement of the owner and included mass-produced items from the potteries and other British industries as well as decorative ornaments and novelties from abroad. *MS*

Top: Tyntesfield, a fine example of Victorian Gothic revival.

Above: The wooden fireplace in the dining room at Sunnycroft.

Above right: Wall decoration from the Indian-style Durber Room at Osborne House.

THE ARTS AND CRAFTS MOVEMENT
1860–1904

As Victorian England embraced industrialization and mass production, a group of artists and designers emerged who valued quality over quantity. They believed in honest materials, traditional craftsmanship and good design and, in reaction to the confusion of revived historic styles in common currency, a return to the functional simplicity of a much earlier period. The inspiration for this style was the art critic John Ruskin, whose interest in medieval architecture influenced many contemporary artists and designers. However, the style's motivating force was William Morris. Morris was a poet, writer, artist, designer, scholar and socialist who believed that good design should be within the reach of all, not just the wealthy. He shared Ruskin's passion

for Gothic, but his interest in architecture encompassed the rustic style of old English manor houses, cottages and barns as well as important ecclesiastical buildings.

The drawing room at Standen, with French doors leading through to the conservatory.

Red House, the first home of William Morris and his wife Jane.

Morris's principles were made manifest in Red House (p 42) in London, designed for him in 1858–60 by Philip Webb. Built from red brick in the vernacular style, it has a steeply

and sometimes the entrance hall, too, it was built from stone or brick and might incorporate patterned tiles, a metal hood and shelves.

Decoration and furnishings in Arts and Crafts houses were particularly distinctive. Based on the simple shapes of sturdy country designs, furniture was made according to traditional methods. Wood was left bare and unpolished and, in contrast to the general Victorian taste for deep, over-stuffed upholstery, chairs were slim and straight backed. Walls were whitewashed or wallpapered, often in William Morris's own designs, and the same patterns appeared on fabrics and carpets. There was nothing tradi-tional or simple, however, in these designs. As individual as handwriting, they were inspired by plants growing in gardens and the countryside and drawn in repeating patterns of great intricacy and fluency. Though they are an integral part of Arts and Crafts decoration, these complex and luxuri-ant patterns have survived for over a century and are still available and widely used today. *MS*

The stone fireplace in the beautiful White Drawing Room at Blackwell.

A stained-glass panel by William Morris from Red House.

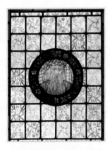

Painted glass by Burne-Jones in the billiard room at Wightwick Manor.

pitched roof, dormer windows, a deep porch and a layout and roofline that suggest that the building has grown and developed over genera-tions. Features of this vernacular style were widely adopted and interpreted in different ways, often taking into account regional variations in build-ing techniques, such as the half-timbering at Wightwick Manor (p 171) in Staffordshire and the harling at Blackwell (p 196) in Cumbria. The medieval influence is always present to a greater or lesser degree. Exterior doors may be made from planked wood with hefty iron hinges or glazed with painted or stained panels; windows are usually casements with leaded lights and wrought-iron fittings. Ceilings might be beamed or plastered with the ribs, bosses and pendants seen in Tudor houses and the chosen materials for floors were flagstones or dark wood.

Of all interior features, the fire-place was the most significant. Very much the focus of the living room,

THE EDWARDIANS
1901–1910

Polesden Lacey, a luxurious villa with opulent Edwardian interiors.

With the start of the 20th century came a new monarch and the beginning of a new era. Though it lasted less than a decade, the reign of King Edward VII saw changes that would dramatically change people's attitudes and the way they lived. The invention of the aeroplane and greater ownership of motor cars broadened the horizons of the better-off, and the campaign for women's suffrage and more relaxed behaviour in society circles signalled a wider social change.

The popular image of the Edwardian era is of a golden age of opulence, luxury and glamour, of debutantes' balls and country-house parties. But for those further down the social ladder, the standard of living was improving in a more modest way, as bathrooms and electricity were installed in new houses for the middle classes. Although these conveniences were enjoyed by the few, they were practical signs of the comfort that epitomized Edwardian aspirations.

By the early years of the 20th century, the competition between classical and Gothic styles had been abandoned in favour of

The parlour at Batemans.

True comfort at Shaw's Corner.

eclecticism, and the architectural style that now dominated was known as Queen Anne revival. Houses built in this style had stone-dressed red brickwork, small-paned sash windows, dormers and white paintwork, as in original Queen Anne houses, but they often incorporated any Gothic, classical, Jacobean or vernacular elements that the architect thought would add picturesque effect. The style, simple but comfortable, was adopted in domestic architecture at every level and dominated the cottage-style houses of the new garden suburbs. Shaw's Corner (p 192) in Hertfordshire is a good example of the comfortable homeliness that prevailed, though the house owes more to the vernacular and Arts and Crafts styles than Queen Anne.

Interiors were much lighter than before, thanks to larger windows and a more informally elegant and airy style of decoration. Walls were still divided horizontally by dado and picture rails, and the space between picture rail and cornice was often filled by embossed or printed wallpaper friezes, often in Georgian designs. The cornice itself was much plainer than before, with straight mouldings taking the place of the now

The main staircase at Castle Drogo.

passé florid Victorian designs. Colours were chosen from a summery palette, with green, yellow, lilac, cream and particularly white bringing a fresher atmosphere to previously sombre rooms. In grand houses such as Polesden Lacey (p 77) in Surrey, these pale colours were enriched with gilding. Draperies were stripped down and in the most progressive Edwardian interiors, pelmets and valances and multi-layered window treatments were dispensed with in favour of simple curtains hung from rings on a brass pole. It was no longer fashionable to crowd every surface with ornaments and clutter and extraneous pieces of furniture were also cleared away, making rooms seem much more open and spacious. *MS*

ART DECO AND THE 20TH CENTURY
1920–1940

After more than a century of styles inspired by the past, Art Deco looked to the future. It celebrated the machine age, as ocean liners, motor cars and aeroplanes became a reality of life, and it reflected the mood of a world changed forever by the First World War. Taking its name from the *Exposition Internationale des Arts Decoratifs et Industriel Moderne* held in Paris in 1925, where the French Style Moderne exhibit stole the show, Art Deco spread quickly to the USA and more gradually to Britain.

The style borrowed references from the geometric forms of Cubist art, colour from the brilliant costumes designed for Diaghilev's Ballets Russes and motifs such as the sunray, chevron and ziggurat from exotic ancient civilizations such as the Aztecs and Egyptians. It also made use of plastics, chrome, glass, mirror and shiny fabrics to create a look that was glamorous and exciting. Art Deco architecture is most visible in cinemas, department stores, office buildings and the domestic houses whose flat roofs and curved steel-framed 'suntrap' windows are characteristic of 1930s suburbia. Inside these houses, stepped architraves, covings and fireplaces, murals, mirrored or metallic wall finishes and parquet floors with rugs in graphic designs set a typical scene.

The living room at The Homewood, designed by Patrick Gwynne.

Art Deco furniture in the dining room at Coleton Fishacre.

The first-floor living room at 2 Willow Road.

A Sanderson fabric, 'Eton Rural', from Mr Straw's House.

In grand houses, Art Deco was usually reserved for interior architecture and decoration. Externally, Coleton Fishacre (p 91) in Devon appears to be Arts and Crafts in style, but the interior displays many Art Deco features, from architectural details to furnishings.

The second significant style to emerge during the 1930s was Modernism. Another European import, the Modern Movement took a more serious, philosophical view of design, shunning the frivolity of Art Deco for a more functional look. The interiors of Modern Movement houses were clean, open and filled with light from large windows, glass bricks and skylights. In some buildings, such as the Hungarian architect Ernö Goldfinger's house at 2 Willow Road (p 47) in London, the living space was made more flexible by the use of hinged wall panels, which could be folded back to open up the space further or closed to create smaller, more intimate rooms. Concrete and steel were valued as modern building materials, interior walls were plastered and painted or clad with laminated timber – pattern was largely restricted to textiles – and parquet was the preferred type of flooring. Built-in furniture added to the streamlined effect and practical style of living. *MS*

Art Deco luxury in Virginia Courtauld's bedroom at Eltham Palace.

LONDON AND SOUTH-EAST ENGLAND

South-East England has been a centre of trade, power and prosperity since the Romans arrived on its soil, and while archaeology gives us a glimpse of those distant times, the area's preserved architecture reveals a colourful, living history of the last 500 years.

The rural landscape of the South-East is studded with the venerable houses of old families, such as the Sackvilles of Knole and the Palmers of Dorney Court, whose homes have passed down through the generations. Some houses, such as Osterley Park, Chiswick House and Kenwood House, originally built in the green spaces around London, now find themselves within an urban environment; others that have always been in the city, such as 18 Folgate Street in Spitalfields and Dr Johnson's House near Fleet Street, have survived intact while the areas they inhabit have changed around them.

The lives and lifestyles of every strata of society are to be seen in the historic houses of London and South-East England. There are buildings with royal connections, such as Ham House and Polesden Lacey. There are the homes of the wealthy such as Waddesdon Manor and Eltham Palace. And there are houses once owned by the exponents of particular architectural styles. Look at Strawberry Hill for a distillation of Gothic, Red House for Arts and Crafts and 2 Willow Road for Modernism.

Rich in their variety, these houses, great and small, stand as monuments to the people, events and ideas that have formed the culture of this old and ever-changing land. *MS*

APSLEY HOUSE

An 18th-century house with Regency interiors

CARLYLE'S HOUSE

A Queen Anne town house with Victorian interiors

One of London's finest residences, Apsley House, also known as 'No. 1 London', has been the London home of the Dukes of Wellington since 1817. Originally designed and built by Robert Adam between 1771 and 1778, the house was enlarged by the 1st Duke. The sumptuous interiors, including the spectacular 90ft (27m) long Waterloo Gallery, house an outstanding collection of paintings by artists such as Velázquez, Van Dyck and Rubens, as well as porcelain, silver, sculpture, furniture and Wellington memorabilia. *SH*

Apsley House is at Hyde Park Corner, London W1. It is administered by English Heritage and open all year.
Tel: 020 7499 5676
www.english-heritage.org.uk

Built in 1708 in Cheyne Row, Chelsea, close to the River Thames, this tall terraced town house was the home of writer and historian Thomas Carlyle, 'The Sage of Chelsea', from 1834 until his death in 1881. When Carlyle moved here with his wife Jane, Chelsea was considered unfashionable, but the intellectual couple entertained many eminent Victorians here, including Dickens, Ruskin, Darwin, Tennyson and

A sample of the wallpaper that hung in the library at the time of Carlyle's death in 1881.

Apsley House, also known as 'No. 1 London', as it was once the first house to be encountered after passing the tollgates at Knightsbridge.

The exterior of Carlyle's House in Chelsea is typical of a Queen Anne terraced town house. Inside, the Victorian decoration remains intact.

A Chelsea Interior, an oil painting by Robert Tait (1858), showing Thomas and Jane Carlyle in their sitting room.

Carlyle's House is in Cheyne Row, Chelsea, London SW3. It is owned by the National Trust and open on selected days from the end of March to the end of October.
Tel: 020 7352 7087
www.nationaltrust.org.uk

George Eliot. Now lying in one of London's most peaceful and fashionable locations, the house still embodies the spirit of Thomas and Jane Carlyle.

The house is set out as it would have been when Thomas and Jane lived here, with relaxed, stylish and comfortable surroundings. Jane's accomplished domestic touches are apparent everywhere: the Victorian period decor, original furnishings, pictures, portraits and books are all still in place.

The kitchen, to which Thomas would often retreat to smoke his pipe, changed little while the Carlyles lived here – it still includes a dresser and old stone sink that were in the house when they moved in. Their scrubbed pine table is also here, as is their cast-iron range. The library, with its William Morris willow-pattern wallpaper, includes Carlyle's green leather

reading chair, his bookcase and a sofa which was bought by Jane in 1835. There is a beautiful screen which Jane created in 1849 using engravings and portraits. Carlyle's desk, made originally for Jane's father, can be seen in the attic study, which also displays an interesting collection of pictures and Carlyle memorabilia. *SH*

THE SAGE OF CHELSEA
Scottish-born Thomas Carlyle is considered one of the greatest essayists and historians of the Victorian age. His reputation as an historian rests with his masterly *The French Revolution*, published in 1837, together with his *History of Frederick the Great*, written between 1858 and 1865. After the death of his witty and intelligent wife Jane in 1866, Carlyle completed his *Reminiscences*, in which he revealed his neglect of his wife, something that apparently weighed heavily on his conscience.

CHISWICK HOUSE
A Palladian mansion

The Red Velvet Room with its classical decor and window. The fluted columns on the window echo the larger ones outside.

Pure white and symmetrical, Chiswick House is a rebuke to those 17th-century architects who departed from the strict classical tradition exemplified in the Palladian style. Lord Burlington, upset by the tumble into baroque that he saw all around him (especially at Castle Howard, p 220), decreed that his new mansion should be a showcase of Palladian design. Beautifully proportioned steps lead to a large entrance portico supported by fluted columns. The whole, finished in white stucco, is topped with a dome, while graceful obelisks disguise the chimneys.

The heart of the building is the octagonal domed saloon, with picture-hung walls and classical busts. Other rooms surrounding this chamber were decorated by architect and designer William Kent, whom Lord Burlington met on one of his Grand Tours and brought back to England to work on his new mansion. Many of them are sumptuous and each has its own classical theme. The ceiling in the Red Velvet Room proclaims the Triumph of the Arts, while the Blue Velvet Room pays homage to classical architecture. The gallery, its ceiling beautifully painted and gilded, was built specifically to display and explore the glories of Italian architecture. *AB*

Chiswick House is in Burlington Lane, London W4. It is owned by English Heritage and open on selected days from the beginning of April to the end of October.
Tel: 020 8995 0508
www.english-heritage.org.uk

PALLADIAN STYLE
Taking its name from the 16th-century Italian architect Andrea Palladio, Palladian architecture and decoration is usually simple and formal externally, more elaborate and decorative within. First brought to England by Inigo Jones, Palladianism was reintroduced by William Kent during the first half of the 18th century, assisted by his powerful patron Lord Burlington. Other fine examples of Palladian style can be seen at Marble Hill House (p 41), No. 1 Royal Crescent (p 114), Houghton Hall (p 185), Wallington Hall (p 233) and Paxton House (p 283).

ELTHAM PALACE

A luxurious Art Deco home

Looking over the moat towards the house.

The circular Art Deco entrance hall.

Eltham Palace is one of the most astonishing and original houses in Britain and a unique architectural treasure. It is a stunning Art Deco house adjoined to the renovated remains of a medieval royal palace and is set within beautiful gardens. Built in 1936 by Stephen Courtauld, millionaire, war veteran and patron of the arts, and his wife Virginia, the house provided the perfect chic setting for their lavish entertaining.

Originally a moated manor house built in the 11th century, Eltham had been developed as a royal palace by

about 1305. It was used by royalty for many years and Henry VIII spent long periods here as a child. However, in later years, Greenwich Palace and Hampton Court were the preferred royal residences, and Eltham was allowed to deteriorate.

By the time Stephen and Virginia Courtauld bought the site in 1933, it was considered that little was worth preserving. They commissioned young architects John Seely and Paul Paget to design a modern home on the site whilst retaining as much as possible of the remains of the medieval palace. The contemporary interiors are the work of various designers, including Italian designer Peter Malacrida and

Swedish designer Rolf Engströmer. The architects and designers used the history of the palace and its inhabitants through the ages as their inspiration – medieval monarchy, sailing, travel and horticulture are all major themes, skilfully interlaced.

As one approaches the house, across a medieval bridge that spans the remains of the tranquil moat, the house rises up before you, a grand and eclectic mix of architectural styles, including Tudor, Georgian and classical. A curved row of temple-like pillars marks the entrance, while H. Carlton Attwood's sculpture *Hospitality*, above the colonnade, greets all guests.

Luxury emanates from Virginia's curved and spacious bedroom, with its delicate marquetry and discreet lighting.

Inside, the lavish Art Deco features include exotic veneers, concealed lighting, large windows and ceilings, marble floors and fireplace surrounds and an emphasis on geometric shapes. There are 'mod-cons', such as built-in electric clocks, an audio system that sent music wafting through the house, underfloor heating and a centralized vacuum cleaner – all demonstrating the comfortable and extravagant lifestyle enjoyed by the Courtaulds and their friends.

Each room has its own theme and individual appeal. The large entrance hall, designed by Engströmer, is a dazzling display of Art Deco elegance combined with the luxury of an ocean liner. Light floods down from a spectacular 23ft (7m) glass dome in the ceiling, highlighting the figurative marquetry on the gleaming curved blackbeam veneer walls. The dining room has a shimmering ceiling of aluminium leaf on a blue background, pale maple walls, chairs upholstered in pink leather, and black-and-silver double doors, inlaid with the Greek key pattern and animals and birds drawn from life at London Zoo. Animals were another passion of the Courtaulds: they had several pets, including three dogs and a ring-tailed lemur, whose centrally heated sleeping area is painted with a tropical frieze.

The Roman-temple theme of the entrance is also used in Virginia's opulent bedroom and bathroom. The bedroom is spacious and calm, with curved, polished maple-lined walls, concealed lighting within the circular ceiling and marquetry of flaming torches, wreaths and garlands. Art Deco fabrics cover the chairs and hang at the large corner windows. Leading off this room is Virginia's glamorous gold-and-onyx mosaic-lined bathroom, with its vaulted ceiling and gold-plated taps. The principal guest bedroom is also sumptuous, decorated with yellow Venetian panelling and *trompe l'œil* books.

Detail of a sculpture relief over the garden entrance.

Virginia Courtauld's bathroom, with gold-and-onyx mosaic tiles and statue of Psyche in the bath alcove.

Throughout the house, large porthole-shaped windows give open views of the gardens and beyond. On the landing near to Stephen's bedroom (relatively modestly decorated, with Sanderson wallpaper), a large round window offers a picturesque view of London. Look out for the leather wall map in Virginia's boudoir – combining a map with topographical views, it resembles a large painted wall hanging in the Art Deco-styled liner, the *Queen Mary,* which completed its maiden voyage in 1936.

But not all is Art Deco. The drawing room, furnished with 'Turkish' rugs, silk damask curtains and pale blue velvet sofas, is more Renaissance in style with its sunny honey-coloured walls, white marble fireplace and dark

green wrought-iron screens in the French windows.

A 12-panelled Chinese sliding screen separates the 1930s house from the medieval Great Hall. The hall was originally built for Edward IV in the 1470s as a dining hall for the court. Light streams through high windows with stained-glass panels, illuminating the magnificent hammer-beam oak roof that was repaired by Seely and Paget in the 1930s. Unusually for such places, this hall is not at all draughty, but pleasantly warm at all times thanks to the underfloor heating installed by the Courtaulds. They intended the Great Hall to be used as a music room and carried out repairs accordingly, installing a minstrels' gallery, entered from upstairs. *SH*

Stephen Courtauld's bedroom, with Sanderson wallpaper depicting Kew Gardens.

Eltham Palace is in Court Yard, Eltham, London SE9. It is owned by English Heritage and open on selected days all year (apart from a few weeks in winter). **Tel: 020 8294 2548 www.english-heritage.org.uk**

FENTON HOUSE

A late 17th-century merchant's house

Fenton House is in Windmill Hill, Hampstead, London NW3. It is owned by the National Trust and open on selected days from March to October.
Tel: 020 7435 3471
www.nationaltrust.org.uk

Set in the winding streets of Hampstead village, this charming merchant's house was built in the late 17th century when Hampstead was a rural area. Even now, behind the wrought-iron gates, Fenton House is an oasis of calm and tranquillity in the heart of London. The house contains an outstanding collection of Oriental and European porcelain, 17th-century needlework pictures and Georgian furniture. There is also a fine collection of early keyboard instruments, most of which are in working order. *SH*

The South Front of Fenton House, seen down the gravel path.

Eltham Palace's Art Deco dining room where Stephen and Virginia entertained lavishly. Dinner was at 8 o'clock, with a menu written in French.

18 FOLGATE STREET – DENNIS SEVERS' HOUSE

A Georgian town house, now an 18th-century time capsule

'You either see it or you don't' is the motto of this extraordinary Georgian town house in Spitalfields. Dennis Severs, the eccentric American artist and collector who acquired the house in 1979, believed that those who 'see it' are fortunate indeed. 'It' is an intangible presence of the past that he hoped visitors would feel as they wander around the house, experiencing the sights, sounds and smells of times gone by.

Growing up in California, influenced by books and old black-and-white films, Dennis Severs fell in love with the quality of what he called 'English light'. Several years later, in a narrow street in London, he found the house that was to furnish his dream, a run-down red-brick Georgian terraced house, built in 1724. Over the years, Severs transformed the house into a fascinating time capsule, with authentic decor and furnishings from the 18th and 19th centuries. He created an imaginary family of Huguenot silk weavers, the Jervis family, who 'occupy' the rooms and shape the house's spirit. Their story, through five generations, unfolds throughout the house and although they can sometimes be heard, they are always just out of sight. There is a sense that the family has been interrupted or that they have just stepped out – a half-eaten meal sits on the table, candles still sputter and fires crackle

(don't wear your best clothes, as it can be quite smoky!).

On entering the house, you will have to adjust your eyes to the darkness of flickering candlelight. Listen for the creak of footsteps, whispers and opening doors, clocks ticking and chiming, a kettle hissing, a dog barking, a baby crying. Personal possessions are strewn about – Mr Jervis's wig, the cook's cap, a pair of spectacles. In turn, each of the ten rooms in the house brings the Jervis family's story to life, stimulating the senses with sounds and scents. The details are surprisingly unnerving – unmade beds, tea slopped in saucers, even half-full chamber pots!

In the parlour, visitors are invited to sit amid the aromas of tallow, wood ash, punch and tobacco smoke.

Flickering firelight and a string of gingerbread men create a homely atmosphere amid the clutter in the kitchen.

The polished dining table, laden with a jug, cascade of fruit, glasses and crumpled napkins.

Gradually it becomes apparent that the scene echoes the William Hogarth painting that hangs over the hearth – the men in the painting have gone and the visitors have taken their places at the table beside the candles, pipes and punchbowl. A critical eye might spot a man's jacket from the painting, slung over the back of a chair, with a newspaper of the day projecting from its pocket. Don't try too hard to question what you see – there may be some slight historical discrepancies.

The elegant drawing room on the first floor and the charming boudoir on the second floor reflect the prosperity of the Jervises in the late 18th century. On the top floor, the story moves on to the Victorian era – the Jervises had fallen on hard times and the attic is 'occupied' by lodgers. There is a smell of damp, washing hangs from ropes over the stairs, the curtains are ragged and paint is peeling from the walls.

Colour is used very effectively throughout the house to evoke different eras and moods: black and brown in the mid 18th-century basement larder and kitchen; warm and spicy olive green and red in the parlour and dining rooms on the ground floor; soft gilded apricots, pinks and blues in the late 18th-century bedrooms and boudoir; and brown once again in the Victorian attic.

Sadly, Dennis Severs died in 1999, but while he was alive he was renowned for ejecting visitors who did not seriously appreciate his renovations. Today, the Spitalfields Historic Buildings Trust and those who knew Severs well are continuing to run the house as he intended. The journey through 18 Folgate Street gives a rare

and fascinating insight into the interiors and lifestyles of those who lived through the 18th and 19th centuries – it is a unique voyage through the frame of time. *SH*

The elegant Georgian drawing room on the first floor.

The Dickens Room on the top floor, with its writing desk and peeling walls, is a wonderful evocation of Victorian poverty.

18 Folgate Street, Dennis Severs' House, is in Spitalfields, London E1. It is owned by the Spitalfields Historic Buildings Trust and is open on selected days all year.
Tel: 020 7247 4013
www. dennissevershouse. co.uk

HAM HOUSE

A Stuart house with lavish late 17th-century interiors

Ham House is in Ham, Richmond-upon-Thames, Surrey. It is owned by the National Trust and open on selected days from April to the end of October.
Tel: 020 8940 1950
www.nationaltrust. org.uk

THE HAUNTING DUCHESS
Described by her contemporaries as 'beautiful, ambitious and greedy', Elizabeth, Countess of Dysart, married the Duke of Lauderdale, an important member of the Court of Charles II. After the duke died the duchess spent a lonely existence embroiled in a bitter legal wrangle with his family. It is said that the duchess's ghost and that of her dog still haunt Ham House!

Built in 1610 on the banks of the River Thames, Ham House was enlarged in the 1670s, when it was at the heart of Restoration court life and intrigue as the home of the extravagant political schemer, Elizabeth Murray, the Duchess of Lauderdale. Luxurious textiles, original furnishings and paintings are on display in 26 rooms. There are three impressive suites of state rooms and a dark, atmospheric Long Gallery. *SH*

The Duchess of Lauderdale's private closet in Ham House, including original japanned chairs, Kingswood cabinet and tea table, dating from about 1675.

DR JOHNSON'S HOUSE

A London town house

Dr Samuel Johnson lived and worked here between 1748 and 1759, and it was here that he worked on the first comprehensive English Dictionary (1755). Today, the restored four-storey house, furnished with 18th-century pieces, evokes Johnson's larger-than-life personality, with descriptions, quotes and anecdotes in evidence all around. Find the house amongst a maze of courtyards and passages and look out for the sculpture of Dr Johnson's beloved cat Hodge outside the house. *SH*

Dr Johnson's House is in Gough Square, London EC4. It is owned by the Dr Johnson's House Trust and open on selected days all year.
Tel: 020 7353 3745
www.drjohnsonshouse.org

Built in 1700, Dr Johnson's House is one of the few residential town houses of its age surviving in the City of London.

KENWOOD HOUSE

A neoclassical mansion with Adam interiors

The fine neoclassical façade of Kenwood House.

Set in 112 acres of landscaped grounds on the edge of Hampstead Heath, Kenwood House, with its graceful and clean-cut façade, epitomizes the golden age of the English country house. Remodelled in the 1760s by Robert Adam, it contains some of his finest interiors. The library or 'Great Room' is outstanding and there is a remarkable 'Chinese' chimneypiece, designed by Adam, in the Upper Hall. The ceilings are by Antonio Zucchi and important works by Rembrandt, Vermeer, Hals, Van Dyck, Landseer, Turner, Gainsborough and Boucher hang harmoniously in the sumptuous surroundings. *SH*

ROBERT ADAM – AN ARTISTIC IMPRESARIO
Hugely energetic, enterprising and entrepreneurial, Scottish-born Robert Adam introduced neoclassicism into England virtually single-handedly and it subsequently dominated interior decoration as a reinterpretation, rather than mere imitation, of the forms of ancient Greece and Rome. Some of Adam's finest interiors can be seen at Kenwood House, but he worked in most of the great houses created at that time – wonderful examples of his consummate taste and unerring eye for colour coordination can also be seen at Osterley Park (p 41), Syon Park (p 47), Saltram (p 117), Kedleston Hall (p 154), Audley End (p 176), Harewood House (p 225), Newby Hall (p 228) and Culzean Castle (p 263).

Kenwood House is in Hampstead Lane, London NW3. It is owned by English Heritage and open all year.
Tel: 020 8348 1286
www.english-heritage.org.uk

LEIGHTON HOUSE MUSEUM
A Victorian artist's residence

This jewel of Victorian elegance and taste was the home of Frederic, Lord Leighton (1830–96), painter and President of the Royal Academy. Built between 1864 and 1879 by architect George Aitchison, it includes Leighton's magnificent studio, which runs along the whole breadth of the house. The sumptuous Arab Hall, with its fountain and mosaic frieze, glitters with 16th- and 17th-century tiles from the Middle East. Throughout, walls and spaces are filled with works by Leighton and other Victorian artists such as Millais and Burne-Jones. *SH*

Leighton House Museum is in Holland Park Road, Kensington, London W14. It is owned by the Royal Borough of Kensington and Chelsea and open all year.
Tel: 020 7602 3316
www.rbkc.gov.uk/LeightonHouseMuseum

A restful alcove at the east end of the library at Kenwood House.

The decorative splendour of the opulent Arab Hall.

LINLEY SAMBOURNE HOUSE

A late Victorian town house

Part of a terrace built in the 1870s in an elegant street in Kensington, London, this five-storey brick house was the home of *Punch* cartoonist Edward Linley Sambourne and his family. Most of the original Victorian decoration and furnishings are preserved, together with many of the family's personal possessions.

Throughout, the walls are covered with early William Morris papers or Linley Sambourne's imitation Spanish leather patches. The windows have coloured panels of stained glass, bringing flashes of brilliant colour and light to the dark interiors. In the entrance hall, one's eyes are drawn to a beautiful stained-glass window in the garden door, depicting an orange tree in a blue-and-white bowl.

The walls and surfaces are crammed with colourful ornaments, framed prints, photographs, drawings, reproductions of Old Masters and Linley Sambourne's own work. The dining room, where the Sambournes frequently entertained, is papered in William Morris's 'Pomegranate' paper, but you can barely see it for the pictures that cover the walls. The sideboard – a 'must have' in a stylish late Victorian home – has painted panels of fruit, inset decorative tiles, mirrors and carved panels. The octagonal oak dining table and the eight dining chairs upholstered in green leather would have been highly fashionable in the mid 1870s. Vivid colours contrast effectively with darker tones in the morning room, with its dark walls, brightly patterned Oriental rugs and colourful cornices.

Within five minutes' walk of the Sambournes' house were the homes of several other successful artists, such as

The entrance hall and staircase, where light filters through from the garden door and first-floor landing.

taste of the time. The dados, ebonized furniture and sunflower motifs, as well as blue-and-white porcelain and Japanese fans, were all highly fashionable at the time, indicating the importance the Sambournes placed on creating the right kind of 'aesthetic' interior. The influence of Japanese art on late 19th-century interior design can be seen throughout the house – see for example the lacquer desk under the window in the morning room and the hand-painted palms on the dining-room door.

The morning-room door that leads through to the dining room.

Cosy Victorian style in the morning room.

Frederic Leighton (*see* Leighton House Museum, p 37) and Luke Fildes. These celebrated painters decorated their homes to impress and when Linley Sambourne and his wife Marion became part of their social circle they also wished to create an interior that would reflect the 'artistic'

Another fashionable feature was the water garden on the first landing. Indoor plants were popular in late Victorian times, and while the house was not big enough for a conservatory, there was room by the landing window for a small display. The light flows up the stairwell and shimmers on the glass box, filled with ferns, shells, colourful minerals and a fountain.

The drawing room takes up the entire first floor and contains a mixture of Regency and Louis XVI furniture. Some pieces are genuine, others are Victorian reproductions. As the house had no studio, a large bay window was built at the back of this room. Light filters through a spectacular stained-glass design of sunflowers in pots under a canopy of verdant foliage. It was here that Sambourne worked at his drawing board to tight deadlines, often well into the night. He used family, friends and servants as his models, taking photographs of them and processing the images in the bathroom. The finished prints were filed away in drawers and cupboards all over the house. Full-length curtains hang at the window here, ready to hide the working area when visitors came.

The principal bedroom, although largely furnished as it was in Linley Sambourne's time, was completely redecorated by his granddaughter, the Countess of Rosse, in the early 1960s. Her choice of a Morris paper was an attempt to maintain the character of the interior. In this room, look out for a fan in a glass case in front of the fireplace. The leaves of the fan are decorated and signed by well-known artists of the period, including Millais, Watts, Frith and Alma-Tadema.

Sambourne's son Roy covered the walls of his bedroom with photographs of his favourite relatives and friends from Oxford. Also on the walls are some of his father's book illustrations, including some Roy had modelled for as a child. He later

Roy Sambourne's bedroom, with its original brass bed and walls hung with photographs and illustrations.

added signed photographs of actresses whom he had escorted as a young man. The stained-glass window in this room is similar to the one in the drawing room. It shows the setting sun and an owl, and features a repeating motif of birds against rays of sunlight.

Along with Sambourne's drawings, tools and photographs and his wife's letters, inventories and detailed diaries, this house gives a unique insight into late Victorian artistic family life. *SH*

Linley Sambourne House is in Stafford Terrace, Kensington, London W8. It is owned by the Royal Borough of Kensington and Chelsea and open on selected days from March to December. **Tel: 020 7602 3316 ext 305** **www.rbkc.gov.uk/ linleysambournehouse**

MARBLE HILL HOUSE

A Palladian villa by the River Thames

Marble Hill House is in Richmond Road, Twickenham, Middlesex. It is owned by English Heritage and open on selected days from the beginning of April to the end of October.
Tel: 020 8892 5115
www.english-heritage.org.uk

This magnificent Palladian villa was built in 1724–29 for Henrietta Howard, Countess of Suffolk and mistress of George II. Here, she extravagantly entertained her friends, including Alexander Pope, Jonathan Swift and Horace Walpole. The perfect proportions of the villa were inspired by the 16th-century architect, Andrea Palladio. The opulent decor of the Great Room, with its architectural paintings by Panini and stunning chinoiserie display, offers a wonderful glimpse into the elegant life of the charismatic Countess of Suffolk. *SH*

Marble Hill House from across the River Thames.

OSTERLEY PARK

Fine Robert Adam interiors

The Etruscan Dressing Room at Osterley Park.

Originally a fine Tudor mansion built in 1575, Osterley Park was transformed by Robert Adam in the 18th century into a grand neoclassical villa. The stunning airy interiors, with tailor-made tapestries, original furniture and exquisite plasterwork, are among the finest examples of Adam's work. With its four turrets, Osterley Park was clearly designed for lavish lifestyles and entertaining on a grand scale. The charming red-brick 16th-century stables remain largely intact and are still in use. *SH*

Osterley Park is in Jersey Road, Isleworth, Middlesex. It is owned by the National Trust and open on selected days from early March to the end of October.
Tel: 020 8232 5050
www.nationaltrust.org.uk

RED HOUSE

William Morris's first family home

Designed by the young architect Philip Webb, Red House was the first family home of William Morris and his wife Jane. It was also a workshop, studio and a meeting place for their friends. The Morris family lived here for six happy years, but in 1866 they moved to Hammersmith and later to Kelmscott Manor (p 101).

The idea of Red House was first conceived by Morris in the summer of 1858, a year before it was built and two years before he and his wife moved in. Webb and Morris were young, idealistic and reformist. The house would establish and embody the Arts and Crafts Movement that they believed in so passionately; it

would be a medieval 'palace of art' where like-minded artists and designers could gather. In its own way, its design represented a quiet revolution, with its Gothic arches, steep-tiled roof and open construction – a dramatic break from Victorian styles.

Red House and its garden were designed as one, and there is a special harmony between the romantic house and its beautiful setting. Through the solid wooden gates, a brick path leads to the L-shaped house with its great barn-like red-tiled roof. Trees, flowers, plants and trellises, so reminiscent of some of Morris's early textile designs, contrast with the mellow red-brick walls of the house. A great

The warm red-brick exterior of Red House in Bexleyheath, with its arched entrance porch, steep red-tiled roof, tall windows and gables.

William Morris, artist, craftsman and poet.

Large 'dragon's blood' lacquered dresser designed by Philip Webb.

The hall, with its oak staircase and bold pattern on the ceiling.

Detail from the painted door at the end of the ground-floor passage.

pointed arched porch leads to a large door, carried on wrought-iron hinges. From inside, look back at Morris's bold, geometric painted patterns on this entrance door.

The light inside is soft and subdued, except on the spacious oak staircase and in the studio, where light floods in through several large windows. Everywhere there are objects, patterns and decoration created by Morris and his friends, some finished and some incomplete. The house is filled with medieval references, including large fireplaces, high ceilings with wooden crossbeams and leaded stained-glass windows.

On the way to the dining room, notice the settle with elaborately painted doors by Morris. He used the dining room as a living room and two things

still dominate it – a red (Morris called the colour 'dragon's blood') dresser, designed by Webb and a great red-brick fireplace.

On the way upstairs, notice the spatial effects of the staircase, the pendulous glass lanterns and sizeable windows, and don't miss the painted embellishments on the turret ceiling above, which were 'pricked out' while the ceiling plaster was still damp.

Upstairs in the studio and drawing room, the shapes of the ceiling are a particularly interesting feature: the sloping roof has been deliberately highlighted and emphasized, with brightly coloured geometric patterns and painted cornices. In Morris's tranquil L-shaped studio, the rounded and rectangular windows on three sides fill the room with light and give views of the well-court and garden, while the walls are papered in Morris's soft green 'Larkspur' wallpaper.

William Morris stained-glass panel of a goose, in the ground-floor passage.

The settle in the drawing room; originally brightly painted, it was designed by Morris, with additions by Webb.

On the first floor is the largest room in Red House, the drawing room, where Jane and her friends made embroidered wall hangings for the house. It has a beautiful oriel window, and because the ceiling is so high, the room could accommodate an enormous piece of furniture designed by Morris: an oversized settle. Webb made a platform and ladder for the settle, so that the loft could be reached from the top and it could also serve as a minstrels' gallery! Morris intended this room to be 'the most beautiful room in the world'. It was originally filled with his brilliant contrasts of colour and pattern: the ceiling was 'pricked out' and painted

with rounded floral patterns and one wall was covered in embroidered panels, while beneath were green hand-painted bushes. Also, the settle was formerly richly coloured, with painted panels by Rossetti. On the walls remain some unfinished frescoes by Burne-Jones, including one depicting William and Jane in medieval costume. It's easy to imagine the Morrises sitting here, relaxed and in accord with each other.

Reacting against the industrial ugliness of the 19th century, Morris relied on modesty and directness of expression, all of which are evident in this idyllic home. *SH*

Red House is in Red House Lane, Bexleyheath, about 3 miles west of Dartford, Kent. It is owned by the National Trust and open on selected days all year (pre-booked guided tours only).
Tel: 01494 755588
www.nationaltrust. org.uk

SOUTHSIDE HOUSE

A 17th-century mansion

STRAWBERRY HILL

A Gothic revival fantasy

This historic family house on Wimbledon Common, built by Robert Pennington in 1687, is a unique piece of living history. Behind the long façade, the rooms still contain much of the furniture that Robert Pennington brought here. The family was associated with many distinguished names, including the descendents of Anne Boleyn's family, Lord Nelson, the Hamiltons, Lord Byron, and Sir Joshua Reynolds. Family portraits and possessions are on display along with some pearls which belonged to Queen Marie Antoinette of France. *SH*

Southside House is in Woodhayes Road, Wimbledon, London SW19. It is owned by a charitable trust and open on selected days from Easter to the beginning of October.
Tel: 020 8946 7643
www.southsidehouse.com

The 18th-century music room, with classical statues in niches.

Strawberry Hill, Horace Walpole's Gothic fantasy.

Filled with horror at the thought of following his father, Sir Robert, into politics, Horace Walpole decided to devote himself to art in general and the Gothic in particular. In 1747 he bought Chopped Straw Hall, renamed it Strawberry Hill and set about rebuilding it ('I am going to build a little Gothic castle at Strawberry Hill'). One of Walpole's friends, John Chute, owned The Vyne (p 84) in Hampshire and designed Gothic interiors for his own establishment. Walpole, whose (Gothic) novel *The Castle of Otranto*

BACK TO THE MIDDLE AGES
Strawberry Hill was considered to be the first instance of Gothic revival in Britain. The style reintroduced medieval design concepts into architecture, interior decoration and furniture. In the 19th century, its principal protagonists were Charles Barry, Augustus Pugin, Norman Shaw and William Burges (*see* p 106) and the movement was championed by the critic John Ruskin. Other key examples of Gothic revival style include Highclere Castle (p 58), Lanhydrock (p 107), Tyntesfield (p 119), Knebworth House (p 187) and Cragside (p 221) .

was published in 1764, started with battlements and a round tower on the exterior before beginning work inside.

The library (designed by John Chute) has a great canopied fireplace, copied from a tomb in Westminster Abbey. The so-called Holbein Chamber, with its decorated ceiling and elaborate fireplace, is where Walpole is said to have suffered the nightmare that spawned *Otranto*. The Long Gallery, with its fan-vaulted ceiling, is cloistered with mirrored alcoves. In Walpole's day the public poured in to visit, eager to see this extraordinary new house; Walpole's housekeeper did well out of this curiosity, charging a guinea a time. *AB*

Exuberant fan vaulting crowns the cloister-like Long Gallery.

Strawberry Hill is in Waldegrave Road, Twickenham, Middlesex, off the A310. It is now part of St Mary's College and open on Sunday afternoons from May to October.
Tel: 020 8240 4224

SUTTON HOUSE
A Tudor red-brick house

Sutton House was built in 1535 for Sir Ralph Sadleir, courtier of Henry VIII and right-hand man of Thomas Cromwell, Henry VIII's Secretary of State. Later, the house became home to merchants, Huguenot silk weavers, Victorian schoolmistresses and Edwardian clergy. Although it was altered over the years, the house retains many of its original features, such as fine linenfold panelling and carved fireplaces. Other highlights include 17th-century wall paintings. *SH*

Sutton House's Linenfold Chamber with original panelled walls.

Sutton House is in Homerton High Street, Hackney, London E9. It is owned by the National Trust and open on selected days from late January to mid December.
Tel: 020 8986 2264
www.nationaltrust. org.uk

SYON PARK

A house with Tudor origins and fine Adam interiors

Syon Park's splendid Great Hall.

Syon Park is between Brentford and Twickenham, Middlesex, off the A4, south-west London. It is owned by the Duke of Northumberland and open on selected days from late March to the end of October.
Tel: 020 8560 0882
www.syonpark.co.uk

Syon Park, the London home of the Duke of Northumberland, has some of Robert Adam's finest neo-classical interiors, commissioned in the 1760s by the first Duke of Northumberland. Highlights include the Great Hall, with its chequered marble floor, and the richly decorated ante-room, with its gilded statues of gods supported on marble columns. The magnificent Red Drawing Room has walls hung with faded crimson silk, a spectacular painted ceiling by Cipriani and an Adam-designed carpet. *SH*

2 WILLOW ROAD

A Modern Movement house

A view of the cork wall and twisting staircase, with a Modernist sculpture at the bottom.

This is the former family home of the architect Ernö Goldfinger, designed and built by him in 1939. It is a three-storey brick-and-concrete rectangle and one of Britain's most important examples of Modernist architecture. Lines are strict and clean, with absolutely no frills or trimmings. The house is filled with furniture designed by Goldfinger specifically for the house. There is also a significant art collection that includes works by Henry Moore and Max Ernst. *SH*

2 Willow Road is in Hampstead, London NW3. It is owned by the National Trust and open on selected days from March to the end of November.
Tel: 020 7435 6166
www.nationaltrust.org.uk

ARUNDEL CASTLE

A castle with Victorian interiors

Arundel Castle, home of the Duke of Norfolk and his ancestors, dates originally from the 11th century, but it was badly damaged during the English Civil War. What we see today owes much to Henry, 15th Duke of Norfolk, who undertook extensive rebuilding work during the late 19th century. There are 23 rooms open to the public, including the Baron's Hall, with its impressive hammer-beam roof, an armoury and the refurbished Victorian bedrooms and bathrooms. **SH**

The Baron's Hall with its huge hammer-beam roof.

Arundel Castle is in Arundel, West Sussex, north of the A27. It is home to the Duke and Duchess of Norfolk and open on selected days from the beginning of April to the end of October.
Tel: 01903 883136
www.arundelcastle.org

BATEMAN'S

The home of Rudyard Kipling with Edwardian interiors

This Jacobean sandstone house (1604), dark and full of Oriental rugs and artefacts, was the beloved home of the writer Rudyard Kipling and his wife Carrie from 1902 to 1936. The rooms retain many of their original features. There is some fine panelling in the hall and the dining room is richly furnished: Rudyard and Carrie always dressed for dinner. Upstairs is Kipling's book-lined study where he wrote works such as *Puck of Pook's Hill*. **AB**

'FIP'
The enigmatic letters 'FIP' are written against some names in the Kiplings' visitor book. This was Rudyard's secret reminder that his guest 'fell in pond'.

Bateman's is half a mile south of Burwash, Sussex, off the A265. It is owned by the National Trust and open on selected days from April until the end of October.
Tel: 01435 882302
www.nationaltrust.org.uk

The parlour or family sitting room.

BEAULIEU: PALACE HOUSE

A medieval house with Victorian Gothic interiors

The dining room, originally the Inner Hall of the 14th-century monastic gatehouse.

Set in the heart of the New Forest overlooking Beaulieu River, Palace House, home of the Montagu family since 1538, was formerly the gatehouse of Beaulieu Abbey, founded in 1204. The house was extended in the 1870s and, while its monastic origins are apparent in features such as fan-vaulted ceilings, the interiors are mainly Victorian Gothic. Many interesting treasures, collected from around the world over the centuries, are displayed inside. Beaulieu is also home to the world-famous National Motor Museum. *SH*

Beaulieu is near Brockenhurst, Hampshire, off the B3054. It is owned by Lord Montagu and open all year.
Tel: 01590 612345
www.beaulieu.co.uk

BLENHEIM PALACE

A magnificent Queen Anne palace

Blenheim Palace was built by Sir John Vanbrugh and presented by Queen Anne and the English nation to John Churchill, 1st Duke of Marlborough, in recognition of his victory at the Battle of Blenheim (1704). The palace is a masterpiece of the English Baroque style and the

The First State Room at Blenheim, with rich gilded decoration.

interiors are inspiring in their splendour, with carvings by Grinling Gibbons, elegant furniture, paintings, frescoes, statues, tapestries and other treasures. Sir Winston Churchill was born here and some apartments are devoted to him. *SH*

The room where Sir Winston Churchill was born in 1874.

THE MASTER WOODCARVER

The Dutchman Grinling Gibbons combined flawless technique with a perceptive eye for nature to produce extraordinarily lifelike carvings – it is said that some birds were once seen pecking at a bunch of his realistically carved lime-wood grapes. He was discovered by the diarist John Evelyn, who introduced him to King Charles II, after which his career blossomed. Gibbons was later appointed Master Carver to George I. His work can be seen at Blenheim Palace and at Chatsworth (p 138), but his masterpiece is the sublime Carved Room at Petworth House (p 76).

Blenheim Palace is in Woodstock, 8 miles north-west of Oxford. It is owned by the Duke of Marlborough and open from mid February to mid December.
Tel: 08700 602080
www.blenheimpalace.com

BROUGHTON CASTLE

A medieval manor house with fine Tudor interiors

The Oak Room, with its superb original oak Tudor panelling which extends from floor to ceiling.

Broughton Castle, standing on an island surrounded by a 3-acre moat, was originally a medieval manor house, built in about 1300 by Sir John de Broughton. It is now the home of Lord and Lady Saye and Sele and has been owned by the same family for over 600 years. The castle was enlarged between 1550 and 1600, and the opulent Elizabethan interiors include intricate plaster ceilings and fine panelling, particularly in the Oak Room. *SH*

Broughton Castle is 2¹/₂ miles south-west of Banbury, Oxfordshire, on the B4035. It is owned by Lord Saye and Sele and open at Easter and on selected days from May to September.
Tel: 01295 276070
www.broughtoncastle. demon.co.uk

CHARLESTON
The farmhouse home of the Bloomsbury Group

Clive Bell's bedroom.

The dining room with its vibrant decoration.

In October 1916, Vanessa Bell, her sons Julian and Quentin, her lover Duncan Grant and his friend, the novelist David Garnett, plus two servants and Henry the dog, moved into Charleston, a farmhouse at the foot of the South Downs, Sussex. Clive Bell, Vanessa's husband, joined them 23 years later, in 1939.

The house was a blank canvas upon which Vanessa and Duncan could apply their artistic creativity. It was isolated enough to provide the tranquillity they craved, yet close to Vanessa's sister, Virginia Woolf, who lived a few miles away.

Charleston is a solid-looking, rectangular house of brick and flint. Before the unusual household took up residence, according to Virginia Woolf, the house had 'all rather run wild'. As soon as they had moved in, Vanessa, Duncan and their Bloomsbury Group friends began to decorate the walls,

furniture and ceramics with brightly coloured paints and home-made stencils, using their own designs inspired by post-Impressionism.

Duncan and Vanessa had been designing interior schemes, furniture and textiles for some time before they moved to Charleston, as members of the Omega Workshop, which Roger Fry had established to help young artists. They continued to develop their ideas and style at Charleston and in later commissions. Over the following half century, members of the Bloomsbury Group flocked frequently to Charleston and relaxed in its welcoming and informal surroundings. Regular visitors included Roger Fry, Lytton Strachey, John Maynard Keynes, T.S. Eliot and E.M. Forster.

To begin with, few structural changes were made to the house, but after Vanessa negotiated a longer lease in 1924, rooms were changed round, a servants' parlour added and a large studio built in the grounds. The house was lavishly and lovingly decorated, mainly by Vanessa and Duncan. Virginia Woolf once observed that she never visited the house without finding it in joyous chaos with pots of paint on the floor. Walls, windows, doors, bath panels and fire surrounds are covered with stylized multi-coloured flowers, bold flowing patterns and figures, animals and objects inspired by nature. Colours are fresh and lush, including soft yellows, russets, greens, lilacs, blues and pinks. Every available surface has been treated to their individual brand of interior design.

Because Duncan and Vanessa did not actually own Charleston, the decor

was not intended to be permanent, and it still gives the impression of spontaneity – welcoming without much expense. Some of the furniture was inherited and some of it second-hand, so there is a real mix of styles and periods.

Despite the individuality of the rooms, Charleston has a remarkably unified look because of the style of painting, the colours and occasionally repeated

The coal-burning stove in the studio, with fireplace surround decorated with caryatids painted by Duncan Grant.

The harmoniously patterned study.

damaged. For example, when the dining table became dilapidated, Vanessa painted over the top and when the mirror in the garden room cracked, a floral panel was added.

Prepare to be amazed by the abundance of patterns, plants and colours everywhere. Cupboards decorated with flowers and foliage, carpets depicting fish and mythical nymphs on doors jostle alongside paintings by Bloomsbury artists as well as by Renoir, Picasso, Derain, Matthew Smith, Sickert, Tomlin and Delacroix.

patterns and motifs. The only exceptions to this are the dining room, with its red lacquer chairs and black walls stencilled in grey and yellow, and the studio, in deep maroon and red. But even in these rooms, the arrangements of paintings and hand-painted pottery give them the distinctive 'Charleston/ Bloomsbury look'. Over time, some original designs were altered and repainted as they faded or became

Although filled with paintings, the house does not feel claustrophobic, but harmonious and restful. In Clive Bell's bedroom, painted by Vanessa, the sunny colours are uplifting and calming, while in the studio, which doubled as Duncan's sitting room, a coal-burning stove surrounded by painted caryatids 'supporting' the mantelpiece gives a welcoming presence. This is a house that was loved and enjoyed by a group of talented, creative and passionate people. *SH*

Vanessa Bell's bedroom, featuring her distinctive circle motifs.

Charleston is 7 miles east of Lewes, East Sussex, off the A27. It is owned by the Charleston Trust and open on selected days from the beginning of April to the end of October.
Tel: 01323 811626
www.charleston.org.uk

CHARTWELL

A Victorian house, home of Winston Churchill

Tall, arched windows in the dining room provide extensive views of the garden.

Churchill's study with his painting of Blenheim Palace over the fireplace and his flag hanging from the ceiling.

In 1922 Winston Churchill acquired a substantial but unassuming Victorian house overlooking the Kent Weald. He transformed it into a warm and loved home where he lived for 40 years. After he became Prime Minister in 1940, hampers of vegetables and fruit from the kitchen garden were sent every Monday to Downing Street.

After his death in 1965, Churchill's wife Clementine wanted the principal rooms to be shown as much as possible as they were in the 1920s and 30s. And so the great man's presence is felt everywhere in the form of cigars, daily papers, fresh flowers cut from the garden, paintings, photographs, furniture and books. There are also sound recordings and collections of memorabilia from his political career.

Despite the house's size, domestic intimacy is apparent the moment one enters the hall – don't miss Sir Winston's disparate collection of walking sticks tucked into an umbrella stand. Throughout his time here, the lights in the upstairs study, with its exposed beams and Tudor doorway, gleamed through the night as he worked on the stream of speeches, newspaper articles and books he produced. From the age of 41, he painted profusely too and the garden studio contains his easel and paint box, plus many of his canvases in various stages of completion. *SH*

> '**I love the place – a day away from Chartwell is a day wasted.**'
> *Winston Churchill*

Chartwell is 2 miles south of Westerham, Kent, off the B2026. It is owned by the National Trust and open on selected days from March to November.
Tel: 01732 866368
www.nationaltrust. org.uk

CHENIES MANOR HOUSE
A fine Tudor manor house

CLANDON PARK
An 18th-century mansion

Chenies Manor House is north of the A404, between Amersham and Rickmansworth, Buckinghamshire. It is privately owned and open on selected days from the beginning of April to October.
Tel: 01494 762888

This red-brick manor house, with its fortified tower, was built in 1460 and added to in 1526 by Sir John Russell (later the 1st Earl of Bedford). Henry VIII and Elizabeth I were both entertained here. Queen Elizabeth's Room has a magnificent oak floor as well as 16th-century tapestries and furniture; the stone parlour, believed to be the Great Hall of the original house, contains some fine 17th-century furniture, and the Blue Bedroom has a Chippendale four-poster bed and other pieces of 18th-century furniture. *SH*

This grand Palladian red-brick mansion was built in about 1730 by the Venetian architect Giacomo Leoni. At the heart of the house is the spectacular light-filled two-storey Marble Hall. The grand theme continues throughout, with an outstanding collection of 18th-century furniture, porcelain, textiles and carpets. There is also the most exquisite Ivo Forde Meissen collection of Italian comedy figures and a series of intricate Mortlake tapestries. *SH*

Clandon Park is in Clandon, on the A247, 3 miles east of Guildford, Surrey. It is owned by the National Trust and open on selected days from late March to the end of October.
Tel: 01483 222482
www.nationaltrust.org.uk

Chenies Manor, with its stepped gables and carved brick chimneys, is set in beautiful gardens.

Giacomo Leoni's airy, ivory-coloured Marble Hall at Clandon Park is one of the grandest 18th-century interiors in England.

CLAYDON HOUSE

A Georgian house with fine rococo decoration

DORNEY COURT

A restored Tudor manor

The unique Chinese room with Luke Lightfoot's elaborately carved woodwork features.

The drawing room at Dorney Court.

Originally a Jacobean manor house, Claydon House was rebuilt in the 1750s, complete with magnificent rococo interiors by Luke Lightfoot and a parquetry staircase unrivalled in the whole of England. The house is perhaps most famous for the aptly named Chinese Room where intricately carved white woodwork on a deep blue background creates a wonderful Oriental landscape, complete with pagodas, birds and nodding China men. Among regular visitors in the past was Florence Nightingale and there are many mementos of her life in the house. *SH*

Claydon House is in Middle Claydon, 13 miles north-west of Aylesbury, Buckinghamshire. It is owned by the National Trust and open on selected days from late March to the end of October.
Tel: 01296 730349
www.nationaltrust. org.uk

This idyllic-looking brick-and-timber Tudor building has been home to the Palmer family for four centuries and it appears unchanged by time. But that is not so. Early 18th-century Palmers 'Georgianized' Dorney Court, giving it a regular three-storey façade. But the Georgian façade was gone and the Tudor look was back by the 20th century, with leaded windows, gables, tall chimneys and brick bays. The house itself dates from the late 15th century.

The Tudor Great Hall has fine linen-fold panelling and includes a collection of Palmer portraits – many painted by Kneller and Lely. The drawing room displays a portrait, in needlework, of family triplets who were amazingly born several days apart from each other in the late 15th century. The luxurious dining

---

MAD LUKE LIGHTFOOT

The riot of rococo that greets a visitor entering **Claydon House** is the work of the talented yet eccentric Luke Lightfoot, 'an ignorant knave with no small spice of madness in his composition', according to Sir Thomas Robinson, Claydon's architect. Difficult and disrespectful towards his social superiors, Lightfoot was dismissed by the owner Lord Verney, but not before he had created the finest collection of rococo rooms in Britain.

Dorney Court is 2 miles west of Eton, off the B3026 near Windsor, Berkshire. It is privately owned and open on selected days in August and on some days in May.
Tel: 01628 604638
www.dorneycourt.co.uk

room, with its painted floor, is of another style altogether – late 17th-century Dutch.

The house, with its almost-attached church, stands protected in a sea of meadow and garden – it seems a whole world away from the noisy traffic pounding up and down the M4, just a mile or so away. *AB*

THE DORNEY PINEAPPLE
The carved stone pineapple in the Great Hall commemorates the very first pineapple to have been grown in England, at Dorney. The fruit was presented to Charles II in 1661.

The Tudor Great Hall at Dorney Court, with its fine linenfold panelling, oak floor and carved stone pineapple.

DOWN HOUSE
The Victorian family home of Charles Darwin

Charles Darwin's desk in the Old Study, recreated as Darwin left it.

Charles Darwin lived at Down House for over 40 years and it was here that he wrote his major works, including *On the Origin of Species by Means of Natural Selection* (1859). The ground-floor rooms have been set out as they would have been in Darwin's time, with Victorian furnishings reflecting the domestic life of the family. Darwin's study, recreated from photographs, includes his chair and desk and is filled with his notes, papers and books. Upstairs there is a museum devoted to Darwin's life and work. *SH*

Down House is off the A21 in Downe, Kent. It is owned by English Heritage and open on selected days from early February to mid December.
Tel: 01689 859119
www.english-heritage.org.uk

GOODWOOD HOUSE

A grand villa with Regency state rooms

Highclere Castle, designed by Sir Charles Barry in the 1830s.

HIGHCLERE CASTLE

A Victorian Italianate mansion

Goodwood House, home to the Dukes of Richmond for 300 years, was originally designed as a hunting lodge during the reign of James I. The opulent gilded state rooms, built for glamour and entertainment on a grand scale, were added by James Wyatt in 1800–06. The house has one of the finest collections of English furniture, Sèvres porcelain and tapestries in England. The walls are adorned with a superb collection of paintings: views of London by Canaletto; sporting scenes by Stubbs; and family and royal portraits by Van Dyck, Lely and Reynolds. *SH*

Goodwood House is 3½ miles north-east of Chichester, West Sussex. It is owned by The Earl of March and open on selected days from late March to early October.
Tel: 01243 755000
www.goodwood.co.uk

Highclere Castle was built by Sir Charles Barry at the same time as he was building the Houses of Parliament. The towering mansion became home to the 3rd Earl of Carnarvon, one of the great hosts of the Victorian era. Throughout the castle, the lavish interiors display various influences, including Moorish, Gothic revival and rococo. The 5th Earl of Carnarvon funded excavations in Egypt which culminated in Howard Carter's discovery of Tutankhamun's tomb and the house includes a unique exhibition of Egyptian discoveries. *SH*

Highclere Castle is 7 miles south of Newbury, Berkshire, off the A34. It is owned by the Earl of Carnarvon and open on bank holidays and on selected days from July to September.
Tel: 01635 253210
www.highclerecastle.co.uk

The Yellow Drawing Room, with beautiful French and English furniture and 18th-century paintings.

THE HOMEWOOD

A unique Modernist country villa

Before they could all move back in again, both of Patrick's parents had died, in 1942.

But Patrick came home to his beloved building. Although a young man when he designed The Homewood, he had become passionate about the Modern Movement while still a schoolboy at Harrow. Later, training as an architect, he had driven his black-and-yellow Austin Seven to Germany to look at early modern houses designed by Le Corbusier, Mies van der Rohe and Eric Mendelsohn. His first job was with the firm of Wells Coates, leading exponents of Modernism, and he absorbed the aesthetic of the style, the flat-roofed plain façades, the enormous windows, the white rendered exteriors and the clean harmony of uncluttered space.

Elevated living is taken to new heights at The Homewood, already on a raised area, but designed so that the living and sleeping rooms are on the upper of the two storeys. A large part of the ground floor is occupied by a four-car garage.

The maple-sprung floor in the living room was perfect for dancing, while the Levanto marble wall is dark and dramatic.

Life was one long party for just over a year in the fantastic new home that young architect Patrick Gwynne built for his parents, his sister and himself on their land near Esher in Surrey. Patrick was only 24 when The Homewood, the Modernist house that created such a stir, was completed in 1938.

Sadly, Patrick's parents, Alban and Ruby Gwynne, who had funded the building ('the temple of costly experience', Commander Gwynne jokingly called The Homewood) did not enjoy the luxurious house for long. The parties and the dancing in the enormous living room, the tennis parties and the dinners on the terrace, all came to an abrupt end when war was declared a year later. Alban Gwynne, a Royal Naval commander, rejoined the services, Patrick enlisted in the RAF, his sister became a Wren and his mother moved to a smaller house.

Tulip light fittings in the entrance hall, designed by Patrick Gwynne.

The focus of the ground floor, entered by a canopied door surrounded by deep glass blocks, is the dramatic spiral staircase, lit from the base and winding into the centre of the house. On one side is the bedroom wing and on the other the magnificent living room with its 12ft (3.7m) deep sash windows, barely keeping the garden at bay. The room, with its sprung

Patrick Gwynne's bedroom, simple but comfortable and practical. The bentwood chair, covered in beaver wool, and the round table are by Bruno Mathsson.

maple-wood floor (perfect for partying) is meticulously designed down to the last detail. The windows have central sections that slide open at a push using a special mechanical device. Opposite, the Indian laurel-veneered wall is in reality a series of built-in units, concealing shelves, a drinks' cabinet, hi-fi equipment and a serving hatch through to the kitchen.

The wall near the staircase hall is covered in a brown fabric on which hangs a large painting by Stefan Knapp. At the far end of the room, polished and veined black Levanto marble is the elegant surround for a gas fireplace. There is a classic Eames chair and ottoman, which once belonged to Gwynne's friend, actor Lawrence Harvey. A beige couch contains a built-in projection screen, while the coffee table, reading lamp and the low black-and-red lacquered chest are all by Gwynne. So too is the desk in white vinyl which converts to a writing table, a drawing board and a typing station. There are fur-covered Bruno Mathsson chaises longues and a Bauhaus chair.

The dining room, reached by a folding screen, is just as full of beautiful utility. The round table of dark glass and plated steel contains coloured lights to match the mood of the diners. A sunken well in the centre of the table means that flowers will not interfere with dinner conversations.

The bedrooms, wood-panelled, uncluttered and comfortable, and the large terrace outside with pool and barbecue, have all been designed, as the rest of the house, with great elegance but with emphasis on the use for which they were made.

Patrick Gwynne died at the age of 90 in 2003, and the house, as he had planned, became the property of the National Trust. *AB*

Detail of a folding screen, decorated with stalks of sweetcorn highlighted in gold leaf.

The exterior of The Homewood, showing the abstract decorative panels on the first-floor wall.

The Homewood is in Portsmouth Road, Esher, Surrey. It is owned by the National Trust and public access is by pre-booked guided tours only.
Tel: 01372 471144
www.nationaltrust.org.uk

HUGHENDEN MANOR

A Georgian house with Victorian Gothic interiors

Hughenden Manor was the home of Victorian Prime Minister and celebrated statesman Benjamin Disraeli from 1847 until his death in 1881. The house is a fascinating testament to his life and to the Victorian age, with its red-brick Gothicized Georgian exterior and Gothic interior, which still contains most of Disraeli's furniture and a great number of his possessions. In the library, there are nearly 2,000 of his books and an autographed copy of Queen Victoria's only published work. *SH*

The imposing red-brick exterior of Hughenden Manor, home of Benjamin Disraeli.

Hughenden Manor is 1½ miles north of High Wycombe, Buckinghamshire, off the A4128. It is owned by the National Trust and open on selected days from March to the end of October.

Tel: 01494 755573

www.nationaltrust.org.uk

IGHTHAM MOTE

A moated medieval manor house

This beautiful moated medieval manor house embraces 650 years of history, from its first owners in 1320 to the 1980s. Its serene quality is enhanced by its watery surroundings and lovely setting at the foot of a wooded cleft in the Kentish Weald. At first sight, the timber-framed building appears almost to float on the moat

Detail of the Chinese wallpaper in the first-floor drawing room.

Detail of the gatehouse door with panels carved in the wood.

Ightham Mote is 6 miles east of Sevenoaks, Kent, off the A25 at Ivy Hatch. It is owned by the National Trust and open on selected days from March to November.
Tel: 01732 810378
www.nationaltrust. org.uk

that surrounds it. As conservation work on the house was undertaken, details of its colourful and complex history were uncovered. Over the centuries, various owners expanded the building as their needs dictated, but always in a manner sympathetic to its medieval origins.

The least-changed part of the original 14th-century building is the crypt, with its vaulted stone ceiling. One of the jewels of the house is the New Chapel, with its unique barrel-vaulted roof displaying painted wooden boards fitted in the early 1530s. The symbols, including the York, Lancaster and Tudor roses, a pomegranate, fleur-de-lis and a portcullis, echo those in the stained-glass windows of the Great Hall and commemorate Henry VIII's marriage to Catherine of Aragon and his claim to the French throne. The drawing room has a fine Jacobean fireplace and a ceiling dating from 1611; the beautiful hand-painted Chinese wallpaper that was put up in about 1800 demonstrates the fashion for chinoiserie at the time. *SH*

JOHN MILTON'S COTTAGE

A Grade-1 listed Tudor cottage

John Milton moved to this cottage in 1665 to escape the Plague in London. It was here that he completed *Paradise Lost* and started *Paradise Regained*. The charming cottage is set out as it would have been in Milton's time, with some of his furniture, including his writing table and a tall-backed chair. The four ground-floor rooms display important editions of Milton's poetry and prose writings and there are pictures of Milton and his family on the walls. *SH*

John Milton's Cottage is in Chalfont St Giles, Buckinghamshire, $1/2$ mile west of the A413. It is owned by the Milton Cottage Trust and open on selected days from the beginning of March to the end of October.
Tel: 01494 872313
www.miltonscottage.org

The courtyard, which still contains stocks and a large dog's kennel. The archway beneath the Gatehouse Tower leads through to the entrance bridge over the moat.

The picturesque 16th-century cottage in Chalfont St Giles, where Milton completed his great epic poem *Paradise Lost*.

KINGSTON BAGPUIZE HOUSE

A Restoration manor house remodelled in Georgian style

The first glimpse of this exquisite small manor house, with its rosy red-brick exterior, stone quoins and elegantly set windows, sets the heart soaring at its sheer Englishness.

Like a neatly built doll's house, Kingston Bagpuize stands prettily against an avenue of beech trees brought to a full stop by a pair of Wellingtonias at what used to be the grand front entrance. The front is now at the back, a new drive bringing visitors into the house through a porch which sits inside, a little uneasily, under the substantial oak and pine staircase, one of the great features of the house.

The site is ancient but the present house is thought to have been built in the 1660s and then remodelled

The panelled library, with black marble fireplace.

The hand-painted Chinese wallpaper in the entrance hall at Kingston Bagpuize.

of the one-time main entrance door on the east front of the house, which matches that at nearby Radley College, known to have been designed by Townsend.

Inside is an elegant, pretty and comfortable house, a family home, with original pine and oak panelling. It has well-proportioned rooms flooded with light from the tall Georgian windows, and a staircase that rises in gentle stages and turns to a panelled gallery, whose focal point is a shell-shaped alcove.

There's a lot of Marlie in the entrance hall – look closely at the hand-painted Chinese paper on the walls, with its light and airy trees, flowers and birds. The paper doesn't quite fit the space – the family believes she brought it back from her foray to China. Unmarried and putting all her energy into the restoration of her house and garden, Marlie Raphael undertook a tour of the northern hemisphere in 1935, collecting pieces such as the Chinese vases and the uncomfortable-looking stone pillow, in the same manner as her male counterparts had done on their Grand Tours of Europe a century or so earlier.

In the present drawing room (once the entrance hall before the house was 'reversed') there are Hepplewhite-style chairs with beautifully stitched seats – look closely to see Marlie's initials. She made these when she was on her travels before she bought the house.

Twin fireplaces, dating from the 1720 remodelling, welcome visitors through the old front door. Two wonderfully worked Queen Anne cabinets of glowing laburnum and walnut face each

60 years later. Although one family – the Fettiplaces and their heirs through marriage – lived here until 1917, the spirit of the house today seems to reside in a remarkable 20th-century woman whose name has a Renaissance ring. Marlie Raphael fell in love with Kingston Bagpuize House and its garden. She bought the house in 1939, and proceeded to fill it with treasures, some inherited, some bought and some gathered during a trip she made to the Far East.

So this is a Restoration house, remodelled in symmetrical early-Georgian style, with a touch of baroque flamboyance in the shape of decorative urns adorning the exterior. The present owner, Virginia Grant (whose late husband, Francis, was Marlie's great-nephew), thinks this remodelling was done by master builder William Townsend, who worked for Nicholas Hawksmoor on some of the Oxford colleges. The clue comes in the shape

The oak-panelled dining room, with a portrait of Marlie Raphael hanging over the fireplace.

other across the width of the room, but what draws the visitor in this and other rooms of the house are the portraits of the children of the family. Here there are 1904 paintings of Marlie's sisters – Dorothy, fingers dabbling in a bowl of goldfish, and Elsie Raphael, later grandmother to Francis Grant – while in the oak-panelled dining room is a portrait of Marlie herself, aged three, painted in 1907. In the library (examine the delicately carved wood framing the black marble fireplace surround), there are equally charming portraits of the next generation as children.

In the entrance hall, owing to another family connection, there is a portrait of Sir Walter Raleigh: Lady Grant married Lord Tweedsmuir, the son of author John Buchan, who just happened to own a painting of Sir Walter.

Marlie died in 1976, leaving the house to her niece, Lady Jean Grant, widow of the 12th Baronet of Monymusk

Detail of a tapestry seat from a chair in the drawing room.

in Aberdeenshire. Lady Grant opened the house to the public for the first time, eventually passing it on to her son Francis, his wife Virginia and their children.

The charm of houses such as Kingston Bagpuize lies much in the generations that have lived in them and adapted them to family needs, while retaining the essential character and period style of the place. While one admires the portraits and the panelling and treads the impressive stairs, there is a tremendous sense of the past but also of the present and future. *AB*

Kingston Bagpuize House is off the A415, 5 miles west of Abingdon, Oxfordshire. The house is privately owned and open on selected days from February to October. **Tel: 01865 820259 www. kingstonbagpuizehouse. org.uk**

The oak-and-pine
cantilevered staircase.

KNOLE

A medieval palace with exceptional Tudor and Jacobean interiors

It's easy to miss the narrow and unimposing entrance of Knole, in the middle of Sevenoaks in Kent, but the drive up to the house, through the glorious undulating medieval deer park, is magnificent. The house rises up ahead more like an ancient college, small village or castle than a family home.

Knole, which gets its name from the knoll on which it stands, is said to be the largest private house in England. It has been an Archbishop's palace and a royal house, but since 1603, when Elizabeth I granted it to Thomas Sackville, 1st Earl of Dorset, it has remained largely unchanged. With its 365 rooms, 7 courtyards and 52 staircases, this vast building has been described as one of the great treasure houses of England.

The austere-looking exterior of the northern entrance belies the cornucopia of riches and splendour inside. The Great Hall, with its superb Jacobean screen, leads on to the magnificent Great Staircase. Upstairs, the Brown Gallery leads to Lady Betty Germain's rooms and the Spangle Bedroom, the latter so-called because of the beautiful satin bed hangings, sewn with thousands of silver-gilt sequins; the sequins have now faded, but they must originally have sparkled in the sun and candlelight. Look out for the Jacobean panelling and plasterwork in this room and don't miss the lovely harpsichord casing at the back of the Spangle Dressing Room. Around the walls are portraits of women from Charles II's court, of which Charles Sackville, the 6th Earl of Dorset, was a notorious member.

The Venetian Ambassador's Room, shimmering in green and gold, takes its name from the Venetian Ambassador to the court of James I.

The family emblem – the Sackville leopard in the Great Hall.

Detail of the satin bed panels that hang in the Spangle Bedroom. The appliqué strapwork pattern is decorated with silver-gilt sequins.

Bourchier's Tower looking across the Stone Court. It was originally the gatehouse to an archbishop's palace and is one of the oldest parts of Knole.

SHINING LIKE A SHELL

Virginia Woolf, a good friend of Vita Sackville-West, daughter of the 3rd Earl of Dorset, made Knole the setting for her novel *Orlando*. Of the Venetian Ambassador's Room she writes: 'The room ... shone like a shell that has lain at the bottom of the sea for centuries and has been crusted over and painted a million tints by the water; it was rose and yellow, green and sand-coloured. It was frail as a shell, as iridescent and as empty.'

The Great Staircase at Knole, constructed in 1605, with its beautiful Renaissance murals.

The Venetian Ambassador's Room with splendid state bed hangings.

The armchairs and stools around the state bed were made for James II in 1688 and the rare Indian carpet and the Venetian window were added in the 18th century.

The ballroom was designed as the solar, chief living room or Great Chamber, to which the early inhabitants and their attendants would have retired from the Great Hall, passing through the doorway at the top of the Great Staircase. Look carefully for this door, as it is cleverly concealed in the panelling. The panelling and decoration in the

Stuart carved walnut chairs upholstered in silk damask. The feet are carved in the shape of dolphins.

music that was no doubt played in this room. A glance out of the full-length windows at the end of the room gives a lovely view of the gardens.

In the Reynolds Room there are no less than eight paintings by Sir Joshua Reynolds and one by Thomas Gainsborough. Notice in particular the charming Reynolds painting of Wang-y-Tong, a Chinese page. The 3rd Duke brought the boy to England and he was educated at Sevenoaks Grammar School. The painting is richly toned, vivid and atmospheric.

The King's Suite, in the heart of the house, includes the King's Closet, a private dressing room for royalty. In here is a crimson velvet upholstered box, a 'seat of easement' or lavatory, which was almost certainly used by Charles II or James II. Next door, behind glass, is the King's Room, containing the splendid Royal State Bed made for James II, with fine gold-and-silver bed hangings. The room has a delicate plasterwork ceiling and contains exquisite tapestries, a famous silver looking glass and 17th-century ebony-and-silver furniture.

Knole's multi-layered atmosphere has been shaped by the strong personalities who have inhabited it. This is a house of potent and enduring charm, of contrasts, surprises, hidden riches and fading magnificence that whisper of affluent times beyond compare. *SH*

ballroom, including a beautiful frieze of ivory-white mermaids and sea-horses, were introduced by Thomas Sackville, 1st Earl of Dorset, in the early 17th century. Look out, too, on the ceiling for the Sackville family emblem of a leopard. The great alabaster and marble chimneypiece in the ballroom is one of the finest works of Renaissance sculpture in England. The decorations, garlands of flowers and musical instruments hint of the

Knole is in Sevenoaks High Street, Kent, off junction 5 of the M25, 25 miles south-east of London. It is owned by the National Trust and open on selected days from the end of March to the end of October.
Tel: 01732 462100
www.nationaltrust.org.uk

The Great Hall, looking towards the magnificent Jacobean oak screen, carved in 1605–08. The fine plasterwork ceiling, with its geometrical pattern of squares and octagons, also dates from the 17th century.

LITTLE HOLLAND HOUSE

The Arts and Crafts home of Frank Dickinson

When artist and craftsman Frank Dickinson and his bride Florence moved into their new house in March 1904, they spent their honeymoon sanding window frames and staining floors. Frank, determined to own an Arts and Crafts home that his mentors John Ruskin and William Morris would admire, built the house himself with the help of a labourer, a bricklayer and two of his brothers. He designed and built the furniture too – the first piece he finished was the coalbox, now in a corner of the dining area. Florence, inspired by her husband's dream, gave up any idea of a wedding trousseau, spending the money instead on green Cumbrian slate tiles for the roof of what was to be their home for the rest of their lives.

'A house with beautiful things inside, a house solid-looking and not showy', was what Frank, a draughtsman at the Doulton factory, wanted. The house is a showcase for his work, including the hand-painted frieze in the master bedroom, the lampshades and the decorative fireplace surrounds. When Little Holland House was finished later in 1904, it became the hub for the couple's artistic, musical and intellectual friends and Frank held exhibitions of his paintings here until his death in 1961. *AB*

The furniture and many of the furnishings at Little Holland House, including the lampshades, were designed and made by Dickinson himself.

A watercolour of Little Holland House, by Frank Dickinson.

Little Holland House is in Beeches Avenue, Carshalton, Surrey. It is owned by the London Borough of Sutton and open on the first Sunday of each month and on bank holiday Sundays and Mondays.
Tel: 020 8770 4781
www.sutton.gov.uk

MAPLEDURHAM

An Elizabethan mansion

The rich red-brick Mapledurham, on the banks of the Thames.

Nestling on the banks of the River Thames, this late 16th-century Elizabethan house has been the home of the Blount family for over 500 years. Highlights inside include an Elizabethan dark oak staircase, a fine strapwork ceiling in the saloon and a superb collection of paintings and furniture. There is a Gothic chapel to the rear of the hall, dating from 1797. Also on the estate is a fully restored and operational 15th-century watermill. *SH*

Mapledurham is 4 miles north-west of Reading, Berkshire, 1½ miles west of the A4074. It is owned by the Mapledurham Trust and open on selected days from Easter to September.
Tel: 01189 723350
www.mapledurham.co.uk

MILTON MANOR HOUSE

A Restoration house with Gothic interiors

This classically inspired brick house was originally built in the 1660s, but two wings were added in 1765, containing a new library and Roman Catholic chapel. At that time Catholicism was still officially banned in England, so the exterior of the wings was kept deliberately plain and inconspicuous. In contrast, the interiors were decorated in elaborate Gothic style. The house also includes some rare examples of medieval English and 17th-century Flemish stained glass, along with some fine porcelain and Mass vestments dating from 1760. *SH*

Milton Manor House is in Milton, off the A34, 3 miles south of Abingdon, Oxfordshire. It is privately owned and open in August and on bank holiday weekends.
Tel: 01235 862321

The classically inspired mid 17th-century façade of Milton Manor House, seen across the lake.

OSBORNE HOUSE

The seaside home of Queen Victoria with opulent interiors

This was the much-loved home of Queen Victoria and her family, where they found some peace and privacy away from public life. The house, completed in 1851, was designed by Prince Albert and the architect Thomas Cubitt, largely in Italian Renaissance style, which is particularly apparent in the statue-lined Grand Corridor. The Royal Nursery remains as it was in 1870. The Indian-style Durbar Room, a state banqueting hall designed by Rudyard Kipling's father John Lockwood, was added in 1890–91 to celebrate Queen Victoria's status as Empress of India. *SH*

Osborne House is 1 mile south-east of East Cowes, Isle of Wight. It is owned by English Heritage and open from the beginning of April to the end of September.
Tel: 01983 200022
www.english-heritage.org.uk

Detail of the wall decoration below the gallery in the opulent Indian-style Durbar Room.

Osborne House, the Italianate villa built on the Isle of Wight by Queen Victoria and Prince Albert.

PARHAM HOUSE

An Elizabethan mansion

Parham House is on the A283, near Pulborough, West Sussex. It is owned by the Parham Park Trust and open on selected days from Easter to the end of September.
Tel: 01903 742021
www.parhaminsussex.co.uk

The approach to this beautiful grey-stone Elizabethan E-plan house, with its varied gables and chimneys, is across a glorious medieval deer park. Inside, the stunning interiors are mainly Elizabethan and Jacobean. The Great Hall has fine panelling and is filled with light from large windows, and the 160ft (49m) Long Gallery stretches the full length of the south front, with wonderful views over the South Downs. The house also contains a splendid collection of embroidery and paintings. *SH*

The Long Gallery at Parham House, with its beautiful painted ceiling.

PENSHURST PLACE

A medieval manor

The Queen Elizabeth Room, used by Elizabeth I to give audience on her visits to Penshurst.

This family-owned house has a history going back six and a half centuries. Despite renovations and additions over the years, there has been no significant rebuilding, so it remains essentially a medieval building. The Baron's Hall, where Henry VIII was once entertained by the 3rd Duke of Buckingham, was built in 1341 and has an impressive chestnut-beamed roof, 60ft (18m) high. The state rooms upstairs include the sumptuous Queen Elizabeth Room and the splendid Long Gallery, which was completed in 1601. *SH*

Penshurst Place is in the village of Penshurst, 4 miles south-west of Tonbridge, Kent. It is owned by Viscount De L'Isle and open from March to the end of October.
Tel: 01892 870307
www.penshurstplace.com

PETWORTH HOUSE

A late 17th-century mansion with an important art collection

This grand country mansion, once the seat of the turbulent Percy family, is now essentially a grand gallery containing the National Trust's largest picture collection, including works by Turner, Van Dyck, Reynolds and Blake. Some paintings are owned by Lord and Lady Egremont who live in part of the house.

The commissioning of works of art started in earnest with the 10th Earl of Northumberland, Algernon Percy. He enjoyed the work of Van Dyck and became the painter's patron. There are 20 Van Dycks at Petworth, including a portrait of the 10th Earl with his first wife Lady Anne Cecil and their daughter Katherine.

When the 10th Earl's granddaughter, Lady Elizabeth, twice-widowed at the tender age of 16, married Charles Seymour, the 6th Duke of Somerset (known as the 'Proud Duke') in 1682, Petworth underwent a renaissance.

Her money and his forcefulness brought about a grand rebuilding, as well as new paintings, sculpture and wonderful lime-wood carvings by Grinling Gibbons.

The Carved Room, with its heady mix of sublime carving by Gibbons and paintings by Turner and Van Dyck, is the star of the show, while the wonderful North Gallery is full of sculpture and paintings to be savoured. *AB*

Petworth House is in Petworth, West Sussex, off the A272/A283. It is owned by the National Trust and open on selected days from late March to the beginning of November.
Tel: 01798 342207
www.nationaltrust. org.uk

Exquisite lime-wood work in the Carved Room includes the arms of the Duke of Somerset.

The 17th-century Grand Staircase sweeps upwards, its walls lined with works of art.

POLESDEN LACEY

A Regency house with luxurious Edwardian interiors

The neoclassical South Front of Polesden Lacey, overlooking the grounds.

If ever a house was designed for entertainment of the most comfortable and luxurious kind, Polesden Lacey, in the Surrey countryside just 25 miles from London, is it. There's been an estate and a house on this well-situated piece of land since the 14th century. Its most famous owner was poet and playwright Richard Brinsley Sheridan, who enjoyed playing the country squire there, but whose unrestrained lifestyle caused it to fall into ruin. It was rebuilt twice (by architects Thomas Cubitt in 1821 and Ambrose Poynter in the first years of the 20th century), before being bought by heiress and society hostess Maggie Greville and her husband Ronnie in 1906.

Maggie Greville, illegitimate daughter of Scottish brewer, philanthropist and art collector William McEwan, and heiress to his millions, inspired passionate loyalty, sneering deprecation or sneaking admiration in all who knew her. No one could be indifferent to this strong and attractive personality, admired and feared for her acid wit and known above all for her skilled hospitality. 'Better a beeress than a peeress,' she is said to have riposted, probably in response to a remark such as that made by Lady Leslie who exclaimed: 'Maggie Greville! I would sooner have an open sewer in my drawing room.'

But it was to Maggie's library, saloon and dining room (all refurbished for her by Ritz designers Mewès and Davis) that royalty, politicians and the titled flocked to enjoy her lavish entertainment, discuss matters of state and

The library is full of photographs of those entertained here by Maggie Greville.

The Tea Room, displaying some of Maggie Greville's French furniture.

also display the privilege of power. King Edward VII, a particular friend of Maggie's husband, was a guest here, while the Duke and Duchess of York (later King George VI and Queen Elizabeth) spent a couple of weeks of their honeymoon at Polesden Lacey.

In those days before the First World War, when the rich were used to extravagance, the standard of entertainment at Polesden Lacey (and at the Grevilles' other establishment, 11 Charles Street in London) became a byword for comfort and opulence. Mrs Greville left Polesden Lacey, with a generous endowment, to the National Trust after her death in 1942. Although all the 'museum piece' furniture was kept, anything deemed to be of secondary quality, and almost all the bedroom furnishings, were auctioned, a move regretted today.

For all that, it is a splendid place to visit, not only for the pleasure of the major rooms, but also for the quality of the paintings, collected by Maggie Greville and her father, the Fabergé trinkets, Chinese and Japanese porcelain, silverware and bronze statuettes. Everywhere there are cabinets displaying these pieces while the paintings (the majority of them Dutch) are hung in the Picture Corridor, which runs along three sides of the central quadrangle. The Jacobean-style plasterwork ceiling here was copied from the Long Gallery at Chastleton House, Oxfordshire (p 90). At the end of the corridor, don't miss the painting of

This 1891 painting of Maggie Greville, society hostess and lavish entertainer, dominates the ground-floor corridor.

Maggie Greville, staring joyfully out of the canvas at what she had created. It was painted by Carolus-Duran at the start of Maggie's short but happy marriage to the Hon. Ronald Greville in 1891. Her husband died in 1908. More paintings in the dining room include English works by Raeburn, Reynolds and Lawrence. The table is laid for the dessert course – the menu is displayed nearby. In many of the rooms, especially in the library and Mrs Greville's study (notice the mirrored blinds, designed so that she could enjoy reflections of the room), there are photographs, many signed, of her rich and famous visitors. *AB*

Polesden Lacey is at Great Bookham, 5 miles north-west of Dorking, Surrey, off the A246. It is owned by the National Trust and open on selected days from late March to early November.
Tel: 01372 452048
www.nationaltrust.org.uk

ROUSHAM HOUSE
A Jacobean house altered by William Kent

Built in 1635 by Sir Robert Dormer, Rousham House and its grounds were extensively remodelled by the Yorkshire-born architect and designer William Kent in 1738. The interior of the house retains some 17th-century panelling and original staircases, but it is the grand Painted Parlour, designed by Kent, that steals the show, with its magnificent painted ceiling, classical motifs and carved wall brackets supporting Italian bronzes. *SH*

Rousham House is near Steeple Aston, east of the A4260, 7 miles west of Bicester, Oxfordshire. It is privately owned and open on selected days from April to September.
Tel: 01869 347110
www.rousham.org

The gardens at Rousham House survive almost unaltered since they were designed by William Kent in the 18th century.

'IL SIGNIOR' OF STYLE

The multi-talented Yorkshire-born designer William Kent, nick-named 'Il Signior', studied painting in Rome and played a leading role in reintroducing Palladian style to Britain during the first half of the 18th century. He also built Holkham Hall (p 182) and designed the interior decoration for Chiswick House (p 26) and Houghton Hall (p 185).

THE ROYAL PAVILION
Oriental fantasy palace of the Prince Regent

The Royal Pavilion, Brighton, was built for George, Prince of Wales, later the Prince Regent and, later still, King George IV. A respectable farmhouse became a neoclassical 'marine pavilion' and then an Oriental fantasy, domed and turreted. George worked

Fire-breathing dragons seem to provide the illumination in the fantastic chandelier in the ornate banqueting room.

THE CHINESE INFLUENCE

The 19th-century fashion for extravagant chinoiserie reached its apogee with the interior designs by Frederick Crace and Robert Jones for The Royal Pavilion, Brighton. The interest in Chinese objects and decoration grew as trade with the East developed in the 17th and 18th centuries. By the mid 18th century, Chinese motifs – exotic scenery, birds, dragons and pagodas – were seen in all forms of interior decoration, including painted and lacquered furniture, hand-painted wallpapers and blue-and-white porcelain. The Pavilion's chinoiserie includes lotus-blossom chandeliers lighting the music room, Chinese hand-painted wallpapers in the Adelaide Corridor and astounding imitation bamboo strips on the South Corridor walls.

Outstanding examples of chinoiserie can also be seen in the Great Room at Marble Hill House (p 41), in the extraordinary Chinese Room at Claydon House (p 56) and in the Chinese Bedroom at Blickling Hall (p 179).

with architect John Nash and designers Frederick Crace and Robert Jones to produce the most extraordinary, most extravagantly sumptuous palace. Look for the Chinese-inspired banqueting room (Jones) lit by fiery dragons and for the music room (Crace) where lotus blossoms provide illumination and serpents are twined in improbable places. The bedrooms are also Chinese in style, with red-and-gold decoration, lacquer work, dragons and bamboo. *AB*

The Royal Pavilion is in the centre of Brighton, East Sussex. It is owned by Brighton & Hove City Council and open all year.
Tel: 01273 290900
www.royalpavilion.org.uk

SQUERRYES COURT

A Restoration manor house

The hall, with its high ceiling, smooth columns and slender-legged furniture.

This beautiful 17th-century manor house has been home to the Warde family since 1731. The mellow brick building looks imposingly across a lake, while the light and airy interior displays several Old Master paintings from the Italian, 17th-century Dutch and 18th-century English schools, including works by Lely, Stubbs, Rubens, Poussin, Giordano and Van Dyck. There are some fine pieces of furniture, tapestries, mirrors and porcelain, which were acquired or commissioned by the family in the 18th century. *SH*

Squerryes Court is ¹/₂ mile south-west of Westerham, Kent, off junction 6 of the M25. It is privately owned and open on selected days from the beginning of April to the end of September.
Tel: 01959 562345
www.squerryes.co.uk

ST MARY'S HOUSE

A Tudor timber-framed house

This enchanting 15th-century timber-framed house, set in picturesque formal gardens, was once a hostel for medieval pilgrims, but later became the home of the real Algernon and Gwendolen, portrayed so vividly in Oscar Wilde's play *The Importance of Being Earnest.* Inside the house, there is some fine Jacobean panelling and the Elizabethan Painted Room, with its fascinating *trompe l'œil* murals, is quite remarkable. Don't miss the traces of medieval wall painting on the walls of the King's Room. *SH*

St Mary's House is at Bramber, West Sussex, off the A283. It is privately owned and open on selected days from Easter to September.
Tel: 01903 816205
www.stmarysbramber.co.uk

St Mary's House, originally a monastic inn for pilgrims travelling to Canterbury.

STANDEN

A Webb-designed Arts and Crafts house furnished by William Morris

There's a feeling that the ghosts of the Beale family, James and Margaret, their seven children, grand-children, innumerable cousins and rela-tives, inhabit the comfortable rooms at Standen, designed by Arts and Crafts architect Philip Webb in 1891 and furnished largely by William Morris.

The interior of this quietly attractive house, with wide views over the Sussex Downs, echoes Morris's view that everything in one's house should be useful or beautiful. The drawing room, with its alcoves and elegant fire-place, was designed by Webb – see his bold sunflower motif worked into the copper 'cheeks'. The Morris 'Sunflower' wallpaper continues the theme. Here and elsewhere in the house are exquisite embroidered Morris-patterned cushions and wall hangings worked by Margaret Beale and her daughters, expert needle-women. Visitors can't get close to their wonderful silk and linen 'Artichoke' wall hanging (1896) in the North Bedroom, but even seen from the doorway, it is lovely.

The green-panelled dining room, where the family gathered for their substantial dinners, has the most beautiful wide fireplace (Webb) surmounted by a fretwork panel. The woven woollen curtains are Morris's 'Peacock and Dragon' design. There are collections of de Morgan lustre-ware and Della Robbia majolica throughout the house. The airy conservatory has been redecorated

The elegant hall at Standen, a quiet introduction to this comfortable Arts and Crafts house designed by Philip Webb.

and replanted by the National Trust who inherited Standen in 1972. *AB*

Standen is 2 miles south of East Grinstead, Sussex, off the B2110. It is owned by the National Trust and open on selected days from late March until the end of October.
Tel: 01342 323029
www.nationaltrust. org.uk

STRATFIELD SAYE HOUSE

A Jacobean house with Georgian interiors

The elegant exterior of Stratfield Saye House.

When the 1st Duke of Wellington returned from the Battle of Waterloo in 1815, a grateful nation granted him £600,000 for a country home. He bought the estate at Stratfield and proceeded to modernize the house (originally built in about 1635), adding outer wings, a conservatory, 'modern' plumbing and central heating – see the two original radiators at the foot of the staircases. The library remains almost as it was in Wellington's time and the hall displays items relating to his campaigns. *SH*

Stratfield Saye House is at Stratfield Saye, Hampshire, between Basingstoke and Reading, 1 mile west of the A33. It is owned by the Duke of Wellington and open at Easter and from early July to the beginning of August.
Tel: 01256 882882
www.stratfield-saye.co.uk

UPPARK

A 17th-century mansion

That Uppark is open to visitors is remarkable, but even more extraordinary is that its famous Grand Tour collection of paintings, furniture and ceramics remains virtually intact. In 1989 fire ravaged this William and Mary house, high on the South Downs, destroying the first floor and its contents. But heroic firefighters somehow managed to salvage nearly all the moveable contents of the ground floor – and the house was gradually restored.

When wealthy and newly titled Matthew Fetherstonhaugh married rich and cultivated Sarah Lethieullier in 1746, the world – or Europe at least – was their oyster. Oil pastels of husband and wife, by William Hoare of Bath, hang in the staircase hall. They were probably painted before the couple, accompanied by family and friends, embarked on their Grand Tour, during which they were all painted in Rome by Pompeo Batoni. Compare Batoni's portraits (in the Red Drawing Room)

The elaborate plasterwork in the Red Drawing Room is testament to the restorers' work after the fire.

with the portrait of their son, Harry, painted 25 years later by the same artist. Harry, incidentally, was briefly entangled with the young Emma Hart (who later became Lady Hamilton, mistress of Lord Nelson). She is said to have danced naked on the table at Uppark and was sent packing, six months pregnant, in 1781.

H.G. Wells's mother was housekeeper at Uppark from 1880 to 1893 and the extensive servants' quarters in the basement are shown as they would have been in Victorian times. The house also includes some fine original mahogany and gilt-wood furniture dating from the 18th century. The saloon, a beautiful room, has a delicately plastered and gilded ceiling and contains two more Batonis – representing two of the Beatitudes. Each of the rooms, all containing rescued and restored treasures, is a triumph of restoration over adversity. *AB*

The beautiful red-brick façade of Uppark, a fine example of a William and Mary house.

Uppark is near South Harting, 5 miles south-east of Petersfield, Hampshire, on the B2146. It is owned by the National Trust and open on selected days from the end of March to the end of October.
Tel: 01730 825415
www.nationaltrust.org.uk

THE VYNE

A fine house with classical interiors

The Staircase Hall at The Vyne, designed by John Chute in 1770.

Built in the early 16th century for Lord Sandys, Henry VIII's Lord Chamberlain, The Vyne later became home to the Chute family, in whose possession it remained for over 300 years. A classical portico was added to the house in the mid 17th century, the first of its kind in England, and a Palladian staircase was built in the late 18th century. Other significant features include a charming Tudor chapel complete with Renaissance stained glass, and an abundance of old panelling, textiles, paintings and fine 18th-century furniture. *SH*

The Vyne is 4 miles north of Basingstoke, Hampshire, between Bramley and Sherborne St John. It is owned by the National Trust and open on selected days from March to the end of October.
Tel: 01256 883858
www.nationaltrust. org.uk

WADDESDON MANOR

A Victorian house built in the style of a French château

WEST WYCOMBE PARK

A neoclassical mansion

Waddesdon Manor was built in 1874–89 for Baron Ferdinand de Rothschild in the style of a Renaissance French chateau. It houses one of the finest collections of 18th-century French decorative arts in the world, including exquisite Beauvais tapestries, Savonnerie carpets and Sèvres porcelain. The interiors include authentic French wood panelling and fireplaces, and some fine furniture, including a marquetry writing table made for Queen Marie Antoinette of France. There is a magnificent silver dinner service made for George III, and the collection of paintings by Gainsborough, Reynolds and 17th-century Dutch and Flemish masters rivals some of the finest museum collections in the world. *SH*

This neoclassical mansion is surrounded by a beautiful rococo landscape garden that was created in the mid 18th century by Sir Francis Dashwood, a founder member of the Dilettanti Society and the Hellfire Club. The exterior is highly theatrical and Italianate, with porticoes on three sides. The richly decorated interior is also neoclassical: highlights include the hall and staircase, modelled on a Roman atrium, and the Blue Drawing Room, with a ceiling depicting the Triumph of Bacchus and Ariadne. There are numerous elegant marble fireplaces, a mahogany, walnut and satinwood staircase as well as fine tapestries, family portraits and exquisite 18th-century furniture. *SH*

Waddesdon Manor, designed by the French architect Hyppolyte Destailleur.

Waddesdon Manor is at Waddesdon, Buckinghamshire, off the A41, between Bicester and Aylesbury. It is owned by the National Trust and open on selected days from the end of March to the end of October.
Tel: 01296 653203
www.nationaltrust. org.uk

The South Front of West Wycombe Park, dating from 1747–51.

West Wycombe Park is at West Wycombe, Buckinghamshire, south of the A40. It is owned by the National Trust and open on selected days from the beginning of June to the end of August.
Tel: 01494 513569
www.nationaltrust.org.uk

SOUTH-WEST ENGLAND

Some of Britain's oldest houses dating back to the earliest times are to be found in South-West England. Subsequently the region has experienced every major architectural movement and style trend, as fortunes made from the wool trade in the Cotswolds and Wiltshire, agriculture in Dorset and Somerset, maritime activities in Devon and tin mining in Cornwall enabled the nation's best architects and most skilful craftsmen to be employed creating homes of taste and distinction.

All period styles from Tudor to the 20th century are well represented in South-West England: Trerice and Cotehele contain robust Tudor exuberance; Chastleton House is a Jacobean time capsule; Dyrham Park exudes Queen Anne elegance; No. 1 Royal Crescent appears gloriously Georgian; Lanhydrock conveys an eminently Victorian air; Castle Drogo, the last castle to be built in England, is impeccably Edwardian within; and inside Coleton Fishacre lies an immaculate Art Deco world. Many of these houses are now in the care of the National Trust, yet a surprising number remain in private hands, much loved, much cared-for family homes.

The one-time remoteness of much of the region, together with little lasting major industry or large-scale urban development, has enabled many of these houses to remain much as they were when first built, their surroundings still unspoilt, transfixed in the memory bank of time. *PB*

ANTONY

An excellent late Queen Anne mansion

Towards the end of Queen Anne's reign, Sir William Carew married a rich heiress and began to create his dream house. Built in soft grey stone, Antony remains an outstanding example of an early 18th-century house in idyllic surroundings, lived in by the Carew family for more than 600 years. Oak-panelled reception rooms cluster around a magnificently grand staircase, and there are many fine paintings, most particularly Edward Bower's powerful portrayal of Charles I at his trial. It's well worth going to Antony for this alone. *PB*

Antony is 2 miles north-west of Torpoint, Cornwall. It is owned by the National Trust and open on selected days from the end of March to the end of October.
Tel: 01752 812191
www.nationaltrust.org.uk

The saloon at Antony where much of the furniture dates from when the house was built in the early 18th century.

ATHELHAMPTON HOUSE

An early Tudor mansion

This house, originally built by a wealthy ship owner shortly after the Battle of Bosworth in 1485, is one of England's earliest-surviving Tudor mansions, remaining in private ownership for over 500 years. It stands amidst Grade I listed gardens containing a large group of pyramid yew topiary – one of the wonders of the horticultural world. Inside, the Great Hall is equally impressive with its magnificent timbered roof, intricately carved 16th-century refectory table, minstrels' gallery and huge tapestry portraying Samson slaying 1,000 Philistines with the jawbone of an ass. *PB*

The façade of the early Tudor house framed by the giant topiary around the Great Court.

Athelhampton House is 5 miles east of Dorchester, Dorset, off the A35. It is privately owned and open on selected days all year.
Tel: 01305 848363
www.athelhampton. co.uk

CASTLE DROGO

An Edwardian fortress

A watercolour of Castle Drogo from the west, painted by Cyril Farey in 1924.

Julius Drewe was an archetypal self-made millionaire who wished to become a country gentleman. He persuaded himself that he was related to a Norman baron named Drogo de Teign, whose descendants lived at Drewsteignton in Devon. Here, in 1910, he began to build a castle looking out over the wilds of Dartmoor, an area of a certain bleak beauty in good weather.

Over the entrance is the Drewe heraldic lion and the family motto.

Drogo is a 'designer' castle, a great country house disguised as a rugged fortress, created by Edwin Lutyens, the most eminent architect of the Edwardian era, and a fastidious, whimsical, intensely romantic man. The house took 20 years to complete in spite of being only one third its originally intended size. By then, Drewe had lost his eldest son in the First World War, suffered a stroke and had only a year to live.

The heraldic Drewe lion proudly guards the entrance in the massive gateway tower. The interior appears somewhat spartan, with its bare granite walls, unpainted woodwork, suitably baronial hall and towering vaulted staircase. Yet Lutyens' immaculate taste and impeccable eye for detail features everywhere. Notice the lion on the iron door-latch in the entrance hall, the kitchen where he designed all the furniture including the circular beechwood table, and the elaborate shower in Drewe's bathroom.

Castle Drogo represents the nation's eccentric side. The last castle to be built in England, at a time when the Chrysler Building and the Rockefeller Centre were appearing in New York, it's hardly directional architecture or cutting-edge design – yet does that really matter? *PB*

Castle Drogo is at Drewsteignton, 5 miles south of the A30 between Exeter and Okehampton, Devon. It is owned by the National Trust and open on selected days from March to November.
Tel: 01647 433306
www.nationaltrust.org.uk

CHASTLETON HOUSE

A fine Jacobean mansion

Robert Catesby, leader of the Gunpowder Plot, once owned the estate at Chastleton. The family subsequently lost all their money in the Civil War, preventing any alterations or adaptations, so Chastleton has remained in a glorious Jacobean time warp, with original 17th-century plasterwork, pictures, tapestries and furniture. It is said to be the most authentic house of its period, externally and internally, to be found anywhere in England. The surrounding countryside represents the Cotswolds at their best. *PB*

Chastleton House is in Chastleton, Oxfordshire, 6 miles north-east of Stow-on-the-Wold. It is owned by the National Trust and open on selected days from the end of March to the end of October.
Tel: 01494 755560
www.nationaltrust.org.uk

CHAVENAGE

A highly unusual mid 16th-century manor house

The view of this mellow grey Cotswold-stone Elizabethan house down a long avenue of trees has changed little since the house was built in the mid 16th century. Only two families have owned this isolated property, a place of mystery, with tales of sinister happenings and headless ghosts. Pride of place goes to the bedrooms where Oliver Cromwell and his Civil War colleague, Henry Ireton, reputedly slept; the walls of both rooms are hung with large and highly decorative 17th-century Mortlake and Flemish tapestries. *PB*

Chavenage is 2 miles north-west of Tetbury, Gloucestershire. It is privately owned and open on selected days between May and September (also at Easter and on bank holidays).
Tel: 01666 502329
www.chavenage.com

The rear exterior of Chastleton on a crisp December morning with frost-covered topiary.

Tapestries cover the walls of Cromwell's Bedroom; these were as much for warmth as decoration.

COLETON FISHACRE

Arts and Crafts meets Art Deco

The South Front, with its slate roof, Dartmoor shale stone walls and leaded casement windows.

The dining room, with its Art Deco furniture.

Coleton Fishacre is set in glorious semi-tropical gardens which slope down to the sea across the estuary from Dartmouth. It was built for Rupert D'Oyly Carte, whose impresario father had made a fortune producing Gilbert and Sullivan operettas. In spring, the scent of the azaleas, bluebells and wild garlic near the seashore is magical.

The house is full of surprises. The exterior is seemingly Arts and Crafts style and appears to be the work of the eminent architect Sir Edwin Lutyens, with trademark mullioned windows, steeply pitched roof and rough stone walls – pure Arts and Crafts Movement. Yet Coleton Fishacre's architect was Oswald Milne, a follower of Lutyens, and it was built in the mid 1920s.

The interior is essentially Art Deco, with bold geometric rugs, tulip uplighters, hexagonal ceiling lights and pictorially tiled bathrooms by Edward Bawden. Everything is decorative and highly directional – interior design had suddenly become high fashion. Semicircular stairs sweep down from the entrance hall under an Art Deco arch into the large saloon – perfect for making a grand entrance in a slinky dress and cloche hat, waving a long cigarette holder. In the corner stands a Bluthner grand piano.

Coleton Fishacre was essentially a pleasure house rather than a permanent home, a fun place where it was perpetually party time. *PB*

Coleton Fishacre is 3 miles east of Kingswear, near Dartmouth, Devon. It is owned by the National Trust and open on selected days from the end of March to the end of October.
Tel: 01803 752466
www.nationaltrust.org.uk

COTEHELE

A fine example of a Tudor home

If the estate agents' mantra 'location, location, location' is true, Cotehele succeeds on all counts, standing high up on the slopes of the tranquil Tamar Valley and looking down through trees at the slow-moving river below.

The original small medieval manor house was considerably enlarged in the late 17th century by Richard Edgcumbe, who had fought alongside Henry Tudor at the Battle of Bosworth and benefited accordingly. Richard's son Piers further extended Cotehele, but by the late 16th century the family preferred to live in their altogether grander property at Mount Edgcumbe overlooking Plymouth Sound, conveniently close to the city and far more congenial to the fashionable society of the day. Thereafter, Cotehele was little used and went into

A view of part of the East Front approached up steep flights of steps.

The interior of the late 15th-century Great Hall with a long refectory table and limewashed walls festooned with ancient arms and armour.

Eurydice, poisoned by a snake, from an Antwerp tapestry dating from about 1700.

A pair of ebony chairs in the Old Dining Room, displayed in front of one of the many tapestries to be found at Cotehele.

virtual hibernation for more than 200 years until it was acquired by the National Trust in 1947, its romantic medieval atmosphere having been preserved by neglect.

The first sight of Cotehele's grey granite crenellated gatehouse, its doorway just wide enough to admit a loaded packhorse, is across a lush meadow strewn with daffodils in early spring, when the extensive gardens are awash with a profusion of primroses, magnolias, rhododendrons and azaleas.

The evocative late medieval atmosphere of Cotehele is immediately apparent as one steps inside the Great Hall with its momentous arch-braced timber roof, which has seven bays in

all, a style traditional to the West Country. The plain limewashed walls are covered with ancient arms and armour, originally placed there as much for defence as decoration. The late 15th-century glass of the windows that light the hall are emblazoned with the arms of other West-Country families into which the Edgcumbes married – a roll-call of the region's great and good, such as the Raleighs, Courtenays, Carews, Tremaynes and Fitzwalters. The long refectory table and elaborately carved oak chairs conjure up visions of the joyous banquets that would frequently have taken place here.

Beyond the Great Hall lie the family rooms, mostly small and rather dark,

approached by steep flights of well-worn steps, through heavy oak doors set in robust granite archways. The walls of many of these rooms are covered with tapestries, mainly Flemish, largely 17th-century; their colours are now much faded, adding to the dim, mysterious atmosphere that prevails throughout Cotehele, particularly on dull days, there being no artificial light in the old rooms. The subject matter of the tapestries varies greatly, ranging from cheerful naked cherubs treading grapes, in the delightful Punch Room on the ground floor, to the violent scene of Romulus murdering Remus, in the Red Room upstairs. A series of

A walnut bed, probably from Goa, in the White Bedroom, which takes its name from the curtains and bed hangings.

Detail from the bed hangings in the White Bedroom – 18th-century crewelwork, embroidered on a linen backing.

Mortlake tapestries in King Charles's Room on the first floor depicts the tragic love story of Hero and Leander, culminating in Leander drowning in the treacherous waters of the Hellespont. This room owes its name to the belief that Charles I slept here in September 1644, while

The Old Dining Room, hung with tapestries depicting the story of Circe.

found at Cotehele, the others being Hall Court, which is inside the gate-house, and Retainers' Court, where Richard Edgcumbe's chapel lies. The chapel contains the oldest-working domestic clock in England, installed on its completion somewhere between 1485 and 1489. The kitchen has enormous height to allow smoke and unwelcome smells to dissipate, and a huge hearth, more than 10ft (3m) wide. The oval-shaped oven is almost as large and there are huge iron cooking pots and kettles dangling from hooks over the fire.

Cotehele's attraction is considerably enhanced by its exquisite, isolated setting. The ideal way to appreciate this is to approach by river as Queen Victoria did in 1865. 'As we proceeded the scenery became quite beautiful – richly wooded hills, the trees growing down into the water, and the river winding so much as to have the effect of a lake.' Gliding upstream on a rising tide, this is just as true today. *PB*

en route from Liskeard to Exeter. If Charles actually slept in all the places quoted, he would have spent most of his life in bed, but this particular tale has some credibility as Charles had successfully campaigned in Cornwall at that time and the Edgcumbes were strongly Royalist. The room contains a substantial four-poster bed and a mirror on the chest by the window with a polished metal plate for reflection – looking glass being extremely rare before the mid 17th century.

Cotehele's kitchen is located behind the Great Hall overlooking Kitchen Court, one of three courtyards to be

'RULES TO BE STRICTLY OBSERVED'
A noticeboard in the kitchen at Cotehele includes the stern instruction, 'Men at breakfast be allowed one pint of Beer or Cyder each, at Dinner and Supper Men and Maids a pint each and Strangers a quart, no other drinking whatsoever in the Hall or any other parts of the House or out Houses under one Shilling forfeit to each offender.'

Cotehele is 14 miles north-west of Plymouth, Devon. It is owned by the National Trust and open on selected days from late March to the end of October.
Tel: 01579 352739
www.nationaltrust.org.uk

COTHAY MANOR

An early Tudor manor house

The manor house little-altered since it was built in the 15th century.

Often described as the most perfect 15th-century house in England, Cothay's real fascination lies in its copious detail. The corbels of the massive trusses in the Great Hall are wingless angels carrying shields. The oak chimneypiece in the dining room contains richly carved figures of Plato's Four Cardinal Virtues, while the stone fireplace carries a rare carving of a six-pointed star, once thought to prevent witches coming down the chimney. The altar cross in the exquisite tiny oratory is 17th-century Spanish colonial and the Gold Room features a medieval fresco of the Madonna and Child. *PB*

Cothay Manor is at Greenham, off the A38, 3¹/₂ miles west of Wellington, Somerset. It is privately owned and open all year (only to pre-booked groups of 20 or more).
Tel: 01823 672283

DUNSTER CASTLE

A Victorian vision of a medieval castle

High up on the edge of Exmoor lies this one-time Norman castle with far-reaching views over Exmoor. Badly damaged when besieged by Cromwell during the Civil War, it was restored by Anthony Salvin as a medieval fantasy castle during the Victorian era. Dunster's most impressive feature is the massive, heavily carved late 17th-century oak staircase, depicting naked cherubs and hunting dogs pursuing the fox through the thick acanthus undergrowth. Dunster epitomizes the romantic Victorian vision of a medieval castle, yet with modern conveniences – its bathroom was supposedly the first in Somerset. *PB*

The Outer Hall looking towards the two stone archways.

Dunster Castle is in the village of Dunster, 3 miles south-east of Minehead, Somerset. It is owned by the National Trust and open on selected days from March to the end of October.
Tel: 01643 823004
www.nationaltrust. org.uk

DYRHAM PARK

A magnificent Queen Anne mansion

William Blathwayt was a high-flyer in the late 17th-century Civil Service, serious, solemn, energetic and ultra-efficient – 'very dextrous in business', according to the diarist John Evelyn. He rose to become Secretary of State after the Dutchman William of Orange became William III, following the Glorious Revolution of 1688. Blathwayt was fluent in Dutch, a language he had mastered whilst working for the British Ambassador in the Hague. He also loved Dutch culture. After marrying the heiress to the Somerset estate of Dyrham, Blathwayt engaged an unknown French architect named Hauduroy, who constructed a simple yet attractive two-storey building, which was completed in 1694.

Blathwayt then obtained a lucrative position at the Board of Trade. He had made the big time and, determined to commission a big-name architect to complete his grand design, engaged William Talman, the architect of Dutch extraction who remodelled Chatsworth. Talman was a court architect, Comptroller of the Royal Works, second only to Sir Christopher Wren – and he was just the man to fulfil Blathwayt's dream.

By 1704 Dyrham was complete and the following year Blathwayt's eagle crest was hoisted aloft for all to see. He filled the house with Dutch furniture, paintings and distinctive blue-and-white Delft china. Blathwayt also constructed an enormous Dutch-style

Detail of the embossed leather hangings in the East Hall. Bought in the Hague, they were hung in 1702 and have darkened considerably with age.

The elegant West Front of Dyrham Park.

water garden in the park containing numerous fountains and a cascade with 224 steps. Sadly, all that is left is a giant statue of Neptune looking slightly out of place high on the hill above the house.

The word 'Dyrham' derives from the Saxon '*Deor Hamm*', meaning an enclosed valley frequented by deer. Today, visitors descend a steep winding drive past a large herd of fallow deer before catching sight of Talman's elegant East Front. The simply proportioned façade, with classical columns and flat roof concealed behind a parapet, echoes Wren's South Front at Hampton Court Palace, yet hardly represents the cutting-edge architecture that Vanbrugh and Hawksmoor were creating at Castle Howard (p 220) at the same time. Nevertheless, Dyrham represents a pleasing example of English Baroque.

Three hundred years later Dyrham remains largely as Blathwayt left it. A unique feature of the house is that it remains so unaltered in appearance, with the majority of the contents dating from the early 18th century when Queen Anne had succeeded to the throne. Blathwayt's portrait and that of his wife Mary hang either side of the fireplace in the Great Hall. Sadly, she died before the new house was begun. Blathwayt never remarried and kept the upstairs Tapestry Room as a shrine to her, complete with her hairbrushes, combs and pincushions.

In the Great Hall, Blathwayt laid a sprung floor of Flemish oak for dancing – its richly polished surface displays a splendid sheen. His bookcases were almost identical to those

of Samuel Pepys – supposedly the inventor of the bookcase. The Great Hall is a lovely room, though what Blathwayt would have thought of the 19th-century flock wallpaper or the panelling, painted white in 1938, is a matter of conjecture.

More satisfying is the walnut staircase that Blathwayt installed, using wood imported from Virginia in the USA, where at one time he had been Auditor General. This staircase leads to the state apartments in the West Range. The concept of a linked suite of formal rooms originated at the court of King Louis XIV of France. By the end of the 17th century this

This late 17th-century parlour chair, one of 14 in the drawing room, is decorated with white-painted putti, a French characteristic typical of the period.

The Diogenes Room, with its superb late 17th-century tapestries, made in either the Soho or Mortlake factories, and distinctive Dutch blue-and-white delftware.

was de rigueur in grand new country houses such as Dyrham.

In the Balcony Room, the eye-catching pair of candlestands supported by chained black slaves indicates another of Blathwayt's sources of income – nearby Bristol being a major port for the 18th-century slave trade. Note the intricately crafted brass door locks decorated with daffodils and tulips, created about 1694.

Beyond the library in the East Range hangs van Hoogstraeten's extraordinary *trompe l'œil* 'A View Down a Corridor', much admired by Samuel Pepys and mentioned in his diary – the birdcage is particularly realistic! In the Damask Bedchamber is a spectacular crimson-and-yellow bed, originally made for an anticipated visit by Queen Anne. Alas, she never came and the bed has never been used. Next door is the Diogenes Room, named after its magnificent late 17th-century tapestry, depicting Alexander the Great encountering the Greek philosopher. Here is a superb pair of Delft urns, presented to Blathwayt by William and Mary, together with two rare pyramid blue-and-white tulip vases – not to be missed!

Blathwayt was considered to be extremely dull and was given the nickname 'the elephant' on account of

being so ponderous. Nevertheless, he created an admirable house whose contents indicate considerable taste. Dyrham is a joy to visit, giving a unique insight into that period of time when the nation went Dutch. *PB*

Dyrham Park is near Chippenham, Wiltshire, 8 miles north of Bath, off the A46. It is owned by the National Trust and open on selected days from the end of March to the end of October.
Tel: 01179 372501
www.nationaltrust.org.uk

This ornate giltwood Georgian mirror and console table can be found in the drawing room at Dyrham.

KELMSCOTT MANOR

The Arts and Crafts country home of William Morris

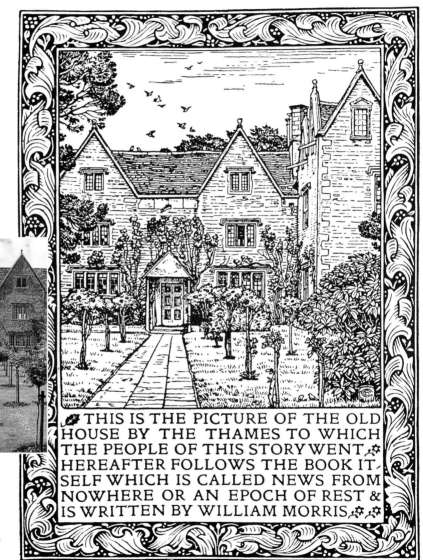

THIS IS THE PICTURE OF THE OLD HOUSE BY THE THAMES TO WHICH THE PEOPLE OF THIS STORY WENT. HEREAFTER FOLLOWS THE BOOK IT SELF WHICH IS CALLED NEWS FROM NOWHERE OR AN EPOCH OF REST & IS WRITTEN BY WILLIAM MORRIS.

The woodcut frontispiece of William Morris's book *News from Nowhere*, engraved in 1892, together with a photograph of the East Front of the manor as it is today.

In 1871 William Morris and his friend Dante Gabriel Rossetti, the charismatic leader of the Pre-Raphaelite Brotherhood, leased a Tudor farmhouse on the outskirts of the small village of Kelmscott, Gloucestershire, close to the dreamy upper reaches of the River Thames. This was to be Morris's idyllic holiday home for the rest of his life.

Here Rossetti set up his easel in the Tapestry Room and conducted a passionate affair with Morris's beautiful wife Jane. See Rossetti's shimmering, romantic portrait of Jane, entitled *The Blue Silk Dress*, now hanging in the Closet, to sense the sheer intensity of their love. Rossetti had first encountered Jane at Oxford when she was only 18, the daughter of a stablehand. Jane's sensual beauty and mystical air completely captivated Rossetti, who drew and painted her obsessively. Their relationship ended after Rossetti suffered a mental breakdown and returned to London.

Approach the manor through the garden gate, across a lawn covered with rose trees, the soft grey limestone house peering out through heavily mullioned windows beneath soaring gables. The gardens at Kelmscott have been much improved in recent years, and are a total delight, with vine-covered pergola, superb herbaceous borders and an enormous ancient mulberry tree – look out for the highly unusual triple-seated water closet in a small building in the back garden, which gives such amusement to visitors. It was in Kelmscott's garden that Morris supposedly saw a thrush stealing a strawberry, inspiring his well-known fabric design 'Strawberry Thief'. Faded chintz depicting this motif now hangs in the house, in the Old Hall.

Kelmscott's interior is cool and intimate, the walls mostly painted white according to the fashion of the late 19th century; only Jane and William's bedrooms feature archetypal Morris wallpaper. Jane's bedroom is decorated with the ever popular 'Willow Boughs' design, first developed by

Philip Webb's ebonized wood settle, the curved hood decorated with flowers painted on hand-tooled leather.

Morris in 1887. This design is also used on the chintz hangings of the early 19th-century four-poster bed, in which Morris had been born in 1834 in Walthamstow. In Morris's room there is an impressive 17th-century oak four-poster bed, with a distinctive valance embroidered by William and Jane's daughter May, who also embroidered the curtains around the bed, using Morris's 1864 'Trellis' design, incorporating birds drawn by Philip Webb. The heavy wooden bookcase was also designed by Webb; beside it is a delicate, sensitive pencil

Jane Morris's bedroom with an early 19th-century four-poster bed.

drawing of Morris on his deathbed, by Charles Fairfax-Murray, which should not be missed.

The workaholic Morris was virtually a one-man design studio – and Kelmscott a show house of his work. In the lobby of the Panelled Room hangs *Cabbage and Vine*, the glorious tapestry designed and woven by Morris in 1878. He firmly believed in the medieval principle that design and craft were synonymous and would not design anything he could not make himself. Thus he taught himself to

weave and embroider. Discover the Green Room where the tiles, wall hangings and sofa covers are all Morris's designs. Philip Webb's sturdy yet stylish furniture is much in evidence here. Webb originally

created the settle in the Garden Hall
for Red House (p 42), the Morris's
first home after their marriage in
1859. Fashioned out of ebonized
wood, the settle has a carved hood
and floral decoration on the panels.
In the Green Room the dining table
demonstrates Webb's preoccupation
with medievalism, a characteristic he
shared with William Morris and
the Pre-Raphaelites.

Morris and his friends in the Arts and
Crafts Movement acutely disliked
modern mass-production techniques
and the inevitable decline in craftsmanship, preferring to take their
inspiration from original domestic
vernacular tradition, much in evidence
at Kelmscott. Don't fail to seek out
Ernest Gimson's wonderful pair of
rush-seated ladder-back chairs, discovered under the stage of Kelmscott's
village hall. The village hall was also
designed by Gimson, as a memorial to
Morris after his death in 1896, and it
was opened by George Bernard Shaw.
The dramatist was then at the peak
of his fame and such were the
crowds that crammed into the hall
that Ramsay Macdonald, the
Prime Minister of the day, had to
stand outside.

Kelmscott is brimming with the
creativity of Morris and his
Pre-Raphaelite and Arts and Crafts
Movement friends. The house exudes
such a profound sense of peace, so
timeless, so redolent with the spirit of
Morris, that if his distinctive bearded
figure suddenly appeared you would
not be the slightest bit surprised. *PB*

The bearded William
Morris surrounded by his
staff at Kelmscott Press,
the firm he founded in
1890 to produce beauti-
fully decorated books.

Kelmscott Manor is 2½ miles east of
Lechlade, Gloucestershire, off the A417. It is
owned by the Society of Antiquaries and open
on selected days from April to September.
Tel: 01367 252486
www.kelmscottmanor.co.uk

A servant's bed in the
attic. The simple furniture
was created by the Pre-
Raphaelite artist
Ford Madox Brown.

KINGSTON LACY

An elegant mansion with Victorian interiors

A view of Kingston Lacy's South Front and distinctive glazed cupola.

The upper marble staircase and top landing.

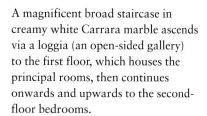

Hugely impressive from the outside, some houses can be acutely disappointing within – not so Kingston Lacy: its façade is delightful, its interior divine. Sometimes when an owner engages one eminent architect to update the work of another, the result can be a disaster. Not true of Kingston Lacy: Sir Charles Barry's addition of a balustrade and jaunty cupola to Roger Pratt's original Restoration building works well, and his transformation of the interior into a Venetian Renaissance palazzo is sublime.

A magnificent broad staircase in creamy white Carrara marble ascends via a loggia (an open-sided gallery) to the first floor, which houses the principal rooms, then continues onwards and upwards to the second-floor bedrooms.

Kingston Lacy's outstanding art collection, accumulated in the mid 19th century by the owner William Bankes, rivals many of the nation's leading galleries: works by Titian, Velázquez, Raphael, Reubens, Van Dyck, Lawrence, Romney and Reynolds all jostle for attention. Awaiting inspection in the dining room is the greatest of them all, Sebastiano del Piombo's superb unfinished masterpiece, *The Judgement of Solomon.*

The true glory of Kingston Lacy is the Spanish Room, which has walls hung in glossy tooled and painted leather, and a lavish gilt and coffered ceiling. Both were copied from palazzos along the Grand Canal in Venice and were intended to enhance Bankes's collection of Spanish paintings. Kingston Lacy remains the perfect English country house – albeit with strong Continental connections. *PB*

Kingston Lacy is 2 miles north-west of Wimborne Minster, Dorset. It is owned by the National Trust and open on selected days from March to the end of October.
Tel: 01202 880413
www.nationaltrust.org.uk

KNIGHTSHAYES COURT

A Victorian house with interiors by William Burges

The library, with its elaborate ceiling and restored walnut shelving.

John Heathcoat-Amory soon regretted engaging William Burges, a fanatical disciple of Medievalism, to create Knightshayes during the late 19th century. Burges's interior design proposals were considered far too flamboyant and costly and he flounced off in high dudgeon, with little of his grandiose Gothic dream realized, leaving behind a detailed portfolio of plans. Today the National Trust is fulfilling Burges's vision, aided by his original portfolio. The attention-seeking technicolour Romanticism of Knightshayes is an acquired taste, yet provides an intriguing insight into High Victorian style. The gardens are simply wonderful. *PB*

Knightshayes Court is at Bolham, 2 miles north of Tiverton, Devon, off the A396. It is owned by the National Trust and open on selected days from the end of March to the end of October.
Tel: 01884 257381
www.nationaltrust. org.uk

MOST GOTHIC OF GOTHICISTS
William Burges was a passionate medievalist driven by a mission to establish a new style of Victorian architecture based on French Gothic style rather than the English version favoured by Augustus Pugin or the Italian Gothic of John Ruskin. Burges pursued this as an architectural Holy Grail, refusing to compromise his beliefs in any way. Burges, like the poet Coleridge, was an opium addict – something which conceivably explains his most hallucinatory designs. He was frustrated by Sir John Heathcoat-Amory, yet indulged by Lord Bute at Cardiff Castle (p 238) and Castell Coch (p 239). Burges created some of the most bizarre and lavish interiors of the 19th century and was totally unconcerned about their cost. Fortunately, Lord Bute was then the richest man in the world.

A view of the Smoking Room, created as 'an apartment specially dedicated to the use of tobacco'.

LANHYDROCK

A late Victorian masterpiece

A view of the East Front, built from local granite.

In the spring of 1881 a disastrous fire gutted much of this large granite-built house – all apart from the North Wing, the two-storey entrance porch and the stylish gatehouse. The owner's wife, Lady Robartes, died of shock; her husband never recovered from the loss of both his home and his wife and passed away the following year. It was left to their eldest son Thomas to rebuild Lanhydrock, a house originally created in the 17th century. Very cleverly, the exterior was fashioned to blend seamlessly with the surviving Jacobean North Wing, whilst the interior incorporated all the modern services that an elegant Victorian country house might require, including central heating, and it fully encapsulates the decorative taste of the era.

Lanhydrock's heyday was essentially the last decade of the 19th century, a time of affluence and self-confidence amongst the most privileged classes.

Inscription on the gate piers at Newton Lodge which stands at one of the entrances to Lanhydrock. The date, 1657, refers to the year that the park was completed.

Thomas, 2nd Lord Robartes, rebuilt the house primarily for enjoyment and entertainment, and Lanhydrock's hospitality was renowned far and wide. There were elaborate dinner parties, fancy dress balls, theatricals and concerts. Games of cricket took place regularly in the extensive grounds together with frequent shooting parties.

Entertainment on such a grand scale required an army of servants and extensive service facilities. 'For housemaid ring once, stillroom and dairymaid twice, kitchen maid three times,' proclaims a helpful notice in the Butler's Pantry Corridor. One of the most fascinating features of Lanhydrock today is how skilfully conditions 'below stairs' have been recreated in the kitchen, scullery, dairy, bakehouse and numerous larders. The kitchen is particularly intriguing, its high gabled roof and large mullioned windows reminiscent

The view down the atmospheric corridor running the entire length of the South Wing. The colourful floor tiles, dating from about 1881, are Minton.

A close-up of the barrel-vaulted ceiling in the Long Gallery, depicting a scene from Noah's ark.

of a college hall at Oxford or Cambridge. The floor is stone flagged, in the centre stands a long wooden table, and around the walls is an impressive collection of implements and utensils. There is also an elaborate arrangement of roasting spits. Here cook could have been assisted by as many as a dozen other servants. Today the kitchen evokes the feeling of early morning in high summer, not long after dawn, calm and deserted, before the first chambermaid bustles

in to boil a kettle for her ladyship's pot of tea.

Her Ladyship's Bedroom on the first floor enjoys a splendid view over immaculately clipped lawns and yew trees to the gatehouse, with Bodmin Moor on the far horizon. Much of the contents of her room, including some fine porcelain, are original. Between her room and His Lordship's Bedroom is the bathroom. The enormous cast-iron bath with its overlarge

A servant's bedroom, fitted out with brass bedstead, armchair, footstool and Victorian washstand.

taps and chunky mahogany rim is so deep that it required steps to climb into and appears even more difficult to emerge from – no wonder the 2nd Lord Robartes preferred to luxuriate in a saucer bath, cosily placed in front of his bedroom fire. Meanwhile, guests had to rely on servants bringing jugs of hot water for hip baths in their rooms.

A particularly evocative room at Lanhydrock is the Jacobean Long Gallery, 116ft (35m) overall, on the first floor of the North Wing; the superb barrel-vaulted plaster ceiling was completed just before the outbreak of the Civil War, in which the then owner, John Robartes, unlike most of the Cornish gentry, fought for the Parliamentarians. Meanwhile Lanhydrock was captured by Royalist troops. The ceiling is embellished with 24 separate panels depicting scenes from the Old Testament – notice how these are surrounded by delightful

The Bakehouse with its red-brick fireplace and ovens which took four days to heat up to the correct temperature.

images of bears, armadillos and porcupines, together with mythical beasts such as centaurs and dragons. The overmantel above the fireplace on the south side also has a plasterwork frieze featuring biblical scenes. Family portraits by artists such as Kneller, Romney and Thomas Hudson line the oak-panelled walls. The Long Gallery was originally intended as a place for taking exercise in bad weather. Today, particularly when sunshine floods through the huge mullioned windows, it is a place of grace and tranquillity, offering excellent views of the formal gardens below, whose colourful parterres are best observed from above.

The 2nd Lord and Lady Robartes produced ten children and Lanhydrock had an entire purpose-built wing devoted to them, together with their attendant nannies and nursemaids. Here can be found the Day Nursery full of Victorian toys, including a Noah's ark and a doll's house, the

Night Nursery, with lace-canopied cots, the nursery scullery, bathroom and nanny's bedroom, well furnished as befitted her status as a valued senior member of the household.

The Robartes divided their time between Wimpole Hall (p 193), then the largest house in Cambridgeshire, their splendid London residence, and Lanhydrock, which they called their 'Cornish country cottage'. Do not be misled by this masterly understatement. Almost 50 rooms are now open to the public at Lanhydrock and plenty of time will be required to appreciate fully this Cornish masterpiece of late Victorian gracious living. *PB*

Lanhydrock is off the A38, 2½ miles southeast of Bodmin, Cornwall. It is owned by the National Trust and open on selected days from the end of March to the end of October.
Tel: 01208 265950
www.nationaltrust.org.uk

IN MEMORIAM

Thomas Robartes, the eldest son of the 2nd Lord Robartes, was killed in action whilst serving with the Coldstream Guards on the Western Front during the First World War. His death devastated the family and they preserved his room at Lanhydrock as a memorial to him, complete with the travelling case and its contents which he took to France.

LONGLEAT

A 16th-century mansion with Victorian interiors

J.D. Crace's saloon created in 1875 from the original Long Gallery. The marble fireplace is a copy of one in the Doge's Palace in Venice.

Built by Sir John Thynne in the mid 16th century and now owned by the engagingly eccentric 7th Marquess of Bath, Longleat is widely considered to be one of the finest examples of English Renaissance architecture. Its Tudor exterior is virtually as conceived by Robert Smythson, while the interior is a riot of Victorian-Italianate grandeur, bringing the glories of Rome and Venice to Wiltshire. The two concepts harmonize surprisingly well together: both are larger than life – just like Longleat's owner. *PB*

Longleat is 5 miles south-west of Warminster, Wiltshire, off the A36. It is owned by the Marquess of Bath and open all year.
Tel: 01985 844400
www.longleat.co.uk

MOMPESSON HOUSE

A Queen Anne town house with Georgian interiors

In 1701 Charles Mompesson, a local lawyer and Member of Parliament, created this elegant baroque town house on the north side of Cathedral Close, Salisbury. The house has remained virtually unchanged for three centuries and its interior features spectacular plasterwork: the ceiling of the Staircase Hall depicts the head of King Midas, whilst upstairs in the Green Room an eagle with outstretched wings awaits take-off. The elegant dining room contains a Hepplewhite table, Sèvres china and 18th-century drinking glasses. *PB*

Mompesson House is in Cathedral Close, in the centre of Salisbury, Wiltshire. It is owned by the National Trust and open on selected days from April to the end of October.
Tel: 01722 420980
www.nationaltrust.org.uk

The dining room with some of Mompesson's renowned collection of 18th-century glasses.

MONTACUTE HOUSE

A typically Elizabethan mansion

Built of local honey-coloured stone, Montacute positively glows when the sun shines. Built in the final years of the reign of Elizabeth I, when all England basked in the glory of the Armada's defeat, it is a magnificent house, whether viewed from the long tree-lined drive or from the landscaped park at the rear.

Montacute is the archetypal Tudor house with tall, delicate chimneys, pinnacles, curvaceous gables and vast glittering windows. In the formal garden, beyond outstanding herbaceous borders, stand a pair of handsome Elizabethan pavilions, originally designed for gambling and dining.

STYLE AND SUBSTANCE

'Elizabethan Great Houses', also known as 'prodigy houses', were the major status symbol of the day, where the proud owners could flaunt their success. Montacute House was built for Sir Edward Phelips, who wanted to show that a fortune could be made by successfully practising the law. At Longleat (p 111), Sir John Thynne demonstrated his rise from a clerk in the royal kitchen to a rich knight of the realm. Bess of Hardwick (*see* Hardwick Hall, p 145) moved via four successive husbands from humble beginnings to become one of the wealthiest and most well-connected people in the kingdom.

The elaborate carved Ham-stone entrance on the West Front.

In the Great Hall, morning sunshine casts coloured pools of light through rich heraldic glass and two rare 17th-century plaster friezes depict village life. In one, a henpecked husband is scolded by his wife for drinking beer whilst minding the baby. Elsewhere there are fine original chimneypieces and plasterwork together with 17th- and 18th-century furniture.

Elm and walnut X-frame folding chair in the dining room at Montacute.

On the second floor is the longest Elizabethan Long Gallery in Britain – it is 172ft (52m) long and displays Tudor and Jacobean pictures. For a penetrating insight into late Tudor style Montacute is essential viewing. *PB*

ODE TO ELINOR

The eminent politician Lord Curzon, former Viceroy of India, leased Montacute in the early 20th century, sharing it for a while with his mistress, the exotic Elinor Glyn. An anonymous wit wrote:

Would you like to sin
with Elinor Glyn
on a tiger skin?
Or would you prefer
to err with her
on some other fur?

Montacute House is in the village of Montacute, off the A3088, 4 miles west of Yeovil, Somerset. It is owned by the National Trust and open on selected days from March to the end of October.
Tel: 01935 823289
www.nationaltrust.org.uk

PENCARROW
An elegant Georgian country house

This graceful Georgian house has been lived in by the Molesworth St Aubyn family since it was built in the mid 18th century. Inside this well-loved family home is an eclectic mix of Victorian glass, period dolls and pushchairs, teddy bears and family portraits by Sir Joshua Reynolds. Another of its treasures is the Pencarrow Bowl, an exquisite piece of porcelain depicting an English hunting scene, created to celebrate the completion of the house. The lovely entrance hall and music room retain their original Georgian panelled walls and embellished ceilings. *PB*

Pencarrow is 4 miles north-west of Bodmin, Cornwall, off the A389 and B3266 at Washaway. It is privately owned and open from late March to late October.
Tel: 01208 841369
www.pencarrow.co.uk

The music room with its rococo ceiling, maple-grained panelling and graceful mouldings.

No. 1 ROYAL CRESCENT
A Georgian masterpiece

Step inside this hugely impressive five-storey town house, one of 30 in the Royal Crescent, and enter the elegant world of Georgian England. This was a time when the cream of society flocked to Bath in order to take the waters, gamble, drink, gossip, and generally have a good time, under the genial eye of Beau Nash, the city's flamboyant Master of Ceremonies and self-appointed arbiter of good taste.

Surprisingly, the Royal Crescent, a Palladian masterpiece completed by John Wood the Younger in 1774,

was originally a speculative property development, created to rent out to wealthy visitors intent on doing the season and willing to pay handsomely for fashionable surroundings. Today, No. 1 Royal Crescent is owned by the Bath Preservation Trust, which has restored and meticulously maintained it as it was in its Georgian heyday.

The graceful simplicity and precise symmetry of the exterior are reflected within, conveying a mood of relaxed elegance. The plasterwork, including cornices, friezes and wall-mouldings, is original throughout. There are

The elegant exterior of No. 1, the first of 30 houses in the sweeping curve of John Wood's Royal Crescent.

fine paintings on display by some of the best 18th-century British artists including George Stubbs, the nation's finest equestrian painter, Thomas Gainsborough, who once lived nearby in the Circus, and Allan Ramsey who had been appointed court painter to King George III in 1760.

Connoisseurs of mahogany furniture from the 18th-century, first popularized by Thomas Chippendale, will particularly admire the dining table laid out for dessert with Worcester porcelain, which was made in 1798 for a Mr Heathcote at No. 20 Royal Crescent. Also in the dining room is an elaborately carved Irish side table with fine ball-and-claw feet and an onyx top. In the study across the hall, a card table, dating from about 1760, is all set up for a game – gambling for high stakes was hugely popular with both men and women in a city which was the 18th-century equivalent of Las Vegas. Don't miss the delicately handpainted chair, discovered to be a Linnell when re-upholstered.

The ground-floor dining room has splendid views of the Royal Crescent.

In the basement, the kitchen is arranged to convey the cooking facilities of a typical Bath town house in the 18th century, displaying numerous Georgian pots and pans together with other period cooking equipment. The roasting spit over the fire was turned by a dog-wheel, with a luckless animal trained to run continuously within the wheel. The poet Robert Southey's laconic description of this barbaric activity was, 'the dog was put in the wheel, and a burning coal with him, he could not stop without burning his legs, and so was kept on the full gallop.' The Royal Society for the Prevention of Cruelty to Animals was not formed until 1824.

The study is painted a distinctive 'Zoffany blue'. The carpet dates from the 18th century and portraits in the the room are by Kneller and Gainsborough.

Arguably the most spectacular room in the house is the drawing room on the first floor – richly decorated as it was principally used for entertainment. The walls are covered with shimmering silk and cotton damask, dyed exactly to match the Axminster carpet, based on an Aubusson design, under an ornate cut-glass chandelier. Precise symmetry and refined harmony, coupled with carefully coordinated colours, are crucial elements in Georgian interior design. Thus the door between the sofa and the Carrara-marble chimneypiece is a false one, placed there purely to achieve balance with the real one on the opposite side. The pianoforte was made in 1798 and represents a superb example of a grand piano of the period. The overall feeling is one of elegant exuberance, combined with a sense of anticipation that the party is about to begin – well-attired gentlemen, witty and gallant, accompanied by glamorous ladies parading in the latest finery, with Jane Austen and Samuel Johnson providing the social soundbites. 'Oh, who can ever be tired of Bath?' noted Austen in her novel *Northanger Abbey*, written in 1798.

The basement kitchen, with the infamous dog wheel at the far end.

Part of the drawing room, with sofa dating from the 1760s and late 18th-century mahogany table laid out with a delicate porcelain tea service.

The bedroom with 18th-century four-poster bed.

From the window of the drawing room there is an unrivalled elevated view of the entire sweep of the Royal Crescent, 'the highest point of the Palladian achievement in Bath,' according to the architectural historian Walter Ison.

For the privileged, the Georgian age was one full of gracious, spacious days, gaiety and glamour. No. 1 Royal Crescent conveys that feeling remarkably well, whilst encapsulating the essentials of Georgian interior design and providing a masterclass in this glorious period of English culture. *PB*

BATH'S HOME COMFORTS
'It is in Bath alone, where People of Fashion can step out of their Coaches after a long journey, into Houses or Lodgings ... as comfortable as their own,' stated the *New Prose Bath Guide* of 1778.

No. 1 Royal Crescent is in the centre of Bath, Somerset. It is owned by the Bath Preservation Trust and open on selected days from mid February to the end of October.
Tel: 01225 428126
www.bath-preservation-trust.org.uk

SALTRAM

In the mid 18th century, having acquired a wealthy wife, John Parker set about transforming this originally Tudor house into an imposing Georgian mansion. The resulting minimalist white Palladian exterior contrasts with the richness of the outstanding Robert Adam interiors. Adam designed almost everything in the suite of state rooms – even the door handles – and they remain a showpiece for his innovative style. The house also includes many fine examples of the work of craftsmen such as Chippendale, Wedgwood and Joseph Rose, as well as excellent paintings by Sir Joshua Reynolds who was born in nearby Plympton. *PB*

Saltram is 3½ miles north-east of Plymouth, Devon, off the A38. It is owned by the National Trust and open on selected days from the end of March to the end of September.
Tel: 01752 333500
www.nationaltrust. org.uk

The saloon, with its sensational chandeliers, has a carpet cleverly designed by Adam to echo his plasterwork design on the ceiling.

TRERICE
An Elizabethan manor house

Trerice (pronounced 'tre-rice') is a little gem of a house – small, intimate, graceful, tucked away amidst the secluded countryside of North Cornwall, and little altered since it was created in 1572 by a prosperous country gentleman, Sir John Arundell.

The first glimpse of the house is through a narrow gateway, its tall, stone pillars crowned by caps and balls. The silver-grey limestone façade, with its highly decorative curly Dutch gables, is most unusual for Cornwall, possibly resulting from Sir John's military service in the Low Countries. The front porch leads to the Great Hall, a magnificent room two storeys high, with a massive mullioned and transomed window and an unusual enclosed minstrels' gallery. The elaborate plasterwork of the ceiling and above the fireplace is superb, Tudor craftsmanship of the highest order.

Even better is the Great Chamber, over 30ft (9m) long and 20ft (6m) wide, facing due south, with light pouring in through the huge bay window. It has a finely detailed plaster barrel ceiling and a magnificent 17th-century Aubusson tapestry. In the nearby Court Chamber, there is a haunting picture of Charles I, wary and careworn. Elsewhere there are more Stuart portraits, oak and walnut period furniture, interesting old clocks and needlework. Those feeling culturally exhausted can always escape outdoors to try their hand at 'kayles', a Cornish version of skittles, on the lawn behind the house. *PB*

Trerice is 3 miles south-east of Newquay, Cornwall, via the A392 and A3058. It is owned by the National Trust and open on selected days from the end of March to the end of October.
Tel: 01637 875404
www.nationaltrust.org.uk

The Great Chamber at Trerice, with its fine detailed plasterwork.

The south end of the East Front of Trerice, with its pretty Dutch gables.

TYNTESFIELD

A Victorian time capsule

The East Front of the house, built in Bath stone, showing the entrance porch and turreted roof.

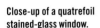

Close-up of a quatrefoil stained-glass window.

George Richard Lawley Gibbs, 2nd Lord Wraxall, the fourth owner of this unique High-Victorian house, died in July 2001. He was a bachelor and, in accordance with his will, it was announced that Tyntesfield was to be put up for sale. Realizing that Tyntesfield was the last major High-Victorian house in private hands that had survived largely unaltered together with most of its original contents, the National Trust decided to try to buy it. This was a brave decision requiring a more than £20 million purchase price to be raised in a short period of time, with massive restoration costs to follow. Against all odds the Trust succeeded and by 31 July 2002 Tyntesfield was theirs.

The National Trust then made another brave move. Rather than conduct a long programme of restoration behind closed doors, they determined to let the public see this for themselves and witness the challenge of bringing Tyntesfield back to life, the first time that the Trust had done this. Thus, the public can enjoy, learn, and even become involved in helping with conservation and refurbishing, becoming part of a huge exciting project, which will continue for some time to come.

Until relatively recently, appreciation of Victorian architecture and interior decoration has been at a low ebb – in an age of minimalism, the style has been considered to be too cumbersome outside, too cluttered within, over-elaborate and assertive. Thus, for some, Tyntesfield at first sight may appear overpowering, gloomy and forbidding – even on a sunny day. Yet the Latin inscription over the entrance translates 'Good will to those who enter, fare well to those who depart' – a warm greeting which may reassure any slightly dubious first-time visitor to the house, which was completed in 1865 for the successful businessman William Gibbs.

Conceivably, the finest room in the house is the library, a beautiful place with an air of scholarship mixed with a sense of fun. Mellow-coloured, gold-tooled books surround the walls, including numerous religious volumes together with all the major works of Ruskin and Pugin, high

priests of the Gothic revival, which Ruskin declared to be 'the proper architecture for an ideal society'. John Norton, the Bristol-born architect of Tyntesfield, was a disciple of Pugin. The library was also a much-loved, much-used family sitting room where excited children enacted plays using the large bay window as a stage. Norton's soaring open oak roof and J.G. Crace's richly coloured carpet add to the appeal of the library, the least-altered room in the house, while large windows give fine views across the Yeo Valley towards the Mendip Hills.

Close-up of a wrought-iron gate in the chapel.

The library is oak panelled throughout and has arched stone windows and fitted oak bookcases.

The Main Hall, with the carved Mansfield-stone fireplace, featuring statues of Fortitude, Truth, Temperance, Justice and Prudence – all classic Victorian values.

View of the Garden Front of Tyntesfield.

A major feature of Tyntesfield is its carving, which appears throughout the house on virtually every surface that lends itself to be carved – wood, stone or metal. Thus an intricately carved stone doorway leads into the dining room, where there is a massive, elaborately carved oak sideboard, together with carved oak side tables and chairs, all by the ubiquitous Crace, doyen of Victorian decorators. Elaborate carving was a key element in High-Victorian style.

Predictably, the main hall is vast, rising three storeys, above which clerestory windows let in an unusual amount of light. The ironwork of the staircase, with a balcony running along three sides of the first floor, is another crucial period style element, as is the craftsmanship shown in the impressively carved fireplace. Looking down from the first floor is Zambrano's towering portrayal of St Laurence, purchased in 1853, when thought to be by the better-known Spanish painter Zurbaran. It is a hall redolent with grandeur and prosperity.

In complete contrast is the billiard room where Anthony Gibbs, William's eldest son, installed a spectacular billiard table, centrally heated and connected to an electronic score board. At the press of a button, a player's score was immediately recorded, something that would have been high-tech in the late 19th century! Around the walls are numerous stags' heads plus an enormous, surprised-looking moose, shot in Canada by the wife of Anthony's eldest son, George, who became the 1st Lord Wraxall.

Adjoining the house is the graceful private chapel built by William Gibbs. William was very devout and deeply committed to the Oxford Movement. His chapel at Tyntesfield is very High Church and was inspired by Sainte Chapelle on the Ile de la Cité in Paris, which it closely resembles. The quality of the mosaics, stained glass and filigree ironwork ensure that the chapel at Tyntesfield is a wonderfully serene ecclesiastical masterpiece.

Construction of the present-day Tyntesfield began after William Gibbs purchased a Regency house outside Bristol in 1843, transforming it 20 years later into the fashionable

This masterly roll-top desk in the Organ Room displays a selection of letter openers and paperweights.

Gothic revival style when he was well into his 70s. William's business, Anthony Gibbs & Sons, founded by his father, had profited enormously from importing guano (solidified bird droppings) from Peru for use as a powerful agricultural fertilizer. 'Anthony Gibbs made his dibs, selling the turds of foreign birds,' was a popular jingle of the day. The National Trust now faces a monumental challenge – to restore Tyntesfield as a showpiece of gracious period country living once more. They deserve to succeed. *PB*

Tyntesfield is off the B3128, 5 miles south-west of Bristol. It is owned by the National Trust and currently only accessible to pre-booked guided tours.
Tel: 0870 458 4500
www.nationaltrust. org.uk

WILTON HOUSE

A Tudor house with Jacobean and Georgian interiors

Wilton House is 3 miles west of Salisbury, Wiltshire, on the A30. It is privately owned and open on selected days from April to the end of October.
Tel: 01722 746720
www.wiltonhouse.co.uk

During the mid 16th century an obscure Welshman named William Herbert became a favourite of Henry VIII. This was a good career move: he went on to marry the sister of Catherine Parr, Henry's sixth wife, was granted the former abbey at Wilton together with a considerable amount of land, and was created the 1st Earl of Pembroke – pretty good for someone who could neither read nor write! Today, more than 450 years later, the present William Herbert, the 18th Earl, continues to reside at Wilton.

Over the centuries the original Tudor house has been much altered – by Inigo Jones, John Webb and James Wyatt – yet it maintains a pleasingly harmonious exterior. The interior is stunning, particularly Jones's glorious Double Cube Room, 60ft (18m) by 30ft (9m), its exuberant opulence equalling that of Versailles.

James Wyatt was branded 'Wrecker Wyatt' following his insensitive alterations to the interior of nearby Salisbury Cathedral, yet his neo-Gothic cloisters at Wilton, containing some excellent classical statuary, look exceedingly graceful. Wilton is indeed unique, one of the nation's finest houses. *PB*

ALL THE WORLD'S A STAGE
In Wilton's front hall stands Peter Scheemakers' marble statue of William Shakespeare. Shakespeare reputedly visited Wilton with his players in order to perform *As You Like It* and *Twelfth Night*, both written in 1600.

Wilton's magnificent Double Cube Room contains brilliant Van Dyck portraits and furniture by Thomas Chippendale and William Kent.

THE HEART OF ENGLAND AND EAST MIDLANDS

The many and varied historic houses in the Heart of England and East Midlands have been shaped through centuries of change in religion, politics, social status and attitudes. Invisible but powerful forces have come together over five centuries to shape the very fabric of the interiors we see today – perhaps best summed up by the cramped priest's holes hidden behind fireplaces and wall panelling at Baddesley Clinton and Harvington Hall and the bold statements of wealth and power represented by the breathtaking interiors of Hardwick Hall and Chatsworth.

In a region so involved in shaping our island's history, it is unsurprising that there is a slight bias towards Tudor, Elizabethan and Jacobean interiors, typified by houses such as Aston Hall, Hellens Manor and Packwood House. But every other era is well represented too, from the later Georgian and Regency periods, through to Victorian at Sunnycroft and Arts and Crafts at Wightwick Manor.

Time and style stand still at Mr Straw's House, where the interiors are largely unchanged from the 1930s. And at Northampton's 78 Derngate, Scottish architect and designer Charles Rennie Mackintosh worked a little piece of pure magic inside an ordinary 19th-century red-brick terrace.

Not only is 78 Derngate a fine example of the visionary skills of this pioneering interior designer, but it also serves as a reminder that we don't need a stately home to provide the space in which to achieve something different. *MD*

THE ANCIENT HIGH HOUSE

A Tudor merchant's house

The Ancient High House is the largest remaining timber-framed town house of its period (1595) in England, standing on four floors with room settings dedicated to the many different periods through which the house has been occupied, from Stuart right through to Edwardian. Of particular interest is the selection of wallpaper fragments around the house, uncovered during restoration work. Look out for the fine Worcester porcelain tea service in the Georgian 'wallpaper room', dating from the early 1760s, before the company received its 'royal warrant'. *MD*

The Ancient High House is in Greengate Street, in the heart of Stafford town centre. It is administered by Stafford Borough Council and open on selected days all year.
Tel: 01785 619131
www.staffordbc.gov.uk

Attention to detail lends authenticity to the recreated rooms at The Ancient High House.

ASTON HALL

A large Jacobean mansion with finely decorated plaster ceilings

Aston was built between 1618 and 1635 by Sir Thomas Holte and was one of the last great Jacobean houses to be built in Britain. It has many fine examples of 17th-century craftsmanship and Jacobean decorative work. Almost all of the furniture was sold off at sales in 1817 and 1849 but Birmingham Museums & Art Gallery have painstakingly refurbished the rooms as they would have been in the 17th and 18th centuries, using old inventories and paintings as sources.

There is a lot to see downstairs and upstairs, including the oak-panelled Great Parlour, the Long Gallery, with its symmetrical arcaded panels that

The Great Parlour with early 17th-century wood panelling and oak table.

date from around 1630, the solid but elaborately carved staircase, and the amazing plasterwork designs in the Great Dining Room. This room in particular demonstrates the 17th-century taste for extravagant ceilings, with its grotesque-style masks, and border frieze showing relief figures standing in niches separated by elaborate strapwork and scrolling. Some of the rooms have given way to some extent to later 18th-century tastes, with wood panelling that is painted instead of plain, flocked wallpaper, elaborately dressed windows and more heavily carpeted floors. *MD*

Aston Hall is 2 miles north-east of Birmingham city centre, off the A38(M). It is owned by Birmingham City Council, forming part of Birmingham Museums & Art Gallery, and open on selected days from Easter to the end of October.
Tel: 0121 327 0062
www.bmag.org.uk/aston_hall

The beautifully carved Great Stairs, known to have been painted white in the 18th century.

STRAPWORK

Strapwork designs, with patterns resembling interlaced ribbons or leather straps, adorn the ceilings of many Tudor and Jacobean properties. Fine examples of strapwork ceiling designs can be seen in the magnificent Long Gallery at Aston Hall, in the upstairs saloon at Mapledurham (p 73) and in the drawing room at Lyme Park (p 204).

The dark red-brick exterior of Aston Hall, an outstanding example of Jacobean architecture and decoration close to the centre of Birmingham.

ATTINGHAM PARK

A late 18th-century neoclassical house with Regency interiors

This house, built in 1782–85 around an older house that was later demolished, stands testament to the incredibly delicate touch of the interior designers (and the skilled craftsmen who helped them) in achieving the elegant gilded 'look' so typical of the Regency period. Throughout Attingham, the decorative plasterwork ceilings with painted roundels, gilt filleted walls, exquisite grotesque wall paintings, and richly coloured window drapes and carpets add to the overall effect. And the effect is enhanced by fine French, Italian and English furniture, paintings, sculptures and books.

This jewel of Regency design came at a very high price for the Berwick family who later felt the full effects of their overspending. Apart from collecting fine things as they travelled abroad, they orchestrated various costly election campaigns, with two

generations of the family becoming MPs, and in 1827 the 2nd Lord Berwick was forced to hold a 16-day bankruptcy sale of Attingham's contents. However, luckily for visitors today, successive generations have helped to 'put right' the house's interior, filling it once more with treasures from around the world.

In keeping with the French vogue for 'male' and 'female' suites of rooms at around this time, Attingham is symmetrically designed with 'male' and 'female' wings on either side of the main entrance hall. It is immediately apparent that the powdery blue drawing room, with its white-and-gold Italian furniture, is part of the feminine side of the house, its theme of *'l'amour'* running through the decorative scheme. The gilt arrows tracing patterns across the Adam-style ceiling are a reference to Cupid, who appears again in the perfectly

George Steuart designed Attingham Park's neo-classical façade.

The dining room with a suite of 24 dining chairs and Axminster carpet from the early 1800s, French tableware and gilded plaster ceiling.

Panels in the Boudoir attributed to French decorative painter Louis-André Delabrière. The side chairs are 19th-century Italian.

shaped Boudoir. The (unfairly named) grotesque wall paintings in this room date from the 1780s, and although there are five doors, three of them are false, showing just how far the designers went to create symmetry in their rooms.

On the male side of the house, the room corresponding to the ladies' Boudoir is the more masculine-shaped Octagon Room, while the dining room (always on the 'male' side of the house!) has a remarkable ceiling, with delicately detailed white plasterwork contrasting starkly with the rich red painted background. The ceiling also has a very apt theme for a dining room – grapes with interwoven vine leaves and wheat sheaths to represent Bacchus, the god of wine, and Ceres, the goddess of the harvest. The wool and velvet gilt-edged curtains are a wonderful (and undoubtedly expensive) copy of the original Regency drapes shown in a watercolour of the dining room by Lady Hester Leeke in 1840. This watercolour still sits on the table at the far end of the dining room – a reminder that a lot of conservation work relies on old paintings and photos, as well as fabric fragments. It is also fascinating to see just how similar the dining room looks now to how it was furnished in the 19th century, and the painting provides a valuable reference for anyone with a home from around the same period.

The vast picture gallery that lies behind the main entrance hall was designed by John Nash in 1805 and has a huge glass-panelled and curved iron roof that echoes the Royal Pavilion, Brighton (p 70), another Nash building, and allows natural light to flood in, showing off the Berwick family's collection of art and sculpture to its best advantage.

The staircase leading off the gallery to the right is not only an amazing feat

of engineering – being cantilevered in design – but also gives an insight into 19th-century taste for all things Eastern and exotic. This appetite for the East is also reflected in the Sultana Room on the 'female' side of the house, named after the Ottoman or 'Sultane' set into the main alcove.

Sadly, there are no bedrooms on show at Attingham as restoration work hasn't extended this far. However, a modest sitting room, reached via the servants' staircase at the end of the picture gallery, deserves a mention for it is a salient reminder of how much work conservation bodies like the National Trust must do to restore properties like Attingham to their former glory … long may their good work continue! *MD*

Detail of an Ionic column on the corner of the portico reflects the 18th-century taste for classicism.

Attingham Park is 4 miles south-east of Shrewsbury, Shropshire. It is owned by the National Trust and open on selected days from March to the end of October.
Tel: 01743 708123
www.nationaltrust.org.uk

The Inner Library, with fitted bookcases dating from about 1810 and fine mahogany furniture.

The drawing room at Attingham, decorated in its present colour scheme by the 3rd Lord Berwick in around 1832.

BADDESLEY CLINTON

*A moated medieval manor house
with Tudor interiors*

Baddesley Clinton is 7 miles north-west of Warwick. It is owned by the National Trust and open on selected days from March to November.
Tel: 01564 783294
www.nationaltrust.org.uk

Baddesley Clinton, dating originally from the 15th century, was completed in the 16th and retains its Tudor style thanks to the original plain oak panelling, painstakingly stripped of centuries of paint in the 1940s. Look out for the rare fragments of Elizabethan wall painting at the end of a corridor near the Great Parlour. Evidence of the manor's staunch Catholic household can be found in the ornate chapel, with its 18th-century Spanish leather wall hangings, and the three priest's holes, used to conceal Jesuit priests in the late 16th century when the house was a refuge for persecuted Catholics.

The armorial stained-glass window designs, dotted throughout the house, date from the late 16th century and are by Henry Ferrers, the owner known as 'the Antiquary', to celebrate the history of his family, and the tradition was continued by later generations. Henry was responsible for a fair proportion of the interior we see today, including several fine 16th-century fireplaces featuring decorative heraldic overmantels.

Although there is a good range of robust English oak furniture, mainly from the 17th century, some of the house's finer (and earlier) pieces were sold in the 1930s to Baron Ash at Packwood House (p 160) where they can still be seen today. *MD*

Far left: The early 17th-century stone fireplace in the Great Hall, decorated with heraldic symbols.

Left: Heraldic glass panel from the Great Hall. The designs celebrate the history of the Ferrers family and were installed by Henry Ferrers in the late 16th century.

BELVOIR CASTLE

A Regency Gothic castle

The splendid Elizabeth Saloon, with its lavish gilded rococo decoration.

This Gothic revival-style castle, which was completed in the early 19th century, seems to have always been here, but it is actually the fourth castle built on the site. Its beautifully preserved Regency interior is typically elegant in style. The Elizabeth Saloon, rebuilt after a fire in 1816, features white-and-gilt rococo panels inset with pale blue silk damask from a French chateau, and a fantastic painted ceiling by Matthew Wyatt, telling the legend of how the peacock got the eyes in its tail. *MD*

Belvoir Castle is 6 miles from the A1 at Grantham, Lincolnshire. It is owned by the 11th Duke and Duchess of Rutland and open on selected days from March to October.
Tel: 01476 871000
www.belvoircastle.com

BERRINGTON HALL

An elegant late-Georgian mansion

Beautifully decorated ceilings by the Italian artist Biagio Rebecca are a particular feature of this graceful Henry Holland house built in the late 18th century. The interior has a delicate feel with elaborate painted ceilings and a spectacular staircase hall with a central glass dome, as well as a handsome collection of French Regency furniture. Look out for the charmingly authentic children's nursery and the fully equipped Victorian laundry. The parkland around the house was landscaped by Lancelot 'Capability' Brown, Henry Holland's father-in-law. *MD*

Berrington Hall is off the A49, 3 miles north of Leominster, Herefordshire. It is owned by the National Trust and open on selected days from the end of March to October.
Tel: 01568 615721
www.nationaltrust. org.uk

The staircase hall showing bronzed balustrading in the form of a lyre.

CALKE ABBEY

A baroque mansion with little-restored 18th-century and Victorian interiors

Sir Vauncey Harpur Crewe's childhood bedroom at Calke Abbey, which over the years became a store room for unwanted household pieces collected by his eccentric family.

Detail from the stunning Chinese silk hangings of the Calke State Bed. Note the warriors on horseback, mandarins and exotic animals.

Maintained in the state in which it was found by the National Trust in 1985, Calke Abbey's decay is the ultimate story of the English country house in decline. While most of the first floor rooms are in a fairly decent state of repair, upstairs on the second floor it is possible to see how the rot finally set in.

These almost derelict rooms, with their cracked plasterwork ceilings, peeling wallpaper, rotten curtains and bare floorboards, are crammed full of discarded furniture, books, children's toys, antiquities and cases of stuffed birds and animals, a particular passion of the 10th Baronet, Sir Vauncey Harpur Crewe.

The cupola and iron weathervane on top of the stable block which was built in 1712–14.

The South Front of Calke Abbey. The house was built in 1701–04 and the central Greek-style portico was added a hundred years later.

Throughout the 19th and 20th centuries, aristocratic families all over Britain found it increasingly hard to maintain the 'old way of life' on their country estates and could no longer afford the spiralling maintenance costs of mansions like Calke, nor the salaries of the many servants and craftsmen needed to keep them running smoothly. The result was that hundreds of houses were demolished and lost forever but somehow Calke Abbey survived, thanks to various grants, a large anonymous donation and public appeals, and it was finally handed over to the National Trust in 1985 and opened up in 1989.

Today the Trust maintains the house, rebuilt in 1701–04 around a much

older Elizabethan house, in the exact same state in which it was found to show us just how bad it could, and did, get in many country houses. It costs more to keep Calke Abbey suspended in this state of semi-dereliction than it would to restore it, but that isn't really the point. By way of illustration, look into the scullery, beyond the kitchen, where vegetation is springing up through the moss-covered cobblestone floor.

But there is much to celebrate here, too, with a wide range of furniture from the 17th–19th centuries and a massive natural history collection put together by Sir Vauncey who was educated at home and seemed to prefer studying animals, insects and

Farrow and Ball pea-green paint and printed borders recreate the 19th-century scheme in the Caricature Room.

The 18th-century main staircase, a fine example of craftsmanship.

birds to socializing with humans! On the first floor, the main rooms include the Victorian-style drawing room, with its beautiful yellow-and-white silk tissue curtains (painstakingly reproduced on special looms) and, under various tatty cotton covers, a sofa and a set of eight English giltwood armchairs, in the same gleaming fabric. Intensely patterned gold-and-white Pugin-style wallpaper was laid over the original Georgian grey watered silk design in 1841–42 and it lends an even richer effect to an already ornate and somewhat over-furnished room.

The curious Caricature Room next to the entrance hall on the ground floor contains an interesting array of *Punch* cartoons, pasted onto the walls by successive generations – a fun variation on the country house print room where architectural engravings and other decorative subjects would have been displayed. The saloon was once Calke's main entrance hall but the steps leading up to it from the outside were dismantled in 1806–08 and the present ground-floor entrance, at odds with the scale of the building, was redesigned for use instead. In the mid 19th century, under Sir John Harpur Crewe, the saloon gradually became something of a museum space, with its neoclassical Corinthian pillars, grand coffered plasterwork ceiling and various wooden display cabinets, containing various specimens and antiquities. All in all, it's a rather unique setting for a game of billiards (the full-size table stands shrouded in cloth in the centre of the room).

On the first floor, the rooms are in various states of decline but even so yield interesting and unanswered questions about Calke and its owners: for example, who put the seemingly modern coloured glass in the Yellow Room's windows and why did Charles Harpur Crewe prefer such a humble bedroom? Not for him the superb 18th-century Calke State Bed that is now displayed (somewhat ironically) behind a glass case in the former Housemaid's Bedroom. The bed's baroque Chinese-design silk hangings are so vivid and the design so intense inside and out (the padded fleur-de-lis bedhead is exquisite), that it provides a welcome antidote to all the decay in the rooms above. Curators found the bed, thought to be a wedding present from Queen Caroline to the 5th Baronet's wife in 1734, packed into boxes and when they pieced it back together, the most stunning example of baroque-style upholstery was revealed in pristine condition. Seeing this makes it easier to imagine the whole house freshly decorated as it was in the late 1790s, with polished plasterwork, rich silk-lined walls and curtains, and gives some sense of scale against which to measure Calke's decline. *MD*

Detailed 18th-century plasterwork in the dining room showing a roundel with painted classical scene.

Calke Abbey is 10 miles south of Derby, on the A514 at Ticknall, Derbyshire. It is owned by the National Trust and open on selected days from the end of March to the end of October.
Tel: 01332 863822
www.nationaltrust.org.uk

CHARLECOTE PARK

An Elizabethan house with Victorian-styled interiors

Elizabethan revival-style wallpaper: crimson-and-blue flock on a gold background, produced by Thomas Willement in the 1830s.

Charlecote Park, an Elizabethan manor, built in 1558.

For the Victorians' interpretation of Elizabethan splendour, look no further than Charlecote Park, where the 1500s and 1800s come together in the mid 19th-century refurbishment of the original 16th-century house undertaken by George Hammond Lucy and his wife Mary Elizabeth. The result is a set of beautifully furnished rooms on a grand scale that mix Elizabethan revival style with Victorian taste and sensibilities.

Among the most impressive Victorian 'fakes' are the Great Hall's massive plasterwork ceiling, painted to look like a solid oak roof, the wooden painted fireplace and panelling with heraldic designs, and the dining room's magnificent stained-glass windows and rich plasterwork ceilings with moulded pinnacles.

Much of the richness in the 'new rooms' – and an effect that is fairly easy to copy – comes from the intense gilt-patterned wallpapers designed by Thomas Willement. Look above the door leading into the library for a glimpse of how vivid the paper would have looked originally. See also the wall coverings in the drawing room – these are silk gold damask, stretched over the walls using batons.

There are some incredibly grand pieces of furniture that lend further weight to the overall effect. The grandest of them all is the huge Charlecote Buffet in the dining room. This was carved from three pieces of oak and depicts the major food groups, with meat on the left and fish on the right. *MD*

Charlecote Park is 6 miles south of Warwick, on the north side of the B4086. It is owned by the National Trust and open on selected days from March to the beginning of November.
Tel: 01789 470277
www.nationaltrust.org.uk

CHATSWORTH

A mainly Georgian mansion with 17th–19th-century interiors

Voted Britain's finest stately home in 2003, Chatsworth is the grand-dame of all country houses, and what comes across most strongly about its interior is that it is a living and breathing house. Its rooms have evolved into what they are now over the last five centuries, and they contain a vast collection of furniture, antiques, art and sculpture, which has been added to in recent years by the late 11th Duke of Devonshire and his wife. Nowhere is this plainer to see than in the Alcove Room where a besom broomstick, signed by the Harry Potter author J.K. Rowling when she presented a literary prize at the house, takes pride of place among other family treasures.

The West Stairs, with stunning painted ceilings by Sir James Thornhill.

The spectacular façade of Chatsworth, home to the Dukes of Devonshire for over 400 years.

The earliest-surviving interiors at Chatsworth date from the late 17th century when the 1st Duke of Devonshire rebuilt the state apartments on the second floor, copying their position from the original Elizabethan rooms built by its 16th-century owner Bess of Hardwick (*see* Hardwick Hall, p 145). The Elizabethan origins of the house have all but vanished under the weight of centuries of rebuilding and changes in taste and decor, but the house still retains what would have seemed a very old-fashioned layout to later generations, with the state rooms at the top of the house.

The second-floor suite of state rooms has retained typical William and Mary period interiors. The 1st Duke was very close to King William and Queen Mary and their palace at Hampton Court is very similar in its interior style to Chatsworth. The Duke hoped that Chatsworth would receive a royal visit (something that didn't happen until almost two centuries later, when Queen Victoria came in 1843). Hence, the lavishly painted baroque ceilings, intricate carved wood panelling and gilded wall hangings are all designed for show – so much so that the huge mirror opposite the State Dining Room door into the State Drawing Room serves to give the effect of doubling the suite in size (when all the other doors are open), as well as giving an important sense of symmetry so desirable around this time.

And for the ultimate in lavish interiors, the State Music Room can't really be surpassed, with its stamped and gilded *cuir repoussé* wall hangings dating from the 1830s, topped by a richly painted frieze and ceiling and by a welcome delicate touch: a *trompe l'œil* violin painted by Jan van der Vaart onto an interior door – it looks real enough to be played at any moment!

The 6th Duke designed his own set of apartments that more suited the 19th-century way of living and this included creating the library by adapting the 17th-century Long Gallery.

Luckily, he retained its glorious gilded stucco ceiling and was thoughtful enough to put in an Axminster carpet that cleverly reflected the painted roundels in the ceiling above. The Long Gallery is large in scale, but even more remarkable is the amazing coffered ceiling in the Great Dining Room, with its symmetrical gilded flower insets. Although the room was redecorated

TROMPE-L'ŒIL

The term *trompe l'œil* derives from the French for 'deception of the eye', and refers to a form of visual illusion in painting which skilfully tricks the eye into thinking an object or detail is three dimensional. Jan van der Vaart's violin, 'hanging' on the door of the music room at Chatsworth, is a fine example. Other examples include Rex Whistler's huge mural at Plas Newydd (p 248), van Hoogstraeten's highly realistic 'A View Down a Corridor' at Dyrham Park (p 97) and the fascinating murals in the Elizabethan Painted Room at St Mary's House (p 71).

Stamped and gilded leather lines the walls of the State Bedroom.

The Great Stairs with panels painted to resemble sculptures. The bronze figure of Mercury was cast for the 6th Duke.

in 1996, the crimson-striped material which has been used on the walls recreates the style of the time (the sparkling crystal chandelier alone has 2,736 pieces) and complements the deep red colour of the beautiful Bohemian cranberry glassware on the dining table perfectly.

In contrast, the delicate hand-painted Chinese wallpapers in the Queen of Scots rooms (not always open) give an insight into the prevailing taste for all things Eastern in the Regency period, with two lovely examples of Polonaise-style beds that have central round canopies and drapes pulled out to each corner of the bed. Look out for the designer's incredible attention to detail in the bamboo-style gilt edging to the wallpapers in the dressing room. For bold Regency stripes, look no further than the Green Satin Dressing Room and Bedroom where the original striped satin, which was rotten, has been copied and faithfully reproduced to stunning effect. But one note of caution here – high ceilings are needed to recreate this powerful look.

Don't miss the late 17th-century chapel, with its excellent examples of baroque wall and ceiling paintings – the alabaster altar curtains hang in front of the paintings while the painted figure to the left of the altar seems to rest his foot on the marble, blending the two mediums together perfectly. And to end on a note of social history: the wall paintings are reserved for the first-floor level where the family would have sat, in the gallery at the back of the chapel, while plainer cedar-wood panelling is used throughout the ground-floor level, where Chatsworth's staff would have gathered. *MD*

Chatsworth is 8 miles north of Matlock, Derbyshire, off the B6012. It is owned by the Chatsworth House Trust and open from March to December.
Tel: 01246 565300
www.chatsworth.org

COTTESBROOKE HALL
A Queen Anne house

The reputed model for Jane Austen's *Mansfield Park*, this Queen Anne house was begun in 1702 and contains many fine examples of 18th-century English and Continental furniture and porcelain. The house is home to the renowned Woolavington Collection of sporting and equestrian paintings, named after their original owner. Also of note are the unusual rococo papier mâché wall decoration in the hall, the wrought-iron staircase and the prize-winning gardens. **MD**

Cottesbrooke Hall is off the A5199, 10 miles north of Northampton. It is privately owned and open on selected days from May to the end of September.
Tel: 01604 505808
www.cottesbrookehall.co.uk

A view of the house from Cottesbrooke Hall's award-winning gardens.

78 DERNGATE
England's only Mackintosh-designed town house

The decorative cohesion inside and outside this seemingly ordinary 19th-century terraced house in Northampton is overwhelming, and the man responsible was the famous Scottish architect, artist and designer Charles Rennie Mackintosh.

Mackintosh's amazingly modern style of architecture and interior design – witness the Continental-style extension on the back of the house and the stunning original interior designs for furniture, fireplaces, doors, soft furnishings and light fittings – was what attracted Northampton businessman Wenman Joseph Bassett-Lowke to commission Mackintosh to completely remodel No. 78 in 1916.

The front door, with its stylized black-and-white porch light and chevron-shaped stained glass, gives a tantalizing glimpse of what is to come behind the door, in the Hall Lounge. Of this room, Mackintosh said he was trying to create 'a sense of mystery and spaciousness' and, oh boy, did he deliver!

The Japanese-style screen, with its square cut-outs and glowing stained-glass panels, is pure magic. The jewelled chevron (or upside-down triangle), the chequer-designed stencils on the wall fabric and the geometric design of the ceiling rose and light fitting are so bold that they distract from the room's size. And there is

A stunning Gothic castle

This impressive 'Norman revival' castle, completed in 1820, was designed to look like a Welsh border fortress. As building work swallowed most of the budget, the interior was left relatively plain, but it was embellished by successive owners. One highlight is the Pugin-designed drawing room in Gothic revival style – the most complete example of Pugin's work outside of the Houses of Parliament. Original furniture includes plain Gothic benches and chairs in the entrance hall and Great Hall, the latter furnished as a grand Edwardian drawing room. *MD*

Eastnor Castle is 2 miles east of Ledbury, Herefordshire, on the A438. It is privately owned and open on selected days from April to October.
Tel: 01531 633160
www.eastnorcastle.com

The rear of the house, showing the Continental extension, with an enclosed balcony to the master bedroom.

more to come in the striking black-and-white striped designs of the Guest Bedroom – look out for the exquisite contrasting light fittings. *MD*

78 Derngate is situated in Northampton town centre, near the Derngate Theatre, and the entrance is via No. 82. It is run by a private trust and open on selected days from March to September (pre-booking is essential).
Tel: 01604 603407
www.78derngate.org.uk

Pugin's Gothic-style drawing room with rich decoration and furnishings.

FARNBOROUGH HALL

A villa with fine Georgian decoration

The dining room at Farnborough Hall, with its fine 18th-century stucco plasterwork by William Perritt.

The 18th-century rococo plaster-work inside this honey-coloured house, home to the Holbech family for over 300 years, is among the best-surviving examples in Britain. In particular, look out for the stucco work in the dining room from around 1745–50, featuring shells, scrolls, fruit and flowers – all designed to complement William Holbech's collection of art and sculpture acquired on his Grand Tour of Italy. **MD**

Farnborough Hall is 6 miles north of Banbury, Oxfordshire, off the A423. It is owned by the National Trust, but occupied and administered by the Holbech family; it is open on selected days from April to September.
Tel: 01295 690002
www.nationaltrust.org.uk

HADDON HALL

A medieval house with Tudor interiors

This castellated manor house oozes Tudor style from every pore. Highlights include the truly stunning minstrels' gallery, added to the great banqueting hall in around 1450, wood panelling on a grand scale in the Elizabethan Long Gallery – said to have been hewn from a single oak tree – and the original 17th-century plasterwork ceiling in the Great Chamber. There are some fine tapestries from the same period and, in the chapel, 15th-century murals that were whitewashed over during the Reformation but rediscovered during renovations undertaken in the 20th century. **MD**

A carved walnut dining chair in the Long Gallery at Haddon Hall.

Haddon Hall is 2 miles south of Bakewell, Derbyshire. It is owned by Lord Edward Manners and open on selected days from April to October.
Tel: 01629 812855
www.haddonhall.co.uk.

HARDWICK HALL
An Elizabethan 'Great House'

The sheer scale of Hardwick Hall has to be experienced to be believed. Towering high on a wind-swept Derbyshire hillside, this 16th-century stone house announces itself proudly with its owner's initials ES (for Elizabeth Shrewsbury) carved out along the roof line. Its numerous windows were another huge status symbol, as the Elizabethans and Jacobeans coveted glass, which was massively expensive around this time, and the well-known phrase 'Hardwick Hall, more glass than wall' sums up the house's extravagant use of what was a precious material.

Known as a 'Great House', the hall truly lives up to its name and demon-strates the status of its builder, Bess of Hardwick, who was a formidable woman. Bess amassed great wealth by marrying four times, lastly the 6th Earl of Shrewsbury. Following his death in 1590, Bess sank a large chunk of her considerable fortune into Hardwick Hall, near the site of Hardwick Old Hall where her family had lived previously. The Old Hall, now a ruin that can still be visited, continued to house lesser members of

The magnificent exterior of Hardwick Hall, often described as 'more glass than wall'.

THE LONG GALLERY
Hardwick's Long Gallery is the largest, although not the longest, surviving Elizabethan Long Gallery in England – it is 167ft (51m) long, 26ft (8m) high and up to 40ft (12m) wide in places. The nation's longest Long Gallery is at Montacute House, Somerset (p 112); it measures 172ft (52m) in length.

The plasterwork frieze of Diana in the forest, and tapestries depicting Ulysses, in the High Great Chamber. The canopy was first erected in the early 17th century.

the family and servants but Bess and her immediate family took up residence on the first floor of the new house, with the second floor of state rooms reserved for visitors.

Wealth and status were everything to the Elizabethans and this is powerfully reflected in the vast scale of the state rooms at Hardwick. The High Great Chamber, reached by wide stone stairs, is an awesome 27ft (8m) high – several modern houses could probably fit within this one chamber!

Throughout the house, the National Trust has laid rush matting, similar to that uncovered at Hampton Court Palace during restoration work, and it's an effect that could be easily copied to lend an authentic atmosphere in domestic homes from around this period. Important guests in the 16th and 17th centuries were expected to process up through the house via the grand entrance hall, with its impressive oak panelling and tapestries, into the High Great Chamber, before being wined and dined there and, afterwards, retiring to talk in the withdrawing room or to exercise in the Long Gallery. And today, walking into the High Great Chamber, completed in 1599, is like stepping back in time. The size of the room and its detailed decoration gives a real sense of how it would have impressed visitors in Bess's day.

The house is blessed with many rare Elizabethan tapestries and Belgian examples are used as wall hangings in the High Great Chamber but, above them and below the perfectly plain ceiling (as was the style up to around 1600), there is an elaborate 'thrown' plasterwork frieze. The name comes from the fact that plaster would have

been 'thrown' onto the walls in layers before being carved to produce a relief. The main subject here is the classical goddess Diana, the huntress (see her above the canopy of state), who was often used allegorically to represent Elizabeth I. Bess dearly wanted Elizabeth I to visit Hardwick but, sadly, she never did. A further public demonstration of Bess's loyalty to the Crown is the huge stone-carved royal coat of arms above the fireplace: the dragon on the right-hand side of the shield was adopted by Henry VII to honour his Welsh heritage.

The Gallery, adapted from the Elizabethan Long Gallery, is indeed long at 167ft (51m) and has a later,

The Cut Velvet Bedroom showing the fireplace with its overmantel decorated with heraldic shields, and a decorated fire screen.

A detail from the Hatton Garden tapestries on the main staircase, showing children and angels.

The magnificent four-poster bed, with its vivid blue hangings, in the Blue Room.

most likely Jacobean, plasterwork ceiling, and some remnants of earlier wall painting above the windows, as well as curtains and much more furniture than it would have had in Bess's time. The Gallery contains many fine portraits, including that of Elizabeth I at the far end of the hall, but don't miss the brass chandelier from around 1600 and the amazing bed canopy, taken from the State Bedroom at nearby Chatsworth (p 138, also owned by the Shrewsbury family at that time). It features 17th-century upholstery and the parts that are now black were originally silver.

In the withdrawing room there are several fine pieces of Elizabethan wood furniture, two of them by the French architect Du Cerceau. His walnut table resting on sea dogs in the middle of the room is so grand that experts think it may have been

a present to Bess from Elizabeth I or Mary Queen of Scots. The lovely spice cabinet, which has lots of compartments, is covered in mythical carved creatures.

On the first floor, the lower ceilings and the more modest sense of scale they give to the rooms, along with far greater furnishings, reveal that this was the part of the house more widely used by later generations, especially in the 19th and 20th centuries, giving them generally a more cosy and lived-in feel. *MD*

Hardwick Hall is 7 miles west of Mansfield, Derbyshire, off the A6175. It is owned by the National Trust (English Heritage care for the ruins of Hardwick Old Hall), and open on selected days from the end of March to the end of October.
Tel: 01246 850430
www.nationaltrust.org.uk

Crimson silk needlework with numerous varieties of oak leaves in the Paved Room's fine display of early embroideries.

HARVINGTON HALL

A moated Elizabethan manor house

The Great Chamber with wood panelling and refectory table, typical of the period.

The largest number of secret priest's holes in the country and rare Elizabethan wall paintings are interesting features of the interior in this moated manor house dating from the 1580s. Hidden behind whitewash until the 1930s, the wall paintings include arabesque drawings in the Mermaid Passage, the figures of the Nine Worthies on the second floor, and white and red drops for the blood and water of the Passion in the Small Chapel, dated to around 1600. *MD*

Harvington Hall is 3 miles south-east of Kidderminster, Worcestershire. It is owned by the Roman Catholic Archdiocese of Birmingham and open on selected days from March to October.
Tel: 01562 777846
www.harvingtonhall.com

HELLENS MANOR

A Tudor and Jacobean manor house

Stepping inside Hellens Manor is like entering a Tudor time warp: half a millennium simply falls away in the stone-flagged hall with its minstrels' gallery, ancient tapestries and huge carved fireplace that bears the Black Prince's crest. James Audley, who rented the manor house for a pair of silver spurs in 1342, was a close confidante of the Black Prince and fought with him at the Battle of Crécy in 1346.

Today, the house retains an impressive collection of furniture dating from Tudor through to Georgian times, as well as paintings – including a Sir Joshua Reynolds and a Van Dyck studio copy of Charles II – armour, furnishings and rare early textiles and tapestries.

Not for Hellens the polished, 'roped off' approach of some grander historic houses: this is a touchy-feely place that encourages visitors to get up-close and personal. Admittedly, some of the decorative additions, such as handmade Turkish carpets, are not centuries old but they add colour and vibrancy to the overall effect of a house that is in tune with its ancient heritage but has been gently adapted by successive generations.

There are many highlights, but one of the most impressive is the sombre-feeling Stone Hall where the local manorial court was held until the 18th century. The walls are decorated with various rare pieces of armoury from the 16th and 17th centuries as well as tapestries – the one on the wall below the minstrels' gallery depicts an ancestor and namesake of Adam Munthe, whose family has lived at Hellens since medieval times.

The Stone Hall, decorated with tapestries and pieces of armoury.

Along the far wall, an impressive stone slab turns out to be a 'mensa' or altar table, dating back to the 12th century. It is thought that the table top was acquired from a local church in the early 1200s – there are five crosses carved into its surface, one for each of Christ's wounds on the Cross.

In the East Hall, there are some fine examples of Tudor carvings almost as fresh as the day they were worked. The staircase carvings with mythical 'wyverns' (similar to griffins) are the work of local 17th-century carpenter

The ancient stone altar table at the far end of the Stone Hall.

Sunlight shines through a leaded window onto the spiral staircase.

Fine Tudor panelling in the music room.

John Abel who also carved nearby Ledbury's market hall.

The White Drawing Room, wood-panelled from floor to ceiling, is now painted white although it would have been limed in Tudor times. On one wall, there is a curious fragment of decorative silk cloth with old letters sewn into the material. Very little is known about it other than the possibility that it might have been part of an Elizabethan bed hanging. Five decorative dining chairs with delicate paintwork are thought to be the work of the 17th-century Swiss painter Angelica Kaufmann. Throughout the house, as in the White Drawing Room, decorative wrought-iron work such as sconces and chandeliers, although designed by a local blacksmith in the 20th century, lend character to the overall effect.

The music room, too, contains fine Tudor wood panelling, while a stucco frieze and plastered ceiling from the Stuart era reminds us how successive generations attempted to update and 'modernize' Hellens.

Upstairs there are many more delights, particularly the leather-lined walls of the Cordova Room. The room was originally decorated in the 17th century, but in the 18th and 19th centuries large sections of leather from Cordova in Spain were added to create a sumptuous effect.

The classical wooden fireplace in the Cordova Room was designed by John Abel. There are also further fine examples of furniture, including several pieces in Bloody Mary's Room, said to have been occupied by Mary I when she visited Hellens in the 16th century. The oak wardrobe has an unusual mixture of bold geometric and floral carvings while the top part of a court cupboard, originally used to store food, sits at the foot of the tester bed, draped with bed hangings and feather plumes. The fireplace shows Mary's coat of arms and the white plasterwork ceiling with fleur-de-lis centrepiece all add up to a bedchamber fit for a queen!

Also upstairs is Hetty Walwyn's room, in which many people feel an 'atmosphere' – even before they hear the story of its unhappy occupant. In the late 17th century, Hetty (or Mehettabel) was locked up here by her father for 30 years following a failed elopement. The room itself contains little of particular note, apart from two inscriptions, one forlornly etched by Hetty on the inside of a barred 17th-century window pane, using her diamond ring, and the other by John Pearcel (possibly her lover), scratched on the outside in 1702. *MD*

The beautiful gardens at Hellens Manor.

> **WINDOW WORDS**
> Etched onto a 17th-century window pane in her bedroom are these words by Hetty Walwyn, imprisoned at Hellens after a failed elopement:
> 'It is a part of virtue to abstain from what we love, if it shall prove our bane.'

Hellens Manor is situated in Much Marcle, 3 miles west of Ledbury, Herefordshire, just off the A449. It is run by a charitable trust and open on selected days from Easter to the beginning of October.
Tel: 01531 660504
www.hellensmanor.com

Hetty Walwyn's bedroom. The length of rope hanging from the ceiling into the room was connected to a bell which she could ring to summon servants.

KEDLESTON HALL

A grand Georgian house

Built between 1759 and 1765, Kedleston Hall has an interior that has particular historic importance because of its connections with the renowned 18th-century architect and designer Robert Adam. The house contains some of the most complete and least-altered series of Adam interiors anywhere in England, and includes large collections of original furniture and paintings in the classically elegant state rooms. Adam also designed the surrounding park, which features a fishing pavilion, a bridge, and a lovely series of lakes and cascades. *MD*

Kedleston Hall is 5 miles north-west of Derby. It is owned by the National Trust and open on selected days from March to October.
Tel: 01332 842191
www.nationaltrust.org.uk

The state bed in Kedleston Hall's State Bedchamber.

LAMPORT HALL

A manor with fine Georgian interiors

Lamport Hall was originally a Tudor manor house but in the 17th and 18th centuries a classical frontage was added. Highlights include the High Room's intact plasterwork ceiling by William Smith dating from around 1740, rare Venetian cabinets with mythological paintings in the early 19th-century Cabinet Room, and a wealth of fine furniture, old books and paintings. Much of the interior restoration was undertaken by the 12th Baronet, Sir Gyles Isham, who bequeathed the estate to a charitable trust in the 1970s. *MD*

The ornately decorated Georgian library, with books dating from the 16th century.

Lamport Hall is 8 miles north of Northampton, on the A508. It is owned by the Lamport Hall Trust and open on selected days from Easter to September.
Tel: 01604 686272
www.lamporthall.co.uk

MOSELEY OLD HALL

An Elizabethan manor house with 17th-century interiors

Mr Whitgreave's Room showing the original wood-panelled fireplace and 17th-century portrait of the owner.

Moseley Old Hall is famous for its connection with Charles II, for it was in one of the house's secret priest's holes that the owner Thomas Whitgreave hid him from Parliamentary troops after the Battle of Worcester in 1651. The house still contains the bed where Charles slept that night. The heavy-beamed ceilings and dark wood panelling all lend atmosphere to the 17th-century interiors, which were faithfully restored by the National Trust in the 1960s. **MD**

Moseley Old Hall is off the A460, 4 miles north of Wolverhampton, West Midlands. It is owned by the National Trust and open on selected days from March to October.
Tel: 01902 782808
www.nationaltrust.org.uk

MR STRAW'S HOUSE

A semi-detached villa, redecorated in the 1920s

Every now and then you come across a house that serves not simply as a reminder of the design styles of a previous age but also as a fascinating glimpse into the real lives behind the bricks, mortar, paint and wallpaper. Mr Straw's House is one such gem! It is a fascinating time warp where hardly anything has changed since Mr Straw senior died in 1932 – the calendar from that time, to the right of the dining room fireplace, is a poignant reminder.

Even in the narrow hall, with its stained-glass doorway and hall table with coat brush and old letters, there is a sense of the daily routines and attitudes of Mr and Mrs Straw's two sons who lived here until their deaths in 1976 and 1990. They felt the loss of their parents so keenly that, touchingly, they kept the house relatively unchanged, especially the rooms most used by their mother Florence – the back parlour and their parents' bedroom, retaining her 1923 decorating scheme and the characteristic clutter of early 20th-century suburban life.

The Straw family were middle-class tradespeople who ran the local grocer's shop. They were relatively well-off compared with many of their contemporaries and the interior of the house reflects this status. However, much of the clutter in the attic rooms, originally for servants, was brought from the shop when Walter Straw shut up shop for the last time in the early 1960s.

The layout of the house reflected the Straw family's middle-class status, with attic rooms for the servants, a formal parlour with large bay window to the front and dining room behind it. Interestingly, Mrs Straw must have preferred the back of the house because she put her parlour there (also choosing the corresponding room upstairs for their bedroom). But the ceiling in the front room gives away the fact that it was designed to be the 'best room', having

a plaster ceiling rose and grander fireplace. The family used this front room as their dining and family room and it feels essentially Victorian in style, with its dark patterned Sanderson wallpaper (their papers were used throughout), heavy furniture and typical clutter. But the parlour or sitting room is much brighter, partly owing to its French window dressed with flowery Sanderson fabric that matches

The back parlour at Mr Straw's House. This room was particularly used by Mrs Straw.

Above left: The hallway showing the wooden staircase and banister, and the Straw brothers' various coats and hats.

Above: Sanderson's 'Eton rural' fabric design was used for the curtains in the back parlour.

the chair covers, white painted skirting boards and picture rails, reflecting Mrs Straw's more feminine tastes. Before heading upstairs, take a closer look at the dining-room door which was given a graining effect to create the illusion that it is made from expensive oak, with a chequered black-and-white paper inlay that looks like marquetry.

Everywhere in the house, the furnishings provide fascinating clues as to the prevailing social attitudes of the time, no more so than in the expensive Egyptian-design Axminster stair carpet which stops just round the corner of the first landing, giving guests the illusion that the whole house is thus carpeted (visitors would not have found this out, never being

One of the delightful green fireplace tiles in the dining room.

Detail of the carpet in the hall, with its fashionable Egyptian design.

Above: The front room, Victorian in style.

Above right: The exterior of Mr Straw's House, a semi-detached villa built in 1905–07.

allowed upstairs). Egyptian designs were very popular around this time, owing to the discovery in 1922 of Tutankhamun's tomb, so Mrs Straw's choice of carpet in 1923 would have been very fashionable and signalled her good taste to visitors. The decorative brass light switches on the ground and first floors of the villa become plain brown bakelite in the attic area where the maid would have slept. It is said that the brothers dismissed their daily maid after their parents died because it would have been improper to have a female in the house with two men! Finally, the funniest and most obvious sign of social delineation is the abrupt ending of the dado rail and its accompanying anaglypta wallpaper on the main landing, just where the stairs wend up to the second-floor attic rooms – they might just as well have put a sign up saying 'Poor wretches, this way'!

The parents' bedroom was lovingly preserved in its original state by the brothers, right down to their father's detachable shirt collars still in their

box on the dressing table and their mother's dresses preserved under layers of blankets and old newspaper on the bed. The pale grey flower Sanderson wallpaper with narrow border around the picture rail and skirting board is typical of the 1920s, as are the pretty Nottingham lace curtains. Interestingly, the handsome gilt mirror is centred according to the wall rather than the fireplace which was fitted off-centre.

Perhaps one of the best reminders of how far we've come since the 1920s in terms of 'modernization' is in the very basic bathroom and kitchen, both of which are perfectly functional and obviously served the brothers well, but are not quite up to the demands of modern living! *MD*

Mr Straw's House is in Blyth Grove, Worksop, Nottinghamshire. It is owned by the National Trust and open by appointment only from the beginning of April to the end of October.
Tel: 01909 482380
www.nationaltrust.org.uk

PACKWOOD HOUSE

A Tudor manor house restored in the early 20th century

The Great Hall at Packwood, showing the oak refectory table brought from nearby Baddesley Clinton (p 131).

When Graham Baron Ash gifted Packwood House to the National Trust in 1941, he left behind a fascinating insight into one Englishman's obsession with all things Tudor. For 20 years or so between the two World Wars, the renovation of Packwood and its interiors consumed all of Ash's time and energy as well as a considerable chunk of his funds before he moved on to his next and final project, Wingfield Castle, a moated castle in Suffolk.

'Baron' Ash, as he preferred to be known, gave himself over completely to restoring this fairly compact Tudor manor house in the 1920s and 30s, using the vast wealth he inherited from the family business in the steel trade, and cleverly employing the architect who had previously restored Shakespeare's Birthplace (p 164) in nearby Stratford-upon-Avon.

A veritable magpie when it came to collecting authentic furnishings, Baron Ash wanted to take the interior of the manor house back to its rightful era, though he couldn't resist adding a few romantic touches, most significantly the Great Hall (converted from a hay barn) and the Long Gallery.

He hunted down and installed genuine 16th- and 17th-century wood panelling and floors, and bought in Tudor and Stuart furniture, tapestries and even stained glass for the mullioned windows from wherever he

An early 18th-century walnut chair against a 17th-century tapestry in the Great Hall.

The Long Gallery, built in 1931 in order to join the new Great Hall to the house, with antique panelling and fireplace brought in and made to fit.

could find it – country-house sales or demolitions, decommissioned churches and cathedral renovations. Many furnishings actually came from Baddesley Clinton (p 131), just down the road. Baddesley's owner, Cecil Ferrers, was trying to avoid having to sell his estate by selling off various pieces to Baron Ash, most notably the stunning oak refectory table in the Great Hall.

Baron Ash's efforts were not in vain because it's hard to believe that Packwood's interior hasn't always been as it is today – a heartening example for anyone trying to recreate Tudor features in their own period property.

On closer inspection, of course, there is something of the *trompe l'œil* in much of Baron Ash's work: the Great

Hall was once an outlying barn and the Long Gallery is a cleverly disguised corridor connecting the Great Hall to the main house, showing off some of the furniture collection at the same time. In the Great Hall, the wine barrels carved into the massive stone fireplace suggest that it, and its accompanying plaster overmantel, once warmed a wine shop. In fact, experts have discovered that the fireplace came from an old wine shop in Stratford-upon-Avon that was open in the 16th century, so Shakespeare himself might have supped wine by this very fireplace.

Much of the Tudor and Jacobean oak panelling and floorboards, so seamlessly fitted into Packwood by craftsmen in the early 20th century, came from country-house sales. For example, the beautiful solid oak floors in the hall and Great Hall both came originally from Lymore Park in Montgomeryshire, sadly demolished in the 1930s. And in the Ireton Room the door in the panelling opposite the bed is a reminder that all is not always what it seems at Packwood. The door opens straight onto a brick wall, rein-forcing the fact that this is recycled panelling. Several fireplaces in the house, including that in the Long Gallery, contain small cupboard doors in their surrounds – the cupboards would have been used to keep spices and salt dry in Tudor times, but the lack of recesses behind them, making them of little use today, is evidence that they, too, have been brought in from elsewhere. The panelling in the corridor outside Queen Margaret's Bedchamber, so named because Queen Margaret of Anjou reputedly slept in the bed in 1471, looks genuine enough, but the odd chip reveals that it is painted plasterwork, an old trick that is still used today to cut the cost of materials.

Apart from the wealth of fine 17th-century furniture on display at Packwood, the soft furnishings deserve a special mention in their own right, particularly the beautifully patterned crewelwork in the Ireton Bedroom. The bedspread alone took some 240 hours to restore. In Queen Margaret's Bedroom, note the red-and-cream bed hangings with their bold geometric design and take a peek under the canopy where the design from the bedhead is continued to even greater effect.

Queen Margaret's Bedroom, with its 15th-century bedstead.

After so much wood panelling, it's a surprise to enter the cool Delft-tiled Ireton Bathroom, with its original Deco-style chrome taps, towel rail and tiny silver butler's bell right by the bath. It's nice to think that Baron Ash allowed himself the odd moment of 20th-century indulgence in this otherwise strictly authentic Tudor interior.

Don't miss Packwood's glorious gardens, including the famous herbaceous borders and the extraordinary 17th-century yew garden, traditionally said to represent 'The Sermon on the Mount'. *MD*

Packwood House is 11 miles south-east of central Birmingham and 2 miles east of Hockley Heath, Warwickshire. It is owned by the National Trust and open on selected days from March to November.
Tel: 01564 783294
www.nationaltrust.org.uk

The Ireton Bathroom, with blue-and-white Delft tiles surrounding the bathtub.

SELLY MANOR

A medieval manor house with Tudor interiors

Selly Manor, one of Birmingham's oldest buildings, is a 14th-century timber-framed manor house rescued from demolition and moved in 1912 by the Cadbury family to Bournville from its original site in nearby Bournbrook. The interior has been faithfully recreated to reflect domestic life as it would have been in Tudor times, with canopied tester beds, solid oak furniture and authentic kitchenware from the period. The site is also home to the medieval hall Minworth Greaves. *MD*

Selly Manor is in Maple Road, Bournville, south-west of Birmingham city centre. It is owned by the Bournville Village Trust and open on selected days all year.
Tel: 0121 472 0199
www.bvt.org.uk/sellymanor

A period tester bed in one of the bedchambers at Selly Manor.

THE SHAKESPEARE HOUSES

Tudor houses linked to William Shakespeare

Shakespeare's Birthplace, where William Shakespeare was born in 1564, is one of the five properties linked to Shakespeare and his family, now owned by the Shakespeare Birthplace Trust. It is a typical provincial merchant's house bought in the mid 1500s by William's father John, a master glover.

The emerging middle classes of 16th-century England, including John Shakespeare, were ostentatious and desperate to show off their new-found wealth. They achieved this by filling their homes with bright wall hangings, Gothic-style carved furniture, tester beds with bright textiles, tapestries and pewterware. The intricate and richly coloured wall hangings in the main parlour and the 'Italian grotesque' textile panels in the first upper chamber are copies from rare fragments of 16th-century wool and linen textiles, discovered behind old panelling in the Golden Cross Inn, Oxford.

The textile-hung bed in the parlour is another faithful copy, from the original 16th-century bed in Anne Hathaway's Cottage nearby, and would have acted as a bold social statement to anyone calling on the Shakespeares. If you were wealthy enough to own a spare bed, you certainly didn't hide it away upstairs but made sure it was on display to visitors!

Shakespeare's Birthplace, a typical provincial merchant's home.

The parlour at Hall's Croft, once the home of Shakespeare's daughter Susannna.

A third set of wall hangings, in the hall where the family would have eaten, provides a fascinating take on *trompe l'œil*. From a distance it looks exactly like wood panelling, something which Tudor folk like John Shakespeare aspired to but could not

The kitchen at Anne Hathaway's Cottage.

necessarily afford. The outer border is designed to look like tortoiseshell and the blue jewel in the centre of each panel like lapis lazuli – both exotic and rare, and a visible reminder of the family's ambitions.

Over the years, the Trust's experts have gathered some fine examples of rare Tudor furniture, such as the beautifully simple stool and bench in front of the Birthplace's hall fire, and the low bench in the kitchen.

In contrast, Hall's Croft (also in Stratford) seems more sparsely furnished, although it still reflects the prosperity of its first owner Dr John Hall, a respected physician who married William Shakespeare's daughter Susanna and lived there in the early 17th century.

Highlights among its original Jacobean furnishings are a 'truckle' bed (copied from an original), an early version of the 'put-you-up'. The bed peeps out from under the 16th-century canopied bed in the main bedchamber. The design of such beds, using rope struts on a chunky frame, gave rise to the bedtime phrase still repeated by parents every night: 'Night-night, sleep tight'. This is because the ropes would have needed tightening occasionally so that a child could indeed 'sleep tight'.

This penchant for practical, adaptable furniture can also be seen in the rare 16th-century seat-table in the back hall at Hall's Croft. At first glance, it looks like a simple monks' bench but closer inspection reveals that it contains storage inside the seat, and the tall backrest flips up and over to become a table or, if you were a monk, a suitably hard bed for the night! For sheer workmanship, look out for the marquetry wall cupboards and the lovely Welsh high-back bobbin chair in the parlour, painstakingly crafted by an apprentice to prove his worth to his master (hence the term 'masterpiece').

In contrast to the 'pure' Tudor and Jacobean styles of Shakespeare's Birthplace and Hall's Croft, the thatched childhood home of Anne Hathaway, who married William Shakespeare in 1582, reflects rural Victorian living, although the furniture dates from the 16th century right through to the 19th century. The most obvious signs of Victorian style include the exposed, stained beams, whitewashed walls, glass-paned windows dressed with curtains, and ceilings in the upstairs chambers which, in Tudor times, would have been open to the roof thatch.

The plain canopied bed in the right-hand upper chamber dates from Anne's time and features homespun cloth hangings. It is a particularly rare example, as only more ornate designs, like the famous 'Hathaway bed' in the main upstairs chamber, usually survived by being handed down as heirlooms. The late 18th-century straw chair in the room to the left of the stairs wouldn't look out of place in any modern-day conservatory and serves as a salient reminder that 'what goes around comes around'! *MD*

Shakespeare's Birthplace and **Hall's Croft** are in the centre of Stratford-upon-Avon, Warwickshire; **Anne Hathaway's Cottage** is in Shottery, just over a mile from the centre of Stratford. The properties are owned by the Shakespeare Birthplace Trust, along with two other houses connected with the bard (Mary Arden's House and Nash's House & New Place). All five properties are open all year.
Tel: 01789 204016
www.shakespeare.org.uk

The parlour at Shakespeare's Birthplace, with its original stone floor.

Anne Hathaway's Cottage in Shottery.

STOKESAY CASTLE

A fortified medieval manor house

The he secret of Stokesay's charm lies in the fact that it was unoccupied after 1750 so hasn't endured centuries of 'modernization' unlike some other historic houses, and its interiors such as the Great Hall and the Solar Chamber have retained their original features. The Great Hall has gabled windows, a fine timber roof, octagonal hearth and medieval timber staircase while the Solar Chamber contains a breathtaking Jacobean fireplace – probably of Flemish origin – with carved overmantel featuring grotesque figures, originally painted gold, pink, red, green and white. *MD*

Stokesay is 7 miles north-west of Ludlow, Shropshire, off the A49. It is administered by English Heritage and open on selected days all year.
Tel: 01588 672544
www.english-heritage.org.uk

One of several gargoyles 'protecting' the 17th-century gatehouse.

Stokesay Castle, with its picturesque timber-framed gatehouse.

SULGRAVE MANOR

A Tudor manor house

SUNNYCROFT

A suburban late Victorian gentleman's villa

Sulgrave Manor is the ancestral home of the family of George Washington, first American president, built back in 1539 by his forebear Lawrence Washington, a prosperous wool merchant and mayor of Northampton. Its interior style is a mixture of Tudor and Georgian, with furnishings from the two periods in authentic room settings such as the kitchen and dining room, and new embroidered bed hangings inspired by Elizabethan designs. **MD**

Sulgrave Manor is at Sulgrave, near Banbury in Oxfordshire, off the B4525. It is privately owned and open from April to October.
Tel: 01295 760205
www.sulgravemanor.org.uk

Sulgrave Manor, built in 1539.

In stark contrast to its grander neighbour Attingham Park (p 128), but still aping some of the same design principles, Sunnycroft is a rare surviving example of the suburban Victorian gentleman's villa, built between 1880 and 1899. Instantly recognizable as a late 19th-century house, with its dado and frieze rails, solid furniture, Maws & Co tiled hallway, elaborate brass light fittings and general clutter, the

Sunnycroft, a classic example of a late Victorian villa, survives remarkably unaltered.

rooms are still fairly well delineated along 'male' and 'female' lines, as in Attingham, but with even more attention to that favoured middle-class occupation … socializing.

The billiard room is intentionally masculine, with its carved wood fireplace, large billiard table and dark patterned wallpaper, while the drawing room feels much lighter and more feminine. This is partly due to the 1970s Laura Ashley wallpaper, gleaming white marble fireplace and white painted woodwork. It also has a 'cosy corner', a built-in seating area fashionable in such houses – originally there would have been a screen that could be pulled across to allow for private conversations.

The so-called 'Jacobethan' inner hall is a Victorian interpretation of old-English style, with elaborate wood panelling and a galleried landing to show off the mainly 19th-century portraits of the family. Take a look, too, at the inner hall's Art Nouveau fireplace with its typical tulip-stem relief, that looks ahead rather than backwards in its design. *MD*

**Detail of a glass skylight
on the upper landing.**

Sunnycroft is off the B5061 in Wellington, Shropshire. It is run by the National Trust and open on selected days from the end of March to the end of October.
Tel: 01952 242884
www.nationaltrust.org.uk

WESTON PARK
*An imposing
17th-century
house*

The elegant dining room at Weston Park.

This 17th-century house has 19th-century additions including the dining room and several salons. Much of it was redecorated and rearranged in the 20th century by Mary, the 6th Earl of Bradford's wife. In the 17th century, the 2nd Earl of Bradford, Richard Newport, and his brother, Lord Torrington, avidly collected art, furniture and ceramics from abroad, much of which forms the heart of the interior today. Look out for the unusual painted 'mock' wood panelling in the library and the wrought-iron main staircase. *MD*

Weston Park is east of Telford on the A5 at Weston-under-Lizard, Shropshire. It is owned by the Weston Park Foundation, a charitable trust, and open on selected days from April to September.
Tel: 01952 852100
www.weston-park.com

WIGHTWICK MANOR

A late Victorian, mock 'old English' style house with Arts and Crafts interiors

Wightwick's richly furnished rooms are breathtaking in their well-balanced proportions, strong sense of style and eclectic content. The furniture, soft furnishings and Pre-Raphaelite paintings complement the scale and architectural features of the house perfectly and were carefully collected by Sir Theodore Mander, a Wolverhampton paint and varnish manufacturer in the late 19th and early 20th centuries, and by more recent generations including the MP, Sir Geoffrey Mander.

In a similar way to Packwood House (p 160), authentic Tudor panelling was recycled from the existing manor house on the site (still seen at the front of the property) and used to line the walls of the interior. This carried through the 'old English' style from the outside of the building. The architect of this 1887 house was Edward Ould, who specialized in new-build, timber-framed houses for the middle classes with 'new money', and he added the east wing with its massive Great Saloon, mock minstrels' gallery and five guest bedrooms in 1893.

What really lends Wightwick Manor its unique style is the marvellous collection of William Morris designs on

Drawing of Wightwick Manor by Edmund Hodgkinson (1889).

Detail of the 'Bird' tapestry designed by Morris, used on the upholstered settee in the Great Parlour.

fabric, wallpaper and carpets, mostly original and in fabulous condition. Apart from designs on curtains, carpets and sofas, Morris's fabric designs have also been used as wall hangings, such as the 'Dove and Rose' silk and wool design in the drawing room.

Morris & Co wallpapers are used liberally throughout the house especially in the bedrooms. Each bedroom is named after the wallpaper design chosen and the designs represent the firm's lifetime output. For example, Morris's first wallpaper was 'Daisy', a pretty but naive design that lends freshness to the Daisy Bedroom, while the progression towards more complex designs can be seen in Acanthus (also upstairs), a pattern which took 20 printing blocks to complete!

Throughout the house on walls, fireplaces and furniture there are beautifully stencilled quotations in carefully chosen typefaces from poets as diverse as Shakespeare, Keats and Ruskin, a

A corner of the Great Parlour showing the late Victorian piano and silk-lined cabinets with wrought-iron doors.

Painted glass by Burne-Jones for Morris & Co., in the billiard room.

simple idea that works perfectly and could easily be incorporated into domestic design schemes. Upstairs, many of the quotes, quite rightly, focus on the theme of sleep while downstairs, nature is strongly represented as might be expected from the age that brought us Morris's incredible flower and leaf print designs and the paintings of the Pre-Raphaelites.

The various pieces of stained-glass work by Charles Kempe deserve a special mention and many of them, such as that on the top panes of the bay window in the drawing room, continue the nature theme, by depicting the four seasons. This creates a subtle link to the garden and is a principle keenly espoused by many of today's designers.

Kempe's most substantial piece of work in the house is the interior of the Great Parlour, including his frieze work depicting the classical story of Orpheus and Eurydice which echoes the Elizabethan frieze at Hardwick Hall in Derbyshire (p 145). The design can be seen up close from the minstrels' gallery. From here there is access to the various guest bedrooms including the impressive but sombre Oak Bedroom, with its writing area and originally separate dressing room. On the way up, take note of the wonderful touchy-feely rush matting used to cover the bottom half of the staircase walls.

The De Morgan tiles (pieces of his lustreware are also on display) in many of the fireplaces add richness to the overall effect, especially in the entrance hall's cosy inglenook, building yet another layer of richness into the overall design.

Here and there in Wightwick, there are reminders that design cannot (and never should) stand still. Perhaps the best example of this is seen in the march towards Art Nouveau that stands in the billiard room – the Voysey chair near the windows seems oddly shaped, but designs such as this heralded the 'next phase'. The two-layered curtain design in the billiard room – a plain green curtain overlaid with a green Morris design – is very effective and practical.

Finally, for an apple-pie slice of pure nostalgia from the 1930s, don't miss the delightful, linoleum-floored Night and Day Nurseries where the children of the house spent the majority of their time, playing with and being educated by governesses, before being fed and tucked up in bed by their nursemaids. In the Day Nursery there are charming Snow White fabric-covered Victorian chairs and in the Night Nursery the fireplace has 'days of the week' Minton tiles. *MD*

Wightwick, not considered a particularly large household, had ten indoor staff around 1900.

Wightwick Manor is 3 miles west of Wolverhampton, West Midlands, off the A454. It is owned by the National Trust and open on selected days from the beginning of March to December. **Tel: 01902 761400 www.nationaltrust. org.uk**

In the drawing room, a late 17th-century walnut marquetry cabinet is topped by a stunning example of De Morgan pottery.

EASTERN ENGLAND

Wild eccentricity is the mark of at least two of the great houses of Eastern England. Knebworth House in Hertfordshire was writer Edward Bulwer-Lytton's Gothic fantasy made reality, while the Herveys' Ickworth, near Bury St Edmunds, with its curved rooms built to house a Grand Tour collection that was snatched by Napoleon, is like no other house in England.

More solid and reassuring are the great estate houses and of these perhaps the most beautiful is Holkham Hall in Norfolk, built in the 18th century to fulfil the Palladian dreams of Thomas Coke who fell in love with the classical world. Nearby Houghton Hall is Palladian revival, too.

An earlier Jacobean splendour reigns at Hatfield House in Hertfordshire, palace and one-time home to the young Queen Elizabeth I. The most expensive building of all was the huge Audley End at Saffron Walden. Once the largest house in the country, it was built with dubiously gotten gains, allowed to fall into ruin and restored, twice, to reflect both the Jacobean and Georgian periods. Blickling Hall near Aylsham and Felbrigg Hall near Cromer each show their Jacobean origins enlivened by 18th-century money and additions.

Eastern England is an area of surprise and style – probably the earliest surprise is the medieval merchant's Dragon Hall in Norwich, while style shines through everywhere, from the fairy-tale turrets of Knebworth House in Hertfordshire to the astonishing entrance hall at Holkham Hall. *AB*

AUDLEY END

A prodigy house with Jacobean and neoclassical interiors

A 'prodigy house' was one built to impress and to entertain royalty and Audley End, once a palace to rival the largest in the land, is one of the greatest prodigy houses in England. But its creator, Thomas Howard, 1st Earl of Suffolk and Lord Chamberlain of the Household, went too far in his attempts to woo James I. He spent the then unbelievable sum of £200,000 on the enormous house, with its double courtyard, state apartments, two porches (one for the king's entry and one for the queen's), Great Hall and all the other reception rooms, family apartments, bedchambers and servants' quarters that were necessary for such a palatial undertaking.

Audley End was built by 1614, the year that James elevated Thomas Howard to Lord Treasurer of England, wryly remarking that the new palace was too great a house for a king, but might suit a lord treasurer. Just four years later, Howard was in deep

disgrace and was flung into the Tower, accused of corruption, extortion and bribery. Although he managed to buy his life and freedom by paying a huge fine, he and his family never really recovered from the burden of debt that he incurred.

The fortunes of Audley End did not improve, even though Charles II bought it in 1666 and briefly held court here. The house came back to the Howards at the beginning of the 18th century but it wasn't until it passed to Sir John Griffin Whitwell (who became Sir John Griffin Griffin to comply with the terms of the will) in 1762 that a renaissance took place here. Sir John (later the 1st Lord Braybrooke) called in Robert Adam to put a neoclassical face on the old Jacobean interior, and Lancelot 'Capability' Brown to landscape the park. At the same time John Hobcroft rebuilt the chapel in exuberant Gothic style, with fan vaulting, ribs, arcading

The Jacobean façade hides a variety of interior styles at Audley End.

and imitation stone columns. The large 'Last Supper' stained-glass window in the chapel was made by William Peckitt in 1771. Audley End was again among the finest houses in the country.

Then, 50 years later, the 3rd Lord Braybrooke, a keen antiquarian and scholar, moved in. He and his wife (when not considering the needs of their eight children) devoted much time and energy to restoring the Jacobean magnificence of the old palace – and they did it very well. But in the process they destroyed much of Adam's work. The extraordinary

The Jacobean style is evident in the Great Hall (right) with its impressive twin flights of stairs, and in the saloon (below).

THE ITALIAN JOB
The artist Biagio Rebecca was of Italian descent but he lived and worked in England. He collaborated with Robert Adam at a number of houses, including Audley End, Kedleston Hall (p 154) and Harewood House (p 225).

chapel was due for conversion too, but they somehow never got round to it.

Visitors today will be relieved to see the exquisite set of Adam reception rooms open for inspection; they will also see Lord Braybrooke's equally impressive Jacobean revival rooms on display. The two sets – thickly plastered Jacobean ceilings and precise and perfect neoclassical beauty – survive because the government, who bought the house after the Second World War, reinstated the Adam rooms in the 1960s.

The Great Hall, with its original carved wooden Jacobean screen, and largely original roof, was the perfect place for Lord Braybrooke's collections of antiquities and family pieces.

It leads, by way of the staircase, to the sequence of rooms created in the 1820s, which are Jacobean in style, with Regency furnishings and wonderful collections of paintings, including a Canaletto (*View of the Campanile and Doge's Palace*) and two fine Van Goyens in the drawing room.

There are two libraries – the smaller used by Lord Braybrooke as a study (look out for the strangely shaped triangular chair, which once belonged to Alexander Pope) and the larger, furnished comfortably for social gatherings, with a splendid view over the garden from a bay window.

Jacobean scrollwork is a feature of all the lavishly plastered ceilings in this set of light and comfortable rooms. The dining room, a large chamber created out of two smaller rooms, has a table laid for ten and portraits on the walls, including one of George II, painted by Robert Edge Pine.

It's hard not to rush headlong to the restored Adam reception rooms but there's a feast of taxidermy in the shape of the 4th Lord Braybrooke's bird and animal collection, the Gothic chapel, a large doll's house, the butler's pantry and bedrooms to see along the way.

The Great Drawing Room, one of two drawing rooms at Audley End designed by Robert Adam.

When one does reach the Adam rooms in the south wing, the contrast could hardly be greater. The Ministry of Works, responsible for the 1960s' restoration, chose to put back the two drawing rooms, the lobby and the dining room. Of these, the Little Drawing Room, to which the ladies would have escaped after dinner, is a perfect neoclassical interior, richly decorated by Biagio Rebecca to Adam's designs in 1773. Fine gilding encloses panels of delicately executed flowers and leaves, cherubs and angels, formal motifs taken straight from the walls of Pompeii. The ceiling, finely wrought floral themes enclosed in gilded loops, could not be more different from the elaborate Jacobean work upstairs. *AB*

Detail of the curtains in the Adam-designed Little Drawing Room.

Audley End is 1 mile west of Saffron Walden, Essex, on the B1383. It is owned by English Heritage and open on selected days from early March to the end of October.
Tel: 01799 522399
www.english-heritage.org.uk

BLICKLING HALL

A Jacobean mansion

This very grand and beautiful Jacobean mansion was designed by the creator of Hatfield House (p 181), Robert Lyminge. The Long Gallery, Jacobean in decoration, with its spectacular original plasterwork ceiling, is not spoiled by the addition of a Victorian frieze and delicate stained glass. The Chinese Bedroom is exotic and beautiful, with its carved ivory pagoda and pretty wallpaper, and there are fine collections of furniture, paintings, books and tapestries. *AB*

The Long Gallery at Blickling – the room is 123ft (37m) long.

Blickling Hall is in Blickling, Norfolk, 1 mile north-west of Aylsham, on the B1354. It is owned by the National Trust and open on selected days from March to the end of October.
Tel: 01263 738030
www.nationaltrust.org.uk

DRAGON HALL

A medieval merchant's hall

A routine roof inspection led to the exciting discovery of this, the only medieval merchant's hall of its type known to exist in Western Europe. Once Norwich City Council had saved the unique roof space they handed the property to the Norfolk and Norwich Heritage Trust, who continued the restoration. The hall, which was used in the 15th century both for trading and domestic purposes by Robert Toppes, a wealthy merchant and Mayor of Norwich, is named after the intricately carved and painted dragon that survives in the spandrel of a tie beam. *AB*

The half-timbered exterior of Dragon Hall, a fascinating legacy of medieval life.

Dragon Hall is in King Street, Norwich, Norfolk. It is owned by the Norfolk and Norwich Heritage Trust and open on selected days all year.
Tel: 01603 663922
www.dragonhall.org

FELBRIGG HALL

A Jacobean mansion with Georgian interiors

'Mad Windham', one-time owner of this great house, with its Jacobean exterior and mainly Georgian interior, would force hapless railway employees to let him drive their trains. He lost his fortune in 1864, but happily the Grand Tour treasures collected by earlier Windhams survive, especially a fine clutch of Italian paintings. Felbrigg also contains its original 18th-century furniture and upstairs there is a fine library. The dining room was redecorated in 1752 by James Paine and includes rococo plasterwork by Joseph Rose the Elder. *AB*

Felbrigg Hall is 2 miles south-west of Cromer, Norfolk, off the A148. It is owned by the National Trust and open on selected days from the end of March to November.
Tel: 01263 837444
www.nationaltrust.org.uk

Plasterwork with a flourish in Felbrigg's dining room.

HATFIELD HOUSE

A Jacobean palace with magnificent state rooms

The gleaming chequer-board floor and shining screen in Hatfield's Marble Hall.

A carved newel post on the Grand Staircase.

Hatfield House is an overflowing showcase of early Jacobean style. It is still the home of the Cecil family, which is why visitors see only the dramatic state rooms. Most arresting is the spectacular Marble Hall, its gleaming chequerboard floor, dining furniture, carved screen and minstrels' gallery all original. Here is Nicholas Hilliard's famous *Ermine Portrait* of Elizabeth I, pale-faced and resplendent in black and gold, a live ermine representing her purity. The so-called *Rainbow Portrait*, at the foot of the Grand Staircase, shows her in revealing red, holding a rainbow of peace. A serpent on her sleeve symbolizes wisdom, while eyes and ears, scattered on her gown, say that the eyes and ears of the world are upon her. On the way up the magnificently carved staircase, look at the topmost newel for John Tradescant, plant hunter and gardener to Robert Cecil. You'll know him by the rake he is holding. *AB*

When the king demands a house swap, there's nothing to be done but to give in gracefully, which is why in 1608 Robert Cecil, 1st Earl of Salisbury and chief minister to James I, found himself owning the Old Palace at Hatfield in exchange for his home, Theobalds, at nearby Cheshunt.

Cecil, physically insignificant and sickly-looking, but a political giant, demolished most of the Old Palace, where Elizabeth I had spent her childhood and held her first council as queen in 1558, and he built an imposing modern mansion next door at a total cost of £38,000.

Hatfield House is in Hatfield, Hertfordshire, off junction 23 of the M25. It is owned by the Marquess of Salisbury and open from Easter to the end of September.
Tel: 01707 287010
www.hatfield-house.co.uk

HOLKHAM HALL
A Palladian revival mansion

Two paintings, hanging in the south dining room at the Coke family's magnificent mansion on the north Norfolk coast, symbolize the great themes of Holkham – classicism and agriculture. Both paintings are of the politician Thomas William Coke – Coke of Norfolk – Member of Parliament, landowner, agricultural reformer and one-time dandy.

Coke as country squire and farmer, painted by Thomas Gainsborough.

The depictions of this far-sighted man couldn't be more different. The mellow portrait by Gainsborough (said to be the last painted by the artist) shows Thomas Coke outside, booted and dressed in country-squire attire, thoughtfully cleaning his gun, while three faithful dogs attend at his feet. The soft evening light falls on the trees and the woodland glade. There is a sense of unbounded acreage. The other

painting is by Grand Tour specialist Pompeo Batoni. The same young Coke, in his fancy-dress finery, pale silks and stockings, fine scarlet cloak and plumed hat casually hung and held, gazes dreamily into the middle distance. Again there is a dog at his feet – and a piece of broken classical pediment. This painting was commissioned by Princess Louise of Stolberg, the 18-year-old bride of the ageing Bonnie Prince Charlie. She fell so heavily for the charming young Englishman that she commissioned the portrait for him. But Coke had other business to attend to. He was just 22 in 1776 when he inherited the Holkham estate and the great house which had been built just a few decades earlier by his ancestor Thomas Coke, 1st Earl of Leicester of the 1st Creation.

FOUNDER OF THE FAMILY FORTUNE
The Coke family fortune was founded in the 16th century by Sir Edward Coke (1552–1634), a successful and brilliant lawyer who became Speaker of the House of Commons and Attorney General to both Queen Elizabeth I and King James I. He was responsible for the prosecution of both Sir Walter Raleigh and Guy Fawkes. He was said to be the only lawyer in the land who could interpret England's often complicated law and some of his judgements are quoted today, more than 300 years after they were pronounced. There's a portrait by Gheeraerts of this uncompromising-looking man in the drawing room.

This Thomas, funded by the family fortunes established by Sir Edward Coke, brilliant lawyer and uncompromising statesman, was also sent on a Grand Tour in the hope that the experience would civilize him and detach him from the pleasures of cockfighting, his all-consuming passion. Travel did

Right: Rich furnishing and decoration in the Green State Bedroom.

Far right: Old Masters hang on the crimson walls of the saloon.

Holkham Hall's astounding Marble Hall – built with English alabaster.

the trick. Young Thomas stayed, mainly in Italy, for six years from 1712 absorbing the ancient culture and, most of all, the architecture. He collected – sculpture, paintings, manuscripts, books – and absorbed classical literature and mythology with a passion. He returned home to Norfolk, determined to design and build a house that would not only pay tribute to the glories of classical civilization but would also be a place in which he could display his collections.

The entrance into the huge space of the coolly classical Marble Hall must be one of the most breathtaking in England. Pale alabaster columns support a frieze, from which rises the magnificent ceiling soaring to 50ft (15m), all decorated panels, a tribute to its inspiration, Rome's Pantheon. White steps sweep to the saloon at the far end while statue-filled galleries allow you to walk behind the colonnade (copied from the Temple of Fortuna Virilis in Rome) and absorb the astounding perfection. The material used is not marble, but alabaster, which was brought from Derbyshire. On the exterior Thomas used, in place of the

Classical style in the library at Holkham Hall.

more obvious stone for his Palladian-style house, locally made bricks which baked to a golden ochre. His design was uncluttered and deceptively simple. A rectangular central block with a clean Palladian portico is enlarged by four wings, one at each corner, containing bedrooms and sitting rooms, for family and guests.

Although succeeding generations may have moved sculptures and paintings around, and some pieces have had to be sold to pay the taxman, the present owner Edward Coke, 7th Earl of Leicester, is intent on ensuring the survival of Holkham Hall and the restoration of the collections to their rightful place. He has restored wall coverings and put in place carpets that visitors can walk across to see the paintings. The blinds are up, so that natural daylight allows the best view of the rooms, their contents and the grounds and park outside.

Walk through the statue gallery to see the trophies that the first Thomas brought home and carefully arranged, building niches to fit the sculptures. Enjoy the high-ceilinged saloon, rich with gilding and hung with paintings, including *The Return of the Holy Family* by Rubens, where the young Jesus is shown as a plump little boy, rather than a baby. Facing the Rubens is a flamboyant painting by Van Dyck of a gallant soldier-duke on his high-spirited horse. *AB*

Holkham Hall is 3 miles west of Wells-next-the-Sea, Norfolk, on the A149. It is owned by the Earl of Leicester and open on selected days from early June to the end of September.
Tel: 01328 710227
www.holkham.co.uk

HOUGHTON HALL
A grand Palladian mansion

Sir Robert Walpole, England's first Prime Minister, spent more than £200,000 creating this grand early 18th-century Palladian mansion in the Norfolk countryside. Architect James Gibbs was responsible for the flamboyant domes on the formal building and much of the interior decoration was by William Kent. The White Drawing Room exudes elegance, while the hugely impressive Stone Hall, with its busts, statues and playful putti, and the Marble Parlour, its gilded ceiling glowing on the marble sideboards and fireplace, are worth travelling a long way to see. *AB*

Houghton Hall is 10 miles west of Fakenham, Norfolk, off the A148. It is owned by the Marquess of Cholmondeley and open on selected days from Easter to the end of September.
Tel: 01485 528569
www.houghtonhall.com

The lavishly furnished Embroidered Bedchamber.

ICKWORTH

An unusual Italianate house

When the colourful and more than a little eccentric Frederick Hervey inherited the Ickworth estate and the Earldom of Bristol in 1779, he went for a career in the Church to secure an income. The Bishopric of Derry and its worthwhile rents became his, so the good Earl-Bishop took himself off to Europe and started to amass a fine collection of classical art. He planned a great oval house back home at Ickworth, with display space for his works of art. Unhappily for him, the whole lot was seized by Napoleon and auctioned off. The 4th Earl died in Italy, his great building in England only just begun.

But his successor, the 5th Earl, restored the family fortunes and, in 1821, took up the trowel, building a great rotunda with curving corridors to house newly bought works of art. You can see his portrait (he became the 1st Marquess of Bristol), painted by Romney, in the dining room.

Other family portraits, painted by Gainsborough and Reynolds, hang on the walls of the library. Probably the most exciting room in this extraordinary house is the Pompeian Room, designed by J.D. Crace in 1879 and commissioned by the 1st Marquess's grandson. It is based on the Villa Negroni in Rome. *AB*

Detail of a plaque hanging in the West Wing.

Ickworth is in Horringer, on the A143, 3 miles south-west of Bury St Edmunds, Suffolk. It is owned by the National Trust and open on selected days from March to the end of October.
Tel: 01284 735270
www.nationaltrust.org.uk

The entrance front and rotunda – eccentricity in the round at Ickworth.

KNEBWORTH HOUSE

A Tudor mansion with Gothic interiors

The richly furnished Gothic-style State Drawing Room.

A detail of the ornate plasterwork in the State Drawing Room.

Soaring turrets and decorated domes, towers embellished with creatures from dreams and fairy-tale fantasy, romantic battlements standing starkly against the well-ordered English skyline, concealing five centuries of rich family history – this is Knebworth House, its exterior like a magician's cape, cloaking not only what is inside the Lytton family home, but also what is hidden beneath the extraordinary Gothic decoration.

Underneath the stucco that covers the three-storeyed house today, with its gargoyles and grotesques, is plain red Tudor brick, the remaining wing of what was a grand four-sided house, built by Sir Robert Lytton at the very beginning of the 16th century.

Lyttons have lived at Knebworth for more than 500 years, and the imprint of each generation is here. But none left greater marks than Mrs Elizabeth Barbara Bulwer-Lytton, a widow of some determination, and her youngest son, the bookish and imaginative Edward, who became a celebrated novelist and Member of Parliament, developing a taste for unsuitable women and for all things Gothic.

Elizabeth, already a widow, inherited Knebworth in 1810. The once-imposing house was a depressing sight after years of neglect and she took the only course that seemed practical. She called in architect Biagio Rebecca and a team of builders who swept away three sides of the house, added eight towers and a porch, changed the windows and the roof line and covered the whole in gleaming white stucco to create a 'Tudor-Gothic' castle. Thirty years later, her son Sir Edward (now referred to at Knebworth simply as 'Bulwer') indulged his own taste by commissioning the highly decorated exterior and High Gothic designs for the interior.

The house has evolved since Bulwer's time – another storey was added by Robert, 1st Earl of Lytton in 1878, and a great deal of good taste was introduced in the early 20th century when Sir Edwin Lutyens became an in-law. But it is hard not to be drawn back to the Gothic features, devised by Bulwer and his decorator J.G. Crace of Wigmore Street. This is most evident in the State Drawing Room, its rich decoration testament to the early Victorian revival in this type of design.

As the carved doors are flung open, the light shining through the enormous stained-glass window at the far end of the room illuminates the glorious red robes of Henry VII, with whom Sir Robert Lytton, Knebworth's first owner, stood shoulder to shoulder at the Battle of Bosworth (1485). The panelling is studded with the Tudor rose, while the elaborate ceiling panels show the 44 armorial quarterings of Bulwer's mother, tracing a noble descent. There is fine Gothic furniture in this room, magnificent wall tables

A detail of a Gothic side table in the State Drawing Room at Knebworth.

CHURCHILL IN LOVE
The numerous family portraits at Knebworth include arresting likenesses of the beautiful Pamela, wife to Victor, the 2nd Earl. The young Winston Churchill fell heavily for her but she refused his proposal of marriage, preferring Victor, also a friend. The friendships survived and Winston was a frequent visitor at Knebworth – his painting of the banqueting hall is in the room itself, hanging below a portrait of Sir Robert Lytton.

The banqueting hall still has a Jacobean feel.

and a fireplace crowned with a sumptuous canopy. The whole effect is one of luxury and warmth.

Just through the Oval Ante-Room, with its pretty painted ceiling, is Bulwer's study. A set of fine beaded tapestries hang here – rejected by Crace as ornaments for the State Drawing Room because they weren't nearly Gothic enough.

The oak staircase, with its impressive carvings.

But both Bulwer and Crace were satisfied with their creation of the oak staircase, decorated with shield-bearing lions and Nubian slaves, the light from the long mullioned windows stained by the coloured glass as it filters through the family coats of arms.

Although the impulsive and often arrogant Bulwer made a marriage against the wishes of his mother, she was always the woman who had the most influence on his life. After her death in 1843, he justified his embellishments of the house by saying that he was carrying on her work: 'But in a more complete form of architecture than a woman could have been expected to have understood.' It is interesting that he did not touch her bedroom with its ivory-painted panelling embellished with pictures of her much-loved Juba, an undoubtedly strange-looking pug dog. The light and airy room is much as she left it, in uncluttered Regency style.

Knebworth is still a family home and that's the joy of this wonderful house – the people and their history shine through in every room. *AB*

Elizabeth Bulwer-Lytton's light and airy bedroom is Regency in style.

Knebworth House is off junction 7 of the A1(M) near Stevenage, Hertfordshire. It is owned by the Lytton family and open on selected days from the end of March to the end of September.
Tel: 01483 812661
www.knebworthhouse.com

OXBURGH HALL
A moated Tudor manor house

A moat still guards historic Oxburgh Hall.

There is an overwhelming sense of centuries of British history as one approaches the magnificent gatehouse guarding this early Tudor moated brick building, built in 1482 by the Bedingfield family, who still live here. Kings and queens have been entertained at Oxburgh, and the house contains some splendid carved oak furniture, embossed Spanish leather wall hangings and a fine collection of early tapestries and embroidery, including precious needlework panels sewn by Mary Queen of Scots. *AB*

Oxburgh Hall is 7 miles south-west of Swaffam, Norfolk, off the A134. It is owned by the National Trust and open on selected days from March to November.
Tel: 01366 328258
www.nationaltrust.org.uk

PECKOVER HOUSE

A Georgian town house

This fine Georgian town house is on the brink – that is the North Brink – overlooking the River Nene. This is where the wealthy merchants and business people of Wisbech built their homes in the late 18th century. The glory of Peckover is the outstanding plasterwork, rococo in the entrance hall and wildly exuberant in the drawing room. There is a large library and a collection of watercolours from the Norwich School of artists, including several works by John Sell Cotman. *AB*

Peckover House is in North Brink in Wisbech, Cambridgeshire. It is owned by the National Trust and open on selected days from March to October.
Tel: 01945 583463
www.nationaltrust.org.uk

Extravagant rococo plasterwork in Peckover's drawing room.

SHAW'S CORNER

The fascinating Edwardian home of writer George Bernard Shaw

A writer's haven – the South Front of Shaw's Corner.

Writer and thinker George Bernard Shaw and his wife Charlotte lived out their celibate marriage at Shaw's Corner for 40 years until her death in 1943. This Edwardian villa (built in 1902) is a shrine to Shaw, who stayed on until his own death in 1950. His collection of hats hangs inside the door, while his study is full of pictures of himself and his friends. The Bechstein piano, which he played downstairs every evening to entertain Charlotte as she lay upstairs, is there too. *AB*

Shaw's Corner is off the B653 in Ayot St Lawrence, 3 miles west of Welwyn, Hertfordshire. It is owned by the National Trust and open on selected days from March to October.
Tel: 01438 820307
www.nationaltrust.org.uk

SOMERLEYTON HALL

A Victorian house with Jacobean Italianate interiors

Somerleyton Hall is 5 miles north-west of Lowestoft, Suffolk, off the B1074. It is privately owned and open on selected days from April to the end of October.
Tel: 08712 224244
www.somerleyton. co.uk

The richly carved domed entrance hall.

Victorian extravagance, afforded by the fortune of property tycoon and builder Sir Morton Peto, turned this Jacobean house into a wonderful Italianate palace, stuffed full of treasures. When Sir Morton's fortunes failed, the Crossley family bought the Hall in 1863. Look for the carving (perhaps by Grinling Gibbons) in the Oak Room – a rich mix of acanthus, sunflowers, cockerels, pomegranates and grapes, and the looking glass originally designed for the Doge's Palace in Venice. *AB*

WIMPOLE HALL

A Jacobean house with Georgian decoration

It is largely thanks to Rudyard Kipling's daughter, Elsie Bainbridge, Wimpole Hall's last private owner, that we can enjoy Cambridgeshire's largest stately home. Wimpole, built by Sir Thomas Chicheley around 1650, has been cursed by owners who lived too well and had to sell their home to balance their books. James Gibbs, Henry Flitcroft, John Soane and Humphrey Repton all had a hand in the design of what is seen today and what Mrs Bainbridge and the National Trust have faithfully recovered. *AB*

The library, designed by James Gibbs to house a collection of 50,000 books.

Wimpole Hall is 8 miles south-west of Cambridge, on the A603. It is owned by the National Trust and open on selected days from late March to the end of November.
Tel: 01223 207257
www.nationaltrust.org.uk

THE LAKE DISTRICT AND NORTH-WEST ENGLAND

Palaces were built and dynasties established on royal gratitude and nowhere is this more evident than at Lyme Park, a mansion constructed on land given for saving the Black Prince at the Battle of Crécy. This palatial house outside Stockport, home to the Leghs, remained in the hands of that one family until 1946. The dynastic theme is also evident at Sizergh Castle and Holker Hall. But although members of the Strickland family still live in parts of Sizergh, it is run by the National Trust, whereas Holker is still very much occupied by Cavendishes.

Our early Tudor buildings represent power of a different sort – that of the feudal lord making the Great Hall of his home his regional power base. We see the picturesque, perhaps forgetting that the fate of communities often depended on business conducted in the halls of such buildings as Little Moreton Hall and Rufford Old Hall, where our ancestors carved out the future.

Even beautiful Levens Hall, hidden behind bizarre yew topiary, is built around a defensive 14th-century pele tower, although their Great Hall, still recognizably Elizabethan, is now carpeted.

Later generations, in a safer world, made poetry their power. Lakeland beauty inspired not only poets but also Arts and Crafts designer Baillie Scott, who built beautiful Blackwell on the shores of Lake Windermere. *AB*

BLACKWELL

A fine example of an Arts and Crafts house

A glazed china cabinet sits above the fireplace in Blackwell's serene White Drawing Room.

Blackwell was completed in 1900 by the Arts and Crafts architect M.H. Baillie Scott and it remains the largest and finest example of his early work. The White Drawing Room, with its (white) woodland frieze, stained-glass oriel window and long views over the lake, must be one of the loveliest chambers in the country. There is another glorious frieze, depicting peacocks, in the hall. Blackwell is full of carving, decorative stained glass, tiles, wood and light. *AB*

Blackwell is 1¹/₂ miles south of Bowness-on-Windermere, Cumbria, off the A5074. It is owned by the Lakeland Arts Trust and open from February to December.
Tel: 01539 446139
www.blackwell.org.uk

HOGHTON TOWER

An Elizabethan manor house

Is this where Shakespeare spent some of the 'missing' years? There is mounting evidence, say the owners, the de Hoghton family, that he did. Whatever the truth, there is no doubt that James I stayed here in 1617, and you can still see the menu for the massive feast at which he is said to have 'knighted' a loin of beef ('Sirloin'). This Elizabethan house underwent interior redecoration in 1862 and there is wonderful carved panelling throughout. *AB*

The impressive front entrance of Hoghton Tower.

Hoghton Tower is 6 miles east of Preston, Lancashire, on the A675. It is owned by the de Hoghton family and open on selected days from April to September.
Tel: 01254 852986
www.hoghtontower.co.uk

HOLKER HALL

A grand Victorian mansion with lavish Crace interiors

'History wants to speak to one, but not dictate,' holds Lord Cavendish. His family home, Holker Hall, set in beautiful countryside near the Cumbrian coast overlooking the north side of Morecambe Bay, communicates its past, but speaks also of a house still filled by a family who have loved it for generations. Holker Hall has been occupied since the early 16th century by successive Prestons, Lowthers and Cavendishes, whose relationships have entwined in such a way that the house has never been bought or sold, but inherited by succeeding generations.

William Cavendish, who became the 2nd Earl of Burlington and, later, the 7th Duke of Devonshire, refused to let history dictate when the entire west wing of his newly Gothicized house

Stained glass showing the ducal coronet.

A Louis XV writing desk in the drawing room.

went up in flames in March 1871. Just 30 years earlier he had called upon the architect Webster of Kendal to alter and reface the entire house, adding fashionable tall Gothic chimneys, mullioned and transomed windows, and gables. Within four years the 'new' wing was in place, occupying the same space as the old, but it was altogether grander, faced in warm red sandstone. It flaunted a square tower with parapets, and a round tower topped with a cupola, projecting bow windows and dormers too. It was designed by architects

Paley and Austin to appear Elizabethan, but it proclaims the best of Victorian workmanship.

The new wing is what visitors see: J.G. Crace interiors with the alterations and additions of each generation. The drawing room walls are hung with the original red silk, while the rich green that decorates the billiard room is hand stencilled – eight layers of paint applied by the present Lady Cavendish and a group of her friends.

Light filters into the hallway through hundreds of small panes of glass, showing off the family arms, including the coiled Cavendish snake, a recurring theme in the furnishings. Their punning motto '*Cavendo tutus*' can roughly be translated as 'Better safe than sorry'. An inlaid marble table depicts birds in fruit-tree heaven, and there are clues to the family's loyalties when England was torn apart in the mid 16th century – a copy of Van Dyck's triple portrait of Charles I (the original is at Windsor Castle) and paintings of his wife, Henrietta Maria, James II as the Duke

The Long Gallery where one could play carpet bowls on a wet day or admire the many treasures displayed along the walls and in cabinets.

A Minton washstand set in Queen Mary's Bedroom.

of York, and Barbara Villiers, mistress to Charles II. The Holker estate was confiscated by Parliament when Thomas Preston was rash enough to entertain Royalist troops here in 1644, but payment of substantial fines saw it restored.

The rebuilding of the main hall after the blaze is marked in two ways on the fireplace – by a carved reminder and by a surround made of fragments of marble rescued from a pedestal, destroyed in the flames.

The library and the drawing room both open off the main hall. These are large, comfortable, light rooms, each with historical tales to tell and each used daily by the Cavendish family. Gazing at each other across the library are portraits of husband and wife, Lord Frederick Cavendish and the beautiful Lucy Lyttleton. Lord Frederick survived the fire, which began in his dressing room, only to be brutally murdered in Phoenix Park, Dublin, on 7 May 1882 – the day he arrived to take up his appointment as Gladstone's Chief Secretary for Ireland. Another striking portrait is the John Sargent pencil drawing of Lady Moyra Cavendish, grandmother to the present owner,

Fireplace tiles, featuring the Cavendish family emblem, a coiled snake.

Hugh Cavendish. The electric light switches by the library door are masked by 'books' with strange titles such as *Nero on the Violin* and *Johnson's Contra-dictionary*.

Four huge, heavily carved twisted columns, each made from a single piece of oak grown on the Holker estate, stand sentinel either side of the fireplace in the dining room. Family pictures line the walls, including a charming painting of brothers Lord Edward and Lord Frederick (the unfortunate Chief Secretary) as boys.

There is a fine cantilevered staircase, each baluster heavily carved with a different design. There are elegant bedrooms, with Hepplewhite-style beds and Minton washstand sets. There is also a magnificent Long Gallery complete with a cabinet of treasures, rocking horses and room to play carpet bowls on wet days. *AB*

Detail of musical instruments carved on a French cupboard in the Gloucester Bedroom.

LEVENS HALL
An Elizabethan mansion

Levens Hall lies almost hidden behind bizarre but endearing yew trees cut, as they have been for 300 years, into the strangest of shapes in the topiary garden. The Elizabethan house, lived in by the same family for hundreds of years, is welcoming. Those who like home comforts will particularly appreciate the fine fireplaces and decorated chimneypieces. The dining room has embossed leather wall coverings from Cordova and upstairs there is some 300-year-old patchwork, the earliest English example, beautifully stitched by dutiful daughters of the house. **AB**

The beautiful façade of Levens Hall, with its remarkable yew topiary.

The Wedgwood Bedroom at Holker, named for the collection of Wedgwood Jaspar ware in the adjacent dressing room.

Holker Hall is in Cark-in-Cartmel, Cumbria, off the B5278, 3 miles west of Grange-over-Sands. It is owned by Lord Cavendish and open on selected days from the end of March to the end of October.
Tel: 01539 558328
www.holker-hall.co.uk

Levens Hall is 5 miles south of Kendal, Cumbria, on the A6. It is owned by the Bagot family and open on selected days from April to mid October.
Tel: 01539 560321
www.levenshall.co.uk

LITTLE MORETON HALL

A fine timber-framed Tudor manor house

L ittle Moreton Hall, all black-and-white timbers, drunken angles and oddly slanted walls, looks like a house of cards about to come tumbling down. But, unmoved even by earth tremors, this picture-book medieval and Tudor timber-framed house has stood secure for six-and-a-half centuries, always in the ownership of one family, until it was given to the National Trust in 1938.

The romantic moated house, a composition of richly patterned timbers, small-paned windows and gabled walls, seems to be the stuff of fairy tales. But it is real enough. Only when one walks, perhaps a trifle gingerly, across the moat and through the gatehouse into the cobbled courtyard, does one realize its extent. The oldest part of the manor, including the Great Hall, was built in about 1440–50 by Sir Richard de Moreton, a quarrelsome man according to contemporary accounts, but one who clearly knew how to employ a reliable builder. Sir Richard's grandson, William (another litigious man, who quarrelled with his neighbour about who should take precedence in ceremonial occasions), later carried

The South Front of this extraordinary Tudor timber-framed house. The Long Gallery runs the length of the top floor.

The spice cupboard or 'cupboard of boxes' in the Great Hall.

Elizabethan timber work, more than 500 years old, around the courtyard doorway.

Little Moreton Hall is off the A34, 4 miles south-west of Congleton, Cheshire. It is owned by the National Trust and open on selected days from March to December.
Tel: 01260 272018
www.nationaltrust. org.uk

on building. Future Moretons extended and modernized the house.

Two beautiful bay windows, one curving out from the Great Hall, the other facing it at right angles, were built in 1559 by Richard Dale for William Moreton and were a cause of great pride. They are inscribed: 'God is Al in Al Thing: This windous Whire made by Williame Moreton in the yeare of oure Lorde M.D.LIX.' Nor was the builder going to be left out: 'Rychard Dale Carpeder made thies windous by the grac of God,' is firmly added. It is the windows, these and others, with their thousands of tiny patterned panes of glass, that complete the picture of Little Moreton. The patterns of the panes vary from room to room – sometimes there is more than one pattern in a single window.

Only three original pieces of furniture survive. Two, a long refectory table and a cupboard that was probably used for storing spices, are on display in the Great Hall. The other, a large round table, stands in the bay window

of the withdrawing room. Apart from these pieces and some display cabinets, the house is unfurnished.

When the artist John Sell Cotman visited Little Moreton in 1807, he drew chickens pecking in the Great Hall; now restoration has taken place, it is possible to see the extent of its imposing space. There are perilous-looking garderobes and fairly recently discovered 16th-century hand-painted panels. There is also a finely tilting Long Gallery, wood-panelled and perching tipsily atop the second floor. It was the huge weight of this room, with its gritstone roof, that caused the National Trust to redistribute the load. It is reassuring to know that the structure is much sounder than it appears. *AB*

LYME PARK

A magnificent Tudor mansion with Georgian interiors

A larger-than-life, darkly brooding portrait of the Black Prince stands watch over the entrance hall at Lyme Park, the mansion built by the Legh family in sweeping parkland outside Stockport.

It is appropriate that the Black Prince has pride of place here. Sir Thomas Danyers, a 14th-century nobleman, rescued the prince and the royal standard from the engulfing French at the Battle of Crécy (1346) and was rewarded with a handsome annuity. Sir Thomas had been dead for 40 years by the time the annuity was converted into a gift of land, received by his granddaughter Margaret and her third husband, Piers Legh, in 1394. There were Leghs at Lyme Park from that time onwards, until 1946 when the estate was handed to the National Trust.

Lyme Park is one of the finest houses in north-west England. Approaching by way of the mile-long driveway through the surrounding deer park, the house may look familiar to those who have watched the BBC TV production of Jane Austen's *Pride and Prejudice* – the exterior of Lyme Park became that of Mr Darcy's beloved home, Pemberley.

Family tradition attributes this wooden carving of a jug to Grinling Gibbons.

The Long Gallery with its restored plaster ceiling and original 17th-century high-backed chairs.

Detail of the baroque plaster ceiling above the Grand Staircase.

Here are layers of history: the Elizabethan frontispiece stands proud in the centre of the north front; the lead statue of Minerva, topping the construction, was added more than a hundred years later. Walk through the entrance archway and suddenly one is in the cool Palladian courtyard of Giacomo Leoni, who was, in the first half of the 18th century, to design and build much of the Lyme that is seen today.

The next great change came in the early 19th century when Lewis Wyatt restored Lyme for explorer, scholar and Egyptologist Thomas Legh, who inherited it in 1797, while still a child. There is a swashbuckling portrait of this energetic traveller on the walls of the grand staircase. He's the dashing figure in Ottoman costume, leaning casually back against a fiery black steed. He was the oldest natural son of the untameable Colonel Thomas Peter Legh, who sired seven children by seven different women – none his wife. Lyme fell into disrepair under the Colonel's ownership. After surviving musket balls, crocodiles, sandstorms and the claustrophobia of Egyptian tombs during his travels, his son must have found the task of restoring a great estate comparatively easy.

But back to the entrance hall where there is more to the Black Prince than meets the eye. The portrait swings away from the wall so that the family using the next-door drawing room (originally the Elizabethan Great Chamber) could look through the 'squint' to keep an eye on proceedings in the hall. The three Mortlake tapestries in the entrance hall were moved here in 1903 from other parts of the house, during extensive redecoration by the fashionable brothers Joubert. The tapestries are part of an original set of six that tell the tragic tale of drowned lovers, Hero and Leander. Another is in the Victoria and Albert Museum. There is a charming painting hanging in the Oak and Acorn Dressing Room: painted in the early 20th century by Phyllis Sandeman, daughter of Thomas Wodehouse Legh, 2nd Lord Newton, it shows a lively servants' ball, full of light and life.

A lithograph dated 1795, showing Lyme Park from the garden.

Detail of the 'augmentation of honours' in the ceiling of the library.

There could hardly be a greater contrast than that between the gilded brightness of the hall and the sombre richness of the Elizabethan drawing room, reached by a small flight of steps. This was the solar, the family

A satyr's head on a radiator cover in the dining-room window alcove.

chamber, where the Leghs sought privacy from the bustle elsewhere. The early 17th-century oak panelling shines with an inlay of holly and bog oak, while the delicate strapworked plaster ceiling is complemented by its deep frieze. Light filters in through windows decorated with ecclesiastical and armorial stained glass.

The male Leghs were staunch Royalists; they and their Jacobite friends would retire to the Stag Parlour to toast 'the king over the water'. This room, named after the carved roundels depicting the life of a stag (the family were fanatical huntsmen), has been redecorated since those days, but there are chairs with embroidered silk velvet covers, said to have been fashioned from the cloak worn by Charles I on the scaffold.

Lyme's treasures include an early copy of the works of William Shakespeare

in the library. Also here – and elsewhere – is the much-prized 'augmentation of honours'. This representation of a dark mailed arm, holding a banner against a sprinkling of stars, was a special honour granted by Elizabeth I, harking back to the glory days of Crécy. In the saloon there are delicate lime-wood carvings, thought to be the work of Grinling Gibbons. There is also the famous light-flooded Bright Gallery, the traditional (but no less beautiful) Long Gallery, for perambulation and picture-gazing, and there is Sir Francis Legh's important collection of clocks, including a musical masterpiece that plays Jacobite tunes. *AB*

Lyme Park is in Disley, Cheshire, 6 miles south-east of Stockport, off the A6. It is owned by the National Trust and open on selected days from April to October.
Tel: 01663 766492
www.nationaltrust.org.uk

King Charles's Bedroom, hung with tapestries. The headboard was made from an overmantel.

RUFFORD OLD HALL

A fine Elizabethan hall with later additions

Even though he was illegitimate, Sir Robert Hesketh managed to lay claim to the rich family estates and build himself a showy new house at Rufford in south-west Lancashire. That was in 1530, and the handsome timber-framed main hall still stands, although its early wings are long gone, replaced by additions dating from the 17th and 18th centuries.

The Great Hall with its magpie quatrefoils and unique oak screen.

What remains of the original building is astonishing and must have been a talking point even when timbered buildings were commonplace. Magpie quatrefoils, worked out of traditional oak panels and set off by black timber on white plaster, decorate the north-west front, with its unusual and elegant five-sided bow-fronted window. The Victorians, over-egging the pudding, imposed a lantern on the roof, but that can be ignored.

The glory of Rufford is its miraculous Great Hall, with its hammer-beam roof, decorated with angels, and unique carved screen virtually intact. It is miraculous because the whole construction, held together by wooden pegs, has survived – with a little help from its friends – for more than half a millennium. Its friends are the National Trust who, when death-watch beetle threatened, unpegged the building with infinite care and craftsmanship, dealt with the deadly beetle and pegged it back together again.

In its layout, the Great Hall follows a conventional late-medieval and early-Tudor pattern, with the outer door opening into a 'screens passage', so that servants were shielded from the view of those in the hall by the screen itself. At the other end of the considerable room were the doors leading to the family chambers, which were in the now non-existent east wing. But the very latest in fireplace design was incorporated, with the stone chimneypiece built into the south wall to avoid the smoky atmosphere inevitably caused by a more traditional central hearth.

The end wall leading to the family chambers reaches up to the richly decorated roof by way of sturdy timbers, finished with the carved flourish of a wide beam below black-and-white quatrefoils. Light from the leaded bay window reveals more intricate carving above the doors that now lead nowhere. Many of the

The Elizabethan North-West Front. The lantern on the roof is a Victorian addition.

hundreds of tiny panes of glass are original, say the National Trust. On one of the panes in the bay window is some graffiti, scratched by a 19th-century gardener.

The roof is massive and stupendous. Each of the eight supporting hammer beams ends in a carved angel – but only one of them is still winged and feathered. It is sad to think of wooden feathers dropping piece by piece over the centuries as wood-worm made their inevitable inroads.

The massive bog-oak screen – the only one of its kind to survive intact in England – is richly carved, with strangely soaring finials exhibiting flights of wild fantasy. It is theoretically moveable but has, wisely, been left where it was for centuries. Hesketh coats of arms and twining vine leaves are linked through the panels. One panel has slightly different decoration to reassure God that the carver was mortal and not presuming to challenge perfection. Perhaps that is why the angel on the passage side has an extra finger. The two outer finials are each hewn from single pieces of timber. The enormous central post sits on top of a sturdy cross-piece carved with shield-bearing angels.

It would be wrong to say that the rest of Rufford Old Hall is an anti-climax, but a change of gear is needed to appreciate the mainly Victorian furnishing in the Georgian rooms. There is much to admire. The armorial glass, set brightly in the gable ends of the long drawing room upstairs, was collected by Sir Thomas Hesketh on his holidays in Europe during the early 19th century. The many fine Flemish tapestries are family property too, loaned to the National Trust. Many of the other rooms are furnished with objects which are correct in time and local to the area, and in the dressing room there is a very fine collection of original watercolour botanical studies, the work of Ellen Stevens of Southampton, made between 1880 and 1904. *AB*

A view of the West Front at Rufford Old Hall. The three-storey brick wing was built for Thomas Hesketh in 1662.

Rufford Old Hall is 7 miles north of Ormskirk, Lancashire, on the A59. It is owned by the National Trust and open on selected days from April to October.
Tel: 01704 821254
www.nationaltrust. org.uk

SIZERGH CASTLE
A fine Elizabethan home

The North-West Front of Sizergh Castle.

Two oak-panelled bedrooms, one with an imposing half-tester bed made from wood recycled from the Strickland family pew removed from Kendal church in the 1850s, are tasters for the magnificent Inlaid Chamber, created by Thomas Boynton and his wife Alice Strickland between 1575 and 1585. The room has unrivalled panelling, sumptuously inlaid with poplar and bog oak, a state bed, domed internal porch and armorial stained glass. Once sold to the Victoria and Albert Museum, the room has now been restored to its rightful home. *AB*

Sizergh Castle is 3 miles south of Kendal, Cumbria, off the A590. It is owned by the National Trust and open on selected days from April to October.
Tel: 01539 560070
www.nationaltrust.org.uk

Do not expect arrow slits and tales of boiling oil. True, the oldest part of Sizergh is a battlemented medieval tower and there are more battlements, added for decoration in the 17th century, on the central part of the building, but this has been a family home for seven centuries, parts still occupied by the Stricklands. The square entrance hall, with its Gothic porch, was designed in the late 19th century to allow a carriage to drive inside. Now a magnificent carved screen, original to the house, forms a second entrance.

The Tudor panelling and carved over-mantels throughout the house are what visitors come to see. But there are also family portraits (three by local artist Romney) and everywhere, in this most comfortable of castles, family collections of china, glass, clocks and porcelain.

The beautiful Inlaid Chamber, with its magnificent panelling and state bed.

YORKSHIRE AND NORTH-EAST ENGLAND

*O*ur medieval ancestors often had to fight for their land, their lives and their homes and nowhere more so than in the north of England. They claimed vast acres, built halls and towers and bred families. As life became easier, the halls, where tough business was done, gave way to more comfortable family living. Sometimes grand new houses, such as Harewood House, were built to replace the old.

Many of the greatest designers and craftsmen in the country came from the North, or from over the border in Scotland. The names Robert Adam, Thomas Chippendale, John Carr of York and Lancelot 'Capability' Brown crop up time and again in association with some of the great showy family homes of Yorkshire and North-East England. Harewood House, Newby Hall, where you'll find one of Adam's best rooms, Fairfax House and Nostell Priory are all fine examples.

An earlier master builder, Robert Smythson, was responsible for one of the loveliest houses in England, Burton Agnes Hall, where, more than 500 years later, the owners are still carrying on the tradition of commissioning works from great craftsmen including furniture maker John Makepeace and tapestry designer Kaffe Fassett.

The tradition of liberal art lives on at Wallington Hall, where the author and art critic John Ruskin was persuaded to add his own contribution to the wall paintings in the extraordinary central hall. *AB*

BRODSWORTH HALL

A carefully conserved Victorian Italianate mansion

Faux marble panels and real marble statues lend extra flourish to the very grand staircase.

Brodsworth in its prime was a dazzle of pattern and colour, with lavishly furnished rooms, faux marble walls and wide hallways lined with white statues.

When Charles Sabine Thellusson came into money from his great-grandfather, Peter (whose extraordinary will decreed that his fortune should accumulate in trust over three generations), he set to with glee,

pulling down the old family house. That was in the 1860s. In its place an Italianate mansion more suited to a prosperous London square than the Yorkshire countryside was designed by architect Philip Wilkinson.

Inside all was luxury. Lapworths of London furnished and decorated. Axminster carpets were laid on Minton tiles, their borders harmonizing. The passages were punctuated with marble statues, distinctly sentimental and most bought as a job lot from Italian dealer Casentini.

Brodsworth was loved by Thellusson, his wife and six children. They entertained in the solid dining room and relaxed in the drawing room, the height of elegance with crimson silk wall coverings and red-and-gilt furniture. The family made music in the South Hall, enjoyed their billiard room and kept more than a dozen servants, housed in a separate wing.

When English Heritage took over in 1990, Brodsworth's glory days were long over, the house ravaged by time. The exteriors were repaired and the lavish interior conserved to give a good idea of the comfort and colour enjoyed by an upper-middle-class Victorian family. *AB*

Brodsworth Hall is 5 miles north-west of Doncaster, South Yorkshire, off the A1 and the A635. It is owned by English Heritage and open on selected days from early April to the end of September.
Tel: 01302 722589
www.english-heritage.org.uk

A view of Italianate-style Brodsworth Hall from the south-east.

BRONTË PARSONAGE MUSEUM

A Georgian parsonage

The dining room, where the Brontë sisters paced each evening as they discussed their work.

Now a museum, the Brontë Parsonage has rooms furnished as they would have been when Patrick Brontë and his wife Maria (who died in 1821 leaving six young children) lived there. Sadly all six children, including writers Charlotte, Emily and Anne and their troublesome brother Bramwell, died before their father. The interiors are simple Georgian, with pale colour-washed walls, unfussy furniture and plenty of paintings and portraits. Most haunting is the dining room where the girls trod round and round the table each evening reading and discussing their writing projects. *AB*

Brontë Parsonage Museum is at Haworth, 8 miles west of Bradford, West Yorkshire. It is owned by the Brontë Society and open all year.
Tel: 01535 642323
www.bronte.org.uk

BURTON AGNES HALL

A magnificent Elizabethan house

Here is the perfect English house – a family home and setting for an ever-evolving art collection that spans six centuries. Burton Agnes is a house where there are few roped-off areas and 'do not touch' signs, and where the blinds are thrown up to illuminate layers of history, revealing pleasure after pleasure.

A gatehouse, four-square, stone-quoined and turreted, is a prelude to the Elizabethan house of russet brick built by Robert Smythson for Sir Henry Griffith between the 15th and 16th centuries. The date 1601 is carved above the entrance.

Burton Agnes has been home to Griffiths, Boyntons and Cunliffe-Listers, always inherited by family. It is lived in and cared for by Susan Cunliffe-Lister, mother of the owner,

Simon, who inherited the house in 1989 when he was just 12. Marcus Wickham-Boynton, the previous owner, opened Burton Agnes to the public in 1949. He was a serious collector of paintings, sculpture, furniture and porcelain. Susan Cunliffe-Lister, daughter of the late Viscount Whitelaw, has assumed his mantle, commissioning craftsmen John Makepeace and Kaffe Fassett to make beautiful furniture and tapestry, while the Elizabethan topiary tradition is carried on through the work of Rupert Till.

The first glory of Burton Agnes is pure Elizabethan. The Great Hall shows off not one, but two matchless set pieces of carved work. At right angles to each other are the sculpted screen and the fireplace. The roof-high screen sings angels, apostles, knights

Above left: Burton Agnes, the 'beautiful house' that poor Anne Griffith did not live to see.

Above : The Great Hall with its two glorious carved set pieces – the screen and alabaster chimneypiece.

and the Evangelists. Fruit, flowers and Elizabethan ladies are all carved in plaster, supported on an oak section, whose frieze shows the 12 sons of Israel. The fireplace's alabaster wise and foolish virgins chorus back. On the left, the wise virgins are busily spinning and scrubbing, while the good-time girls on the right of the fire-place, careless of the oil lost from their lamps, sing and dance through the centuries. In an alcove at the far end of the Great Hall is a bronze head, *Sunita*, by Epstein – the 20th-century adding voice.

The Inner Hall, through a splendid doorway, displays a triple portrait by Geerhardts of the daughters of Sir Henry Griffith, for whom Burton Agnes was built. Anne, the youngest, says family legend, was obsessed with the beautiful house in which she was to live. She thought of little else. Sadly, she was attacked by robbers and so badly hurt that she died within days. She begged that her head be interred in some part of the Inner Hall, but she was buried, untouched, in the churchyard. Anne's ghost raised hell, scaring the family half to death until they did as she asked, bringing her inside to watch over the lovely building.

There is more Elizabethan carving in the drawing room, which glows red and gold with decorative panelling.

Detail of the elaborately carved chimneypiece.

Above the fireplace is a Dance of Death, the skeleton trampling meaningless symbols of earthly pomp while the just receive their rewards and the unjust their deserts.

The paintings at Burton Agnes are not of uncertain ancestors staring gloomily from murky backgrounds. Marcus Wickham-Boynton enjoyed 19th- and 20th-century works, and these are displayed throughout, especially in the Garden Gallery, the Upper Drawing Room, the library and the Long Gallery. They amaze and delight. From Augustus John's depiction of his son, David, as *The Archer* to works by Renoir, Corot, Pisarro, Sickert, Manet, Matisse, Derain and Cézanne, the paintings are the collection of a discerning man and they are hung to be enjoyed.

Room styles change: lacquered Chinese panels, fashionable in the mid 18th century, cover the walls in one small sitting room while the dining room, used daily, is elegant and Georgian. The Upper Drawing Room, a cool pale space, understated with furniture by Georgian craftsmen, has 20th-century French paintings on the walls.

The staircase, ingeniously designed with a thickly carved double newel to fill a narrow space, but at the same time to afford a sweep wide enough for a lady wearing a farthingale to make an entrance, leads to bedrooms and reception rooms.

The ceiling in the Queen's Bedroom drips thickly with plasterwork honeysuckle that appears as if about to twine its way down the walls. The library, a perfect place to sit and read or reflect, is another fine room. But the climax, every bit as exciting as the first view of the decorated Great Hall, is the Long Gallery. Here is an apricot-and-white space filled with

Visitors are welcome to sit and enjoy the books in the library.

The lavishly carved staircase, ingeniously built into a narrow space.

Burton Agnes Hall is in the village of Burton Agnes near Driffield, East Yorkshire, on the A614, 7 miles west of Bridlington. It is owned by the Burton Agnes Hall Preservation Trust and open daily from the beginning of April to the end of October. **Tel: 01262 490324 www.burton-agnes. co.uk**

light and art. Works collected by the family are displayed in a room as ancient as many of them are modern. Enjoy the embroidery, by Janet Haigh of Burton Agnes, with lost sheep wandering around the maze. When the maze was planned the gardener was warned to expect several hundred yews. He thought they were the sort

that required shepherding, and was disconcerted and unprepared when he had to plant them. The artist has stitched woolly ewes jumping through the yew maze to represent this.

If anyone doubts that a great house can improve with age, Burton Agnes will prove them wrong. *AB*

BURTON CONSTABLE HALL

A mansion with Georgian interiors

Constables still live in one wing of this huge house, built by their ancestors during the reign of Elizabeth I. But is it Tudor or is it Georgian? The character of the rooms was determined by an 18th-century Constable, William, who not only called in decorators to make over the house in Georgian style, but who also collected classical ornaments and scientific instruments, the latter displayed in ranks of cabinets. Be sure not to miss the Long Gallery and the dazzling Chinese Room, with its exquisite wallpaper. *AB*

The grand Staircase Hall, with bright-yellow colour scheme dating from 1972.

Burton Constable Hall is 7 miles north-east of Hull, East Yorkshire. It is owned by the Burton Constable Foundation and open from Easter to the end of October.
Tel: 01964 562400
www.burtonconstable.com

CASTLE HOWARD

A magnificent early 18th-century baroque palace

Looking upwards into the roof of the splendid Marble Hall.

When playwright John Vanbrugh was approached at the end of the 17th century to build a 'castle' for the Howard family on the North Yorkshire moors, he set to with a will, despite the fact that he was new to architecture. Castle Howard – more of a palace than a castle – is huge, theatrical (and will be forever Brideshead to many, after the TV filming). Its massive walls, crowned by the central dome, shelter a marvellous Marble Hall, as well as fine paintings, tapestries, antiquities, china, sculptures and other collections. *AB*

Castle Howard is 15 miles north-east of York, off the A64. It is owned by the Howard family and open from March to October.
Tel: 01653 648444
www.castlehoward. co.uk.

CRAGSIDE

An extraordinary Victorian mansion

When, in 1882, Prince Edward and Princess Alexandra, the Prince and Princess of Wales, announced their intention to visit Lord Armstrong at his Northumbrian home, they gave nearly two years' notice. This was as well, because it allowed Lord Armstrong time not only to refurbish the tower suite of bedrooms, but also, with architect Norman Shaw, to design a stupendous new drawing room, with carved marble inglenook fireplace, itself the size of a small room. The marble

A decorative lampshade with orange tassels and wrought-iron rim, in the library at Cragside.

The South-Front entrance.

The cosy inglenook fireplace in the dining room with deep settles to the sides.

Emmerson's portrait of Lord Armstrong, dogs at his slippered feet, reading by the fireplace in the dining room.

(some ten tons of it) was hastily ordered from Italy, carved in London by the Arts and Crafts designer W.R. Lethaby, and shipped to Amble. From there it was transported by horse and cart to Armstrong's extraordinary mansion built into the hillside, overlooking the craggy countryside.

No wonder the royals wanted to visit: they'd heard all about this 'palace of a modern magician', wrought by this most energetic of men, whose engineering works turned out ships and armaments for armies and navies across the world. At home, the 1st Lord Armstrong was more concerned with domestic matters. He harnessed water power to run a new-fangled lift in the house and a roasting spit in the kitchen. In the butler's pantry there is a wall telephone (powered by electrically charged batteries) connected to the pump house – in case more power was needed. Central heating (coal-fired) was vented through the floor and walls by hot-water pipes. When he wanted to convert the turbines to

run on gas, he simply bought the gas works in nearby Rothbury. But, perhaps most interesting of all, Cragside was the first house in the world, in 1880, to be lit by hydro-electric power. Electricity was also used for fire alarms and dinner gongs.

Downstairs the spirit of ancient Rome was recreated in the men-only baths – a Turkish bath, a tepid tile-lined plunge bath and a shower – all hugely innovative. 'Was this the world's softest Geordie?' ask advertisements, promoting Cragside, now owned by the National Trust. But William Armstrong was no softie: he was through and through a gadget man who would never be satisfied until he'd made something work – and then improved it.

This romantic stone mansion with gabled and timbered turrets is glimpsed through a leafy mantle of trees – millions of them were planted in 1,700 acres of bare landscape by Armstrong. His fondness for untamed Northumbria stemmed from his memories of being cured of childhood illness by the good air. Cragside started small, a weekend retreat, constructed modestly in 1863.

The Owl Bedroom, built for a royal visit, with a bed made of American black walnut.

But he wanted bigger and better and he needed somewhere to experiment with electricity. Architect Norman Shaw had a job for life, designing an ever-expanding stone castle with mullioned windows. Before the trees grew up and the conservators pulled the blinds down, Cragside would have had long views over the ravine and Simonside Hills. Now its heavy stone, wood and thickly tiled interior seems dark, a masculine home for a wealthy businessman to hold court.

The walls of the ground-floor corridor are decor-ated with these poly-chrome tiles.

The library is Victorian Gothic at its best, with stained glass from Burne-Jones and Ford Madox Brown. The onyx fireplace came from a business

trip to Egypt. 'East or West, Hame's Best', proclaims an inscription over the huge inglenook fireplace in the dining room, smug in its cosiness. A portrait by Henry Emmerson shows Armstrong, domestic and slippered, dogs, including his favourite collie, Silkie, at his feet in that room. Here, too, is a rare capstan table which expands as it is twisted open.

If these two rooms are masculine, concession to female taste is seen in the boudoir upstairs. The furniture is on loan from the Victoria and Albert Museum. Also upstairs, the Gallery saw a change of character before the Wales came to visit. Once it had been an area where Armstrong carried out his electrical experiments. Now pictures are displayed (although the bulk of Armstrong's fine collection has been dispersed).

The extraordinary 'Owl Suite' is in a tower opening off the Gallery – carved owls on the bedposts gave the name. Decorated for the royal couple, it was the height of luxury at the time, centrally heated with a sunken bath, hot and cold running water and a flush lavatory.

Even when Cragside was officially completed, Armstrong came up with plans for alteration – the billiard room was the last addition before his death in the first year of the 20th century. *AB*

Cragside is near Rothbury, 13 miles south-west of Alnwick, Northumberland, off the B6341. It is owned by the National Trust and open on selected days from the begin-ning of April to the end of October.
Tel: 01669 620333
www.nationaltrust.org.uk

FAIRFAX HOUSE
A fine Georgian town house

A room steward at Fairfax House remembers her yoga classes there in the late 1960s. Lying prone, she would gaze up at the ceiling of the keep-fit studio, wondering what lay under all those layers of paint. Now she shows visitors the restored plaster-work, displaying the finely worked figure of Amicitia, representing friendship, which survives all trials and tribulations.

The exquisite restoration of this Georgian gentleman's town house is another triumph of survival over tribulation. Thanks to the work of the York Civic Trust and architect Francis Johnson, the building – which had slipped into use as a dance hall, the yoga studio, and café – is now proba-bly the finest example of a Georgian town house in England.

Designed by John Carr of York (whose portrait hangs in the library) for Viscount Fairfax and his daughter, Anne, the house was built in 1745 and decorated in the following decade. You'll see the outstanding plasterwork of Joseph Cortese, now full of classical allusion, now swirling with rococo flourish.

By one of those happy chances, the York Civic Trust was given a stupen-dous collection of clocks, porcelain, paintings and Georgian furniture, collected by the late Noel Terry, the confectioner. Much of the furniture is Chippendale, all of it is rare and valuable – the unique collection fits Fairfax House perfectly. *AB*

The kitchen at Fairfax House as it would have been in about 1765.

Fairfax House is in Castlegate in the centre of York. It is owned by the York Civic Trust and open all year.
Tel: 01904 655543
www.fairfaxhouse.co.uk

HAREWOOD HOUSE

A Georgian mansion with Adam interiors

Edward Lascelles, who inherited the Harewood estate, acquired by his father in 1738.

The small sitting room used by the present Earl of Harewood and his wife. The room is filled with paintings and sculptures; the bronze bust by the fireplace is of Lady Harewood.

When Edwin Lascelles, in possession of a fortune from the family sugar plantations in Barbados, decided in the 1750s to build himself a new home at Harewood, he hired the 'A team' of the time to do the work.

Lascelles, Lord Harewood, chose a lordly site for his new mansion on a hill overlooking the rolling Yorkshire landscape. He dammed a river to form a lake and appointed John Carr of York, Robert Adam and Thomas Chippendale to design the house, its interior and the furniture. Adam engaged his favourite crafts-people, Joseph Rose and William Collins, to carry out the plasterwork and he hired Angelica Kauffmann, her partner (later her husband) Antonio Zucchi, and Biagio Rebecca to provide decorative paintings and bas-relief decoration. And who better to manage the wide sweep of landscape in front of this new palace than Lancelot 'Capability' Brown?

The house was built for show: grand state rooms interspersed with family-sized chambers. One of these smaller rooms is now a comfortable sitting room, furnished and used to display work collected by George Lascelles, the 7th Earl of Harewood, and his wife, Patricia. Lord Harewood, cousin to HM Queen Elizabeth II and one-time director of the English National Opera, and Lady Harewood have filled this room with paintings and sculpture. There are sculptures by Jacob Epstein and Henri Gaudier Brzeska. Paintings include works by Picasso, Sickert and Sidney Nolan; the three small gouaches of Harewood are by John Piper.

The Lascelles have collected paintings and sculpture with percipience: the entrance hall, an elegant space designed by Adam, its pilasters and frieze picked out in chocolate in contrast to the cool blue-and-white walls, is dominated by another mighty Adam. Epstein's model for mankind, gazing heavenwards, is carved from a single piece of alabaster. Delicate Chippendale chairs – for show rather than use – are spaced against the walls.

Lord Harewood's mother, the late Princess Royal, Princess Mary, was the daughter of King George V; she lived at Harewood from 1930 until her death in 1965. There is an inter-esting exhibition, including her wedding dress, miraculously preserved bouquet and touching photographs of her and her five brothers. Her dressing room shows her collection of amber, rose quartz and jade, and chairs used at corona-tions, given to the family.

But it is doubtful if even the Princess Royal slept in the impressive state

The Spanish Library, with its solid bookcases, was designed by Sir Charles Barry.

Epstein's mighty statue of Adam dominates the entrance hall.

Robert Adam chose these colours for his ceiling to match the yellow silk wall covering in the Yellow Drawing Room.

was made Victorian by Sir Charles Barry, who also designed the famous terrace in the mid 19th century, under instruction from Louisa, Lady Harewood. Barry also designed the mahogany bookcases in the main library – but look up to see Adam's exquisite ceiling giving an altogether lighter feeling. Gaze, too, at the ceilings in the yellow and cinnamon drawing rooms, where Adam gave full rein to his decorative imagination. In the latter room is the portrait of Edwin Lascelles, for whom Harewood was built. Sir Joshua Reynolds's painting shows a forceful personality.

The charm of Harewood lies much in the small rooms, used as galleries to show off fine collections of china and paintings. But the best is to come. The Gallery, which extends the length of the house, was designed by Adam and altered by Barry – but it is still magnificent. Light floods in to make the wooden floor gleam and the exquisite ceiling, which took Joseph Rose two years to complete, glow. The painted panels, showing Greek gods in love and at war, are by Biagio Rebecca, while Angelica Kauffmann's oval paintings top the mirrors. The red-and-gold draped pelmets will not sway in the breeze – they were carved and decorated by Chippendale. And everywhere there are outstanding paintings – one of the finest private collections in the country including works by Titian and El Greco. *AB*

bed, displayed in all its carved, gilded and silk-hung glory, situated in splendour between massive pillars. Chippendale's domed masterpiece has been restored to the house after languishing for years in a stable. The restoration cost nearly a quarter of a million pounds. It vies for attention with another of Chippendale's best pieces, the 'Diana and Minerva' satinwood commode with its ivory inlay.

The splendid Spanish Library, named after its Spanish leather wall covering,

Harewood House is at Harewood, 8 miles north of Leeds, Yorkshire, on the A61. It is owned by the Earl of Harewood and open from March to November.
Tel: 0113 2181010
www.harewood.org

KIPLIN HALL

A mansion with Victorian interiors

Built in 1622 for George Calvert (who later became the 1st Lord Baltimore and disappeared to America to found Maryland), Kiplin Hall is constructed of mellowed red brick. Its tall domed towers stand in the centre of each side, making an interesting outline. It blossomed as a family home in the 19th century and its interiors are Victorian and welcoming. There are some fine paintings and furniture on display and the handsome late-Victorian library has Jacobean-style panelling. *AB*

Kiplin Hall is off the B6271 between Scorton and Northallerton, North Yorkshire. It is owned by the Kiplin Hall Trust and open at Easter and on selected days between May and September.
Tel: 01748 818178
www.kiplinhall.co.uk

The Admiral's Study, filled with memorabilia of Admiral Carpenter, a one-time inheritor of Kiplin Hall.

NEWBY HALL

A 17th-century mansion with Adam interiors

Boucher's 'Loves of the Gods' were the inspiration for the rare Gobelins tapestries. This detail shows the goddess Venus on a dolphin.

A portrait of William Weddell, young and rich, the world (and a piece of classical sculpture) at his feet, hangs by the stairs at Newby Hall. William Weddell was just 24 when he was painted by Pompeo Batoni in 1760. Newby had been bought by his father in 1748 specifically for William and future generations of Weddells.

It was the young man's predilection for collecting objects of beauty that

A MASTER OF MYTHOLOGY
The Venetian Antonio Zucchi had travelled widely in Italy studying paintings and antiques with Robert Adam. Adam invited him to come to England where he enjoyed huge success with his mythological scenes, painted in the neoclassical manner, at houses such as Newby Hall, Kenwood House (p 36), Osterley Park (p 41), Harewood House (p 225) and Nostell Priory (p 232). He worked on many projects in conjunction with the Swiss painter Angelica Kauffmann, love blossomed and they later married.

shaped the house we see today. Off he went on his Grand Tour, his booty including 86 paintings, 19 chests full of sculpture from Rome and a set of priceless tapestries, made at the famous Gobelins tapestry factory in Paris. Soon after his return he employed Robert Adam to create space to show off his treasures in the house which had previously been

Old French sayings decorate the Motto Bedroom at Newby Hall.

remodelled by the architect John Carr of York in the 1750s.

It is hard not to compare Newby, shaped by Carr, Adam and that other Yorkshire craftsman, Thomas Chippendale, with nearby Harewood House (p 225), where the same designers wrought their miracles. Where Harewood shouts grandeur, Newby whispers elegance; where Harewood keeps you on your toes to seek out the next glory, Newby's beauty is quiet. But, like Harewood, it was built for show. Proud of his fine paintings and sculpture, Weddell devised a subtle routine to amaze his friends and fellow members of the Dilettante Society, a group of wealthy amateurs devoted to art and antiquarian societies – and to lengthy dinners discussing their collections.

Ancient Rome was the inspiration for Adam's elegant entrance hall, the panels showing martial trophies now picked out in cool Wedgwood blue and white. The plasterwork, marble floor, fat round Chippendale chairs and granite-topped tables are original. The date 1771 can be seen on a panel.

Visitors leave the hall by way of the Red Passage, but Weddell's guests, already impressed, would have been ushered into the Tapestry Room, a fairy-tale room with walls hung with Gobelins tapestries, tapestry-seated Chippendale chairs echoing the floral background, and ceiling panels painted by Antonio Zucchi. Roundels on each tapestry show how the gods conducted their love affairs.

And so to dine. Today Weddell's dining room is a library, but this is where his guests would have satisfied

The central rotunda in the Statue Gallery built to house William Weddell's Grand Tour collection.

GOBELINS TAPESTRIES
The Gobelins tapestries at Newby Hall are not only extremely lovely, they are important. Made specifically for William Weddell at the Gobelins factory in Paris, they are one of only five sets made for English patrons and the only entire collection still in its original setting. They were woven by Gobelins works manager, Neilson, to designs by François Boucher – a favourite of Madame de Pompadour, Louis XV's mistress. The Tapestry Room was created by Robert Adam as the perfect setting for the tapestries.

in Roman style, it was designed to be seen at night, dramatically lit by lamps and candles as if the marbles really were placed in an ancient Roman temple. But the room is not forbidding: the pink-and-green plastered walls and the flower- and bird-filled Florentine scagiola tables add to its warmth.

Cool Adam gives way to solid Victorian in the billiard room; prints of nudes (not for the very prudish) hang in a bathroom while the 'Motto' bedroom with its French furniture bears sayings (in French) on every surface and the 'Print' bedroom was once known as the 'best lodging room'. Wealthy Robert de Grey Vyner, who inherited Newby in 1892 and who, in his own way, was as avid a collector as Weddell, could not resist picking up chamber pots during his travels in Europe – they (and some of them are extremely rare) are housed in a small room in the Victorian wing. Nearby, above the stairs, hangs a framed 'IOU' to his ancestor, goldsmith and banker, Sir Robert Vyner. It is signed by King Charles II and acknowledges a debt amounting to £416,724. 13s 1½d – it is dated 1677 and was never paid.

The library, once the dining room, with its fine Adam ceiling; the central oval painting of Bacchus and Ariadne is by Angelica Kauffmann.

their hunger pangs before their aesthetic senses were once again sated when the great doors to the Statue Gallery were flung open and a series of niches set in a long wing revealed Weddell's Grand Tour acquisitions. The Gallery is the icing on the classical cake. Although the sculpture looks splendid with natural sunlight streaming through the central rotunda, built

The staircase is an elegant sweep, while everywhere from the windows are glimpses of the world-famous gardens for which the present owners, the Comptons, direct descendants of the Weddells, are justly renowned. *AB*

Newby Hall is 3 miles south-east of Ripon, North Yorkshire. It is privately owned and open on selected days from the beginning of April to late September.
Tel: 01423 322583
www.newbyhall.com

NOSTELL PRIORY
A Georgian mansion

Nostell Priory was built by two great Georgian designers, James Paine and Robert Adam. Its fine interiors include delicate plasterwork and an outstanding collection of furniture. The Adam-designed Top Hall is the place to marvel at the glorious design on the walls and ceiling, and to admire the wheelback chairs by Chippendale. On a smaller scale, but still containing Chippendale furniture, is the famous Nostell doll's house with its original 18th-century contents and decoration. *AB*

Nostell Priory is in Nostell, on the A638, 5 miles south-east of Wakefield, West Yorkshire. It is owned by the National Trust and open on selected days from late March to early November.
Tel: 01924 863892
www.nationaltrust.org.uk

The dining room at Nostell Priory, with its elaborate rococo decoration.

TEMPLE NEWSAM HOUSE
A Tudor-Jacobean mansion

Confiscated by two monarchs (Henry VIII and Elizabeth I) during its first century, Temple Newsam, built around 1500, was 'rescued' in 1622 by the entrepreneur Sir Arthur Ingram and rebuilt as a glorious home. Each generation added something, inspired by the original Jacobean features. The women of the family enthusiastically built and decorated – see the drawing room, hung with hand-painted Chinese wallpaper, and the Moses tapestries, which were given to the Marchioness of Hertford by her friend the Prince of Wales in the 1820s. *AB*

The oak staircase at Temple Newsam, made in 1894 by C.E. Kempe out of John Carr's stairs.

Temple Newsam House is 4 miles east of the centre of Leeds, West Yorkshire, off the A63. It is administered by Leeds City Council and open on selected days all year.
Tel: 0113 2647321
www.leeds.gov.uk/ templenewsam

WALLINGTON HALL

A 17th-century house with Georgian and Victorian interiors

The East Front of Wallington Hall, with griffin heads on the lawn.

An illustrated lesson in Northumbrian history, social and natural, is the unexpected bonus of a visit to Wallington Hall, the home of the Blacketts and, later, the Trevelyans. The 17th-century house was one of the first to be given, entire, to the National Trust, but the Trevelyan family still lives in this surprising place, which has been enlivened over generations by clever, artistic and idealistic men and women.

At the heart of the house is the central hall, an atrium where children played, music was made, ideas were discussed, tea was taken and visitors entertained. It was planned by one-time mistress of the house Pauline Trevelyan. Small, bright-eyed and intelligent, Pauline and her lugubrious husband Walter Calverley Trevelyan (referred to as 'Calverley'), a noted geologist, scientist and philosopher, set up a brilliant (although mainly teetotal) household. They lived in Edinburgh before moving to Wallington in 1849 and spent much time in Rome and Greece where Pauline bought paintings, and spent days at a time sketching and drawing. Back in Northumbria they set up a radical and artistic household.

The richly coloured scenes in the central hall, painted by Pre-Raphaelite disciple Walter Bell Scott, tell of Northumbrian history. Grace Darling is here, rowing through the storm, while the Venerable Bede lies on his deathbed in another. Hadrian's Wall, St Cuthbert, marauding Danes and a scene depicting Newcastle's iron and coal industry are here too. Pauline, who had become friendly with Ruskin, Swinburne, the Rossettis and Ford Madox Brown,

Detail of a needlework screen in the East Gallery, completed by Julia, Lady Calverley.

commissioned and planned the unique space, which was designed by John Dobson (with a little help from Ruskin) in 1853.

Pauline and her friends decorated the tall piers supporting the arches with paintings of native wild flowers. Ruskin (reluctantly) completed one of the pier paintings choosing wild oats, yarrow, wheat and cornflowers as his subjects. On the spandrels of the ground-floor arches (painted by Scott) are 'medallions', depicting famous Northumbrians, from Hadrian to George Stephenson. Crane your neck and you'll see

dramatic battle scenes on the upper spandrels. These tell the story of the Battle of Otterburn (1388) – Scott designed the panels after reading the 'Ballad of Chevy Chase', which recounts the famous fight. The two sculptures here, the lovely *Paolo and Francesca* by Alexander Munro and *The Lord's Prayer* by Thomas Woolner, were dearly loved by the Pre-Raphaelite Brotherhood.

Because the central hall is compelling it would be easy to forget the rest of the house, mostly decorated before the Trevelyans arrived. Walter Blackett remodelled Wallington in the mid

The great colonnaded central hall at Wallington, painted with murals depicting scenes from Northumberland's history.

18th century on Palladian lines. Italian plaster craftsman Pietro Lafranchini set to with a will, adding rococo swirls, swags and flourishes. It is said that by the time Lafranchini left Wallington the cook produced the best Italian food in the north of England.

In the dining room, double-headed eagles and exuberant garlands frame mirrors while a portrait by Thomas Gainsborough of 'Sukey' Trevelyan, the second daughter of Sir George Trevelyan, was so disliked by her uncle, who commissioned the painting, that he had it redone – by Sir Joshua Reynolds, says the story. The library contains blood-stained books belonging to Lord Macaulay, related to the family by marriage. He was fond of reading while shaving with an unsteady hand.

Upstairs is more evidence of industry by ladies of the household – the Needlework Room contains ten panels of tapestry worked by an earlier Calverley, Lady Julia, in 1710.

They were brought to Wallington in 1755. And Lady Wilson's Cabinet of Curiosities contains a stuffed porcupine fish, narwhal tusks, stuffed birds and their eggs and an assortment of antiquities. The entrance hall is lined with cabinets containing a nationally important collection of china and porcelain. *AB*

The study at Wallington, with a copy of *The Times*, letter scales and spectacles on the desk.

Exuberant plaster swags by Pietro Lafranchini adorn the chimneypiece in the dining room.

Wallington Hall is in the village of Cambo, Northumberland, 12 miles west of Morpeth, off the A696. It is owned by the National Trust and open on selected days from April to October.
Tel: 01670 773967
www.nationaltrust. org.uk

WALES

A visitor crossing the Severn bridge into Wales will be immediately conscious of entering a different country with a different language. '*Croeso i gymru*' proclaims a huge sign, 'Welcome to Wales,' an ancient kingdom Celtic in origin, whose properties reflect a long and sometimes turbulent history. Welsh historic houses fit into Britain's main stylistic periods, yet they possess a distinctive quality that sets them apart from their English counterparts.

Plas Mawr on the northern-most coastline seems to be transported from northern Continental Europe, a Tudor Renaissance town house of exceptional quality, with exuberant and colourful plasterwork. Plas Newydd and Erddig represent the best of Georgian elegance, the latter containing paintings, furniture and silverware highlighting the quality of that gracious age.

In the centre of the nation, Powis Castle is typical of the rugged fortresses a visitor expects to see in Wales. Inside it metamorphoses into a glittering stately home full of Jacobean splendour. In South Wales, the fairy-tale-like fantasies of Cardiff Castle and Castell Coch, designed for the fabulously wealthy Marquess of Bute, represent extreme examples of the extravagance of the 19th-century Gothic revival.

Moreover, the interiors of these diverse buildings can often be full of wonderful surprises. Across the whole country are room after room of the most staggering artistic merit, created by some of the greatest designers of the ages – from the nameless plasterers, painters and upholsterers of the Tudors to more recent luminaries such as William Burges and Rex Whistler. *PB*

CARDIFF CASTLE

A Norman castle with lavish Victorian neo-Gothic interiors

The architect and designer William Burges began remodelling the original Norman fortress at Cardiff shortly after he first met the prodigiously wealthy 3rd Marquess of Bute in 1865. The impressionable young Bute's riches enabled William Burges to indulge his fanatical medieval fantasies to the full. The castle became Bute's main residence whenever he was in South Wales and work at Castle Coch soon followed. Perhaps Burges's finest achievement at Cardiff Castle is Bute's private oratory, a dramatic vaulted space decorated with rich religious murals. *PB*

William Burges's exotic design for the Summer Smoking Room, typical of his extravagant use of colour and form to achieve dramatic effect.

The Summer Roof Garden, inspired by a Roman villa.

Cardiff Castle is in Castle Street, in the centre of Cardiff, South Wales. It is owned by the City and County of Cardiff and open all year.
Tel: 029 2087 8100
www.cardiffcastle.com

CASTELL COCH

A Victorian fairy-tale castle

Castell Coch stands high on a hillside, turrets topped with steep conical roofs rising up from thick beech woods, a Transylvanian castle brought to Wales. The richly decorated vaulted interiors display all the drama of a Hollywood film set built for a medieval extravaganza – bring on the shining knights and shrieking damsels in distress! Castell Coch is extraordinary, exuberant and larger than life, posing the intriguing questions – what sort of architect would create it, and who would be happy to finance it and actually live here? The Victorians, however, were fascinated by the Middle Ages: other architects

Viewed from the air, the heavily buttressed towers peep out from the extensive beech woods that surround the castle.

such as Salvin and Pugin were building castles; Sir Walter Scott had published *Ivanhoe*; and the Pre-Raphaelites were painting their medieval fantasies. In the context of the time there was nothing very unusual about Castell Coch – today it seems incredible and therein lies its fascination.

When the eccentric William Burges was introduced to the young 3rd Marquess of Bute, it was a meeting of like-minds. Burges was infatuated by the Middle Ages: he even wore medieval costume and was dubbed the 'most Gothic of Gothicists' among his fellow 19th-century architects. Bute was scholarly and passionate about antiquarianism, archaeology and building. Deeply religious, he shocked Victorian society by converting to Catholicism. He was also reputedly the richest man in the world. United by their love of medievalism, this unusual pair happily set about creating the fairy-tale Cardiff Castle (p 238) and Castell Coch.

Castell Coch, Welsh for 'the red castle', was built on the ruins of a genuine old medieval fortress; it is entered over a drawbridge and through a gatehouse complete with portcullis, both fully operational. On the way in, glance upwards to see the painted statue of Madonna and Child, by the Italian sculptor Ceccardo Fucigna. Notice, also, that Lord Bute's medieval obsession did not inhibit him from installing a metal bell-pull for his visitors. Indeed Bute had many

VICTORIAN VINEYARD

When Castell Coch was completed in 1891, Lord Bute informed his bemused head gardener that he intended to establish a vineyard and dispatched him to France for an instant course in viticulture. Three acres of vines were planted near the castle and they flourished, producing 3,000 bottles of perfectly acceptable sweet white wine following the first vendage. A scoffing article in *Punch* magazine declared it would take four men to drink it – two to hold the victim, and one to pour the wine down his throat!

creature comforts incorporated at Castell Coch, such as central heating, lighting and plumbing.

The courtyard features cantilevered galleries and wall-walks linking towers topped with spiky copper-gilt weather vanes. A covered staircase leads to the first-floor banqueting hall, with its lofty boarded and stencilled ceiling, and murals reminiscent of illustrated medieval manuscripts. The statue on the tapered chimneypiece is that of St Lucius, considered to be the first Christian British king. The adjacent drawing room, with its dramatic, steeply vaulted ceiling, remains Burges's pièce de résistance at Castell Coch. The two-storey chimney-piece, with its trio of statues designed by Burges, depicts the Three Fates, Greek goddesses possessing the power of birth, life and death over all mankind. Murals show scenes from *Aesop's Fables*, while painted stone vault ribs radiate from a golden sunburst with a central orb at the apex. This room encapsulates Burges's romantic vision of the Middle Ages.

Elsewhere in Castell Coch, Lord Bute's rather spartan bedroom contrasts with that of Lady Bute, which could be straight out of the *Arabian Nights*, with its Moorish-looking dome, maroon-and-gold painted furniture and large, low bed decorated with glass crystal orbs. The crenellated towers either side of the wash basin conceal cisterns for hot and cold water. Over the fireplace, a winged statue of Psyche, personification of the soul and wife of the Greek god Eros, carries a heart-shaped shield bearing the arms of Lord and Lady Bute. Bute had married Gwendoline Fitzalan-Howard, the granddaughter of the

Lady Bute's richly decorated bedroom, with its domed ceiling.

Duke of Norfolk, who lived at Arundel Castle (p 48), which was also much altered in the Victorian era but in a rather more orthodox manner.

Castell Coch is highly theatrical, yet well crafted as a building; the quality of the external construction is particularly meticulous, the newer building integrating seamlessly with the remains of the original 13th-century castle. Inside, Burges's recreation of a lost medieval world sometimes risks becoming mere pastiche, but those who question his strong colours may be unaware that the stonework of ecclesiastical medieval masterpieces, such as Salisbury Cathedral, was once brightly painted. Certainly Castell Coch is not bland and boring like many modern buildings, but vibrant, thought-provoking and full of surprises. *PB*

The figures over the striking chimneypiece in the Octagonal Drawing Room are The Three Fates.

Castell Coch is 5 miles north-west of Cardiff, South Wales, off the A470. It is in the care of Cadw and open from February to December.
Tel: 029 2081 0107
www.cadw.wales. gov.uk

ERDDIG

A fascinating Georgian country house

The majority of the nation's historic houses open to the public focus on the principal rooms traditionally used by the owners. Erddig, on the other hand, gives particular emphasis to the servants and their quarters. Indeed, the visitor is not welcomed at the front door, but ushered around the back, through the stableyard, past the laundry and the bakehouse, where bread is regularly baked once a week, to the servants' passage. On display here is a wonderful group of servants' photographs, including one taken in 1911 of Harriet Rogers, a formidable cook and housekeeper. This fascinating 'below-stairs world' includes the servants' hall, housekeeper's room, butler's pantry and the New Kitchen (early 1770s). The kitchen is architecturally one of the most impressive rooms in Erddig and was so famous that when Queen Mary visited in 1921 she insisted on seeing it.

Successive owners of Erddig maintained an unusually close relationship with their staff, treating them so well that the servants often stayed for many years. In the servants' hall there is a painting of a housemaid aged 87 and another of a 75-year-old estate carpenter. The panelled housekeeper's room appears very agreeable and the laundry maid's attic bedroom well appointed for the time. No wonder Erddig's owners were regarded by their neighbours as being 'rather soft'. Nevertheless, the servants' records are remarkably detailed, giving a fascinating insight into

the daily running of a great country house in its heyday.

Perhaps one of the most remarkable of all the servants at Erddig was an 18th-century lady's maid named Betty Ratcliffe, nicknamed 'Betty the little', who displayed a particular talent for drawing and modelling. Her work can be seen in rooms throughout the house, including the Gallery, the State Bedroom and the Red Bedroom. Particularly notable is her detailed model of a Chinese pagoda, which was based on the one at Kew Gardens and fashioned out of mother-of-pearl,

Harriet Rogers, housekeeper and cook at Erddig; this is one of the many fine period photographs on the walls of the servants' passage.

Above: The library featuring an 18th-century mahogany library table.

Above right: This Chinese painted wallpaper was hung in the State Bedroom during the redecoration of the house in the late 18th century.

formal gardens. The quality of the interior furnishings and decoration, including the fine early-Georgian furniture and mellow panelling, comes as a welcome surprise.

mica and fragments of glass carefully glued onto vellum.

The exterior of Erddig is architecturally unremarkable. The original late 17th-century central block was extended either side in a somewhat uninspiring way during the early part of the following century, whilst the rather bland 1770s neoclassical West Front contrasts unfavourably with the warm brickwork of the Garden Front– see how well the latter appears when looking at the house from beyond the long canal, shaded by rows of lime trees in the extensive

The well-presented appearance of Erddig today is remarkable considering the house's more recent history. After a period of gradual decline, the house became virtually derelict during its last 20 years of private ownership. It was acquired by the National Trust in 1973, by which time only two rooms were occupied and there was no modern heating or lighting. Rather surprisingly, there had been no disposal of family treasures in order to ease mounting debts. Thus such gems as the large Delft vase in the Tapestry Room, bearing the arms of William and Mary, the marvellous Georgian silverware kept in the butler's pantry, and Kneller's portrait of Bloody Judge Jeffreys – apparently

The saloon, with its George III cut-glass chandelier.

A detail of the carved and gilded gesso hawk's head on the tester bed in the State Bedroom.

The Garden Front at Erddig, originally built in 1684, looks out over the canal and formal garden.

a local man – displayed in the entrance hall, all remain in situ.

It is equally remarkable that the poor state of the house had no lasting detrimental effect on its contents. The Georgian furniture in the saloon still retains its original covers, and in the State Bedroom there is a fine six-panel Chinese lacquered screen, said to be a gift of Elihu Yale, the benefactor of the American university named after him. Other objects of considerable interest in this Aladdin's cave of a house are the curious-looking 19th-century portable shower in the bathroom and hundreds of small blue Victorian bottles, apparently an early form of fire extinguisher. Poems, written by the owners, accompany the portraits of family retainers in the servants' hall. The entrance hall was

used as a music room after the mid 19th century, and the eclectic collection of musical instruments on display includes a splendid chamber organ, an early 19th-century harp lute and a Victorian brass euphonium.

Erddig is such an absorbing place largely because of its enormously varied contents, ranging from one of the best collections of early 18th-century furniture to be found anywhere in Britain to family toys and the vintage agricultural tools in the outdoor workshops. Erddig also highlights the value of the National Trust. Without their timely intervention and careful conservation work this hugely fascinating house would probably have been consigned to oblivion along with Harriet Rogers and 'Betty the little'. *PB*

IN CASE OF FIRE ...
The numerous small blue glass bottles to be found at Erddig came from the Harden Star Hand Grenade Extinguisher Company and originally contained a mixture of water, salt and ammonium chloride. When hurled into a fire this supposedly heated to boiling point and extinguished it. Thankfully they were never put to the test at Erddig.

Erddig is off the A483, 2 miles south of Wrexham, Clwyd, North Wales. It is owned by the National Trust and open on selected days from March to the end of October.
Tel: 01978 315151
www.nationaltrust.org.uk

PENRHYN CASTLE
A Regency fantasy fortress

Not many people would demolish an architect-designed house barely 30 years old in order to build a neo-medieval castle, yet this is precisely what George Hay Dawkins-Pennant did during the short-lived Norman revival early in the 18th century. He was in good company: Robert Smirke was then building Eastnor Castle (p 143) in Shropshire and Robert Adam had constructed a series of Scottish castles. These were the halcyon days when men of taste and discernment commissioned new homes, just as dedicated followers of fashion purchase the latest designer outfits today.

Penrhyn enjoys a glorious location: westwards lies Snowdonia, to the north, Anglesey and the sea. It became the largest castle in Wales, festooned with so many towers and turrets that the owner's son-in-law joked that the architect came in after breakfast simply to ask permission to add another tower.

The Grand Hall and Grand Staircase are aptly named – take time to examine the abundance of stone carving, bosses, corbels, friezes and gargoyles of bewildering complexity. Beyond lies a forest of slender columns, a myriad of Romanesque arches and countless long stone-flagged corridors stretching as far as the eye can see. Penrhyn is truly designed on a grand scale.

There is more. Penrhyn's art collection is magnificent – the castle is rightly called the 'Gallery of North Wales'. In the breakfast room alone hang works by artists such as Rembrandt, Guardi and Canaletto. *PB*

Above left: The stained-glass windows in the Grand Hall feature signs of the zodiac in a convincing 13th-century style.

Above: The castle library has an elaborately carved ceiling together with four limestone fireplaces.

Penrhyn Castle is on the A5122, 1 mile east of Bangor, Gwynedd, North Wales. It is owned by the National Trust and open on selected days from the end of March to the end of October.
Tel: 01248 371337
www.nationaltrust. org.uk

PLAS MAWR

A well-preserved Elizabethan town house

The exterior façade of Plas Mawr.

Early plasterwork at Plas Mawr is dated 1577, the year Francis Drake began his celebrated voyage around the world. By then an Englishman's home was no longer his castle but had become a status symbol representing success, wealth and position in society. So, having made his fortune, the Welshman Robert Wynn came to Conwy and built Plas Mawr, which is Welsh for 'great hall'. Wynn had travelled extensively and the lime-washed house reflects the Renaissance in Northern Europe. The gatehouse's crow-stepped gables, pedimented windows and faceted finials echo buildings in Antwerp or Bruges, cities familiar to Wynn.

The dominant feature inside is highly ornamental plasterwork, sometimes brilliantly painted – see the overmantel in the hall, with its vivid display of Tudor roses, caryatids and the Wynn coat of arms. The hall was the first room visitors would have encountered and Wynn wished to impress them immediately and flaunt his wealth and status. Exuberantly decorated ceilings, friezes and overmantels also feature in the parlour, the chambers over the parlour and brewhouse, and the Great Chamber. The latter, on the first floor, was the place where Wynn lavishly entertained important guests, being renowned for keeping 'a worthy plentiful house'.

Adjacent are the two chambers, one Wynn's bedroom, the other that of his much younger second wife, by whom he fathered two sons and five daughters within six years when in his 70s. In the late 16th century, Plas Mawr was hugely impressive and highly innovative. Today it is considered to be one of Britain's best-preserved Elizabethan town houses. *PB*

The Great Chamber, with overmantel displaying Garter arms, caryatids and a Tudor rose.

Plas Mawr is in the High Street, Conwy, Gwynedd, North Wales. It is in the care of Cadw and open on selected days from the beginning of April to the end of October.
Tel: 01492 580167
www.cadw.wales.gov.uk

PLAS NEWYDD

An 18th-century Gothic mansion

ew places in Britain enjoy such glorious views as Plas Newydd on the Isle of Anglesey, standing on the shore of the Menai Strait, looking across to the mountains of Snowdonia on the Welsh mainland. The view is particularly fine on a bright clear day when the peaks are covered in snow, gleaming in the sunshine.

He also tried to become involved with the building work, suggesting a pavilion joined to the Octagon Room, 'which would tempt us to walk out by moonlight, to enjoy the murmur of the waves and the perfume of those plants which are most fragrant at that time'; this purple prose failed to impress Lord Uxbridge.

The South and East Fronts of Plas Newydd.

Plas Newydd is Welsh for 'new place' or 'new mansion', and so it was when the powerful Griffith family built the original hall house at the beginning of the 16th century. The present building is largely the work of James Wyatt and Joseph Potter, whose neoclassical and Gothic designs were commissioned by Lord Uxbridge after inheriting Plas Newydd in 1782. Further alterations were undertaken by the 6th Marquess of Anglesey between the two world wars, including remodelling the North Wing and creating the long dining room which features Rex Whistler's famous mural. Between these two periods of development, Humphrey Repton remodelled the grounds.

Wyatt's influence is immediately apparent upon entering the Gothic hall, where the slender vaulting echoes his cloisters at Wilton House; the adjacent music room is reminiscent of his chapel at Magdalen College, Oxford. Look out for the 20 late 18th-century mahogany chairs displaying the family crest, which line the walls of the hall. Above them hang three Flemish portraits of the intrepid William, 1st Baron Paget, a wily Tudor statesman who, unlike many of his compatriots, managed to keep his head firmly on his shoulders. 'Be affable to the good and sterne to the evill,' he advised, 'thus God will prosper youe, the King favour youe and all men love youe.' This was sound advice

Rex Whistler's mural in the dining room which portrays a fictional Mediterranean scene.

The artist Rex Whistler working on his mural. The young girl seated at the foot of the ladder is Lady Katherine Paget, twin of the present Marquess.

and he lived to a ripe old age. The Paget family continue to reside at Plas Newydd to this day.

Wyatt's work is also in evidence in the Ante-Room, designed in 1795, and in the saloon, where the semi-circular bay window provides the stunning view across the water, which is such a feature of the house from so many of the rooms. Look out for the elaborate marble chimneypiece purchased by Lord Uxbridge in 1796.

More recent are the interesting signed photographs of visiting royalty including George V and Queen Mary, who was godmother to the present Marquess of Anglesey, together with a picture of the latter with the Duke of Edinburgh.

Part of Plas Newydd's charm lies in the fact that it reflects the changing tastes and requirements of successive generations of Pagets through the centuries. Lord Uxbridge progressively converted Plas Newydd from a medieval manor house to an 18th-century neoclassical and Gothic mansion. While the decor remains essentially Georgian, the pale pink-and-white colour scheme of Lady Anglesey's Bedroom, together with the floral chintz and muslin bed hangings, are the work of Sybil Colefax, a leading interior designer of the inter-war years and founder of Colefax & Fowler, the well-known interior decorating company. The long rectangular dining room, built in the 1930s and now known as the Rex Whistler Room, contains Whistler's remarkable 58ft (18m) *trompe l'œil* masterpiece covering the full length of the room. Notice the young man with a broom on the left – it's a self portrait of the artist. On the right, Lady Anglesey's spectacles look so real that you want to pick them up! Whistler is said to have conducted an intermittent love affair with Lady Caroline Paget, the eldest daughter of the 6th Marquess of Anglesey. His sensitive drawing of her is in the saloon. Whistler joined the Welsh Guards early in the Second World War and was tragically killed in France in July 1944, aged 39.

The Octagon Room which occupies the ground floor of the South-East Tower. The painting above the fireplace portrays the Menai Bridge, which links the Isle of Anglesey with the mainland.

The frieze in the saloon was designed by James Wyatt and the furniture is Georgian.

The 5th Marquess with his theatrical company. Fascinated by the theatre from an early age, he converted the private chapel into a theatre where he staged lavish productions.

The most eminent member of the Paget family was the 1st Marquess, who had an extremely distinguished military career and commanded the cavalry at the Battle of Waterloo. A portrait of him as a dashingly handsome Lieutenant Colonel in the 7th Light Dragoons hangs in the music room. The Cavalry Room contains a wonderful collection of paintings, uniforms, weaponry and medals of the period.

Plas Newydd is a place of great historic interest and natural beauty. It is not a great architectural masterpiece, but it has a unique atmosphere. *PB*

Plas Newydd is on the A4080, 3 miles west of Bangor, Gwynedd, North Wales. It is owned by the National Trust and open on selected days from the end of March to the beginning of November.
Tel: 01248 715272
www.nationaltrust.org.uk

PLAS YN RHIW

A Tudor manor house with Georgian additions

This small Tudor manor house, lying on the tip of the Lleyn Peninsula in North Wales, enjoys spectacular sweeping views south-eastwards across Cardigan Bay to Cader Idris. In 1938 this three-storey farmhouse was rescued from 20 years of neglect and lovingly restored by the three Keating sisters. Their possessions are still strewn around the house, which has granite walls up to 8ft (2.4m) thick in places. The homely interior and small terraced gardens sloping to the sea combine to make Plas yn Rhiw an idyllic place to visit. *PB*

Plas yn Rhiw is 16 miles south-west of Pwllheli, Gwynedd, North Wales. It is owned by the National Trust and open on selected days from late March to the end of October.
Tel: 01758 780219
www.nationaltrust. org.uk

Plas yn Rhiw, seen from the end of the beautiful sunlit garden.

Kitchen implements form a still life on a table by the kitchen window.

POWIS CASTLE

A medieval castle with Jacobean interiors

The battlemented outline of Powis Castle rises high on a narrow ridge with far-reaching easterly views across the Severn Valley towards England. This is the Welsh Marches, the ancient battleground of warring English and Welsh armies – Plantagenet kings against Llywelyn Ap Gruffydd and Owen Glyndwr.

In more peaceful times, the original 13th-century fortress was transformed into a grand stately home under the powerful Herbert family, who were ennobled after William Herbert had become a royal favourite, having married Anne Parr, the sister of Henry VIII's last wife, Catherine. The majority of the work at Powis Castle was carried out by the 3rd Lord, later the 1st Marquess of Powis, in the late 17th century; then much of the interior was remodelled in the early 20th century, also in the Jacobean style. Today, John George Herbert, 8th Earl of Powis, continues to reside at the castle.

Visitors to Powis first cross a courtyard, passing a dramatic lead statue of a figure astride a prancing horse, then enter the castle between twin drum towers, which survive from medieval times. Experience a different world, as spartan castle metamorphoses into luxury stately home. The ornate Grand Staircase was created around 1670, leading to the first-floor state rooms, also dating from the reign of Charles II. Look upwards to see the flamboyant painted ceiling by Antonio Verrio, whose work can also be found at Burghley, Chatsworth (p 138) and Hampton Court Palace. The walls were painted by his pupil, Gerard Lanscroon, who also decorated the ceiling in the library, an allegorical composition depicting the 2nd Marquess's daughters, with Lady Mary Herbert as Minerva, Roman goddess of wisdom. This represents a misjudgement of character by the artist, as she later almost ruined the family by recklessly speculating on the French stock market, causing the marquess to be imprisoned in Paris. The library contains one of the castle's greatest treasures, a miniature by the Elizabethan artist Isaac Oliver, depicting Lord Herbert of Chirbury as a melancholy knight. It is considered to be one of the nation's most exquisite miniatures.

A view of the West Front of Powis Castle, showing the twin drum towers and the statue of *Fame* by Andries Carpentiere.

In the State Dining Room, look out for the unusual horseshoe-shaped wine table, designed for comfortable fire-side drinking! Sir Joshua Reynolds's portrait shows Lady Henrietta Herbert. She was the last of the original Herberts of Powis and married Edward, the 2nd Lord Clive, son of Clive of India. After the marriage, Powis passed to the Clive family. The Clive Museum contains some 300 items from India and the Far East,

including the fabulous painted chintz state tent belonging to Tipu Sahib, late 18th-century Sultan of Mysore, together with his jewelled slippers and a gold tiger's head.

Perhaps the most impressive room at Powis is the State Bedroom, the only one in Britain where the bed is still in an alcove separated from the rest of the room by a balustrade. This derives from the time when British aristocracy loved to imitate the formal etiquette of the French Court of Louis XIV. With its 17th-century tapestries and its profusion of gilt, this is a room of unashamed opulence and it provides an interesting insight into lordly living during the late 17th century.

In contrast, the adjacent Long Gallery exudes a wonderfully romantic atmosphere and is the only room at Powis surviving from the Tudor era. The gleaming oak floor, elaborate plasterwork and chimneypiece all date from the late 16th century. Take a close

The horseshoe-shaped wine table in the State Dining Room.

A detail of the Charles Rex cypher above the bed in the State Bedroom.

The library, originally fitted out in about 1665, contains Gerard Lanscroon's decorated ceiling.
The Venetian painting over the fireplace was purchased by Clive of India in 1771.

look at the delicate 'Adam and Eve' plasterwork on the overmantel, a particularly fine example of Tudor craftsmanship. The Long Gallery provides a perfect setting for classical marble sculpture, amongst which is the brilliantly executed ancient Roman statue of a ferocious cat attacking a snake, which was originally purchased in Rome by Clive of India. Don't miss the unusual late 17th-century clock, used to measure the accuracy of clocks and watches during manufacture.

Elizabethan plasterwork also features in the Duke's Room, named after the early 18th-century titular Duke of Powis, who used it as a bedroom. This is a glorious room, with an intricately carved Jacobean four-poster bed and richly panelled walls hung with finely woven 17th-century Brussels tapestries. Adjacent are a surprisingly intimate group of bedrooms, which

The Grand Staircase leading to the impressive first-floor state rooms.

include the Walcot Room and the Lower Tower Bedroom. This part of Powis Castle is particularly enjoyable to visit, for it has the most wonderful homely atmosphere.

Before leaving Powis, be sure to step out into the celebrated terraced gardens. Originally laid out in the 1680s, they remain one of the few baroque gardens to have survived largely in their original form and contain superb topiary, excellent classical statuary and huge, well-trimmed lawns. Best of all, the gardens provide a view of the castle that will remain with you long after visiting one of the finest historic buildings in Wales. *PB*

Powis Castle is off the A483, 1 mile south of Welshpool, Powys, Mid Wales. It is owned by the National Trust and open on selected days from late March to the end of October.
Tel: 01938 551944
www.nationaltrust.org.uk

A detail of the overmantel in the Long Gallery, depicting the elaborate 'Temptation of Adam and Eve' plasterwork.

CLIVE OF INDIA

Robert Clive went to the sub-continent as a young clerk in the East India Company. He discovered he had an unexpected military expertise and returned home some years later having made India part of the British Empire – whilst amassing a personal fortune in the process. He survived accusations of abuse of power and was ennobled, but died in 1774, aged only 49.

THE TUDOR MERCHANT'S HOUSE

A late 15th-century town house

The Tudor Merchant's House is in Quay Hill, Tenby, Pembrokeshire, South Wales. It is owned by the National Trust and open on selected days from the beginning of April to the end of October.
Tel: 01834 842279
www.nationaltrust. org.uk

By the end of the Middle Ages, Tenby had become a thriving commercial port and this narrow three-storey late 15th-century town house, overlooking the harbour and located up a cobbled alleyway, is just the sort of house that a successful merchant would have owned at the time when the Welshman, Henry Tudor, had seized the English Crown. By 1586, a Thomas Jurdan is recorded as living here.

This house was not just a place to live in, as the merchant conducted his business in a room close to the entrance, off the street, while his servants prepared food for all the family using the huge fireplace that dominates the ground floor.

The huge fireplace on the ground floor.

In the oak-beamed room upstairs, the family ate, relaxed and entertained, perhaps offering their guests some *piment*, a medieval drink still popular in Pembrokeshire during the Tudor age – a rough, piping-hot red wine spiced with ginger, cinnamon and honey. This might be accompanied by *civeles*, small biscuits made from ground almonds, egg, sugar and wine, cooked in butter.

At night the merchant and his family retired to the only bedroom on the second floor, leaving the servants to sleep around the fire downstairs. The bedroom's lofty ceiling clearly shows the original jointed roof trusses. The walls are plain limewashed, like the rest of the house, which in Tudor times would be typical of this part of town, but has now become rather special. *PB*

The living room on the first floor is late 15th-century.

SOUTHERN AND CENTRAL SCOTLAND

The many picturesque ruined castles and abbeys in the Scottish Borders bear witness to the turbulent history of the region prior to the beginning of the 17th century. With more peaceful times, after James VI of Scotland succeeded Elizabeth I as James I of England, castles began to seem old-fashioned, and classical country houses, from the palatial new house at Floors to the neat little Palladian villa at Paxton, were built along the banks of the beautiful River Tweed. Suites of public rooms designed for entertaining, decorated with Italianate plasterwork and elegant furniture, looked out over rolling acres of landscaped gardens.

By the mid 18th century, the warring times seemed far enough away for Robert Adam's castellated fantasy architecture at Culzean Castle to combine the new fashion for the picturesque with a discrete reference to ancient Scottish lineage.

Edinburgh developed as a medieval burgh: Gladstone's Land, with its Flemish-inspired detailing is typical of a 17th-century Scottish merchant's house. By the 18th century, Edinburgh had broken the bounds of its medieval plan, and The Georgian House demonstrates the elegance of the new, bourgeois lifestyle. Glasgow, in contrast, developed in the 19th century, its phenomenal expansion fuelled by industry. The confident Glaswegian nouveaux riches employed cutting-edge architect-designers such as Alexander 'Greek' Thomson (*see* Holmwood House) and Charles Rennie Mackintosh (*see* The Hill House) to build comfortable, innovative houses in the suburbs, designed for business entertainment and family relaxation away from the hubbub of the city. *KB*

ABBOTSFORD HOUSE

The farmhouse home of Sir Walter Scott

In his historical novels and narrative poems, Sir Walter Scott can be said to have single-handedly invented the Romantic vision of Scotland, which many of Scotland's present-day visitors still come to seek. Scott's works were phenomenally successful in the 19th century: *Waverley*, published in 1814, was the most popular novel in the English language.

Scott was born in Edinburgh, but was sent to his grandparents' farm near Smailholm, in the Scottish Borders, in the hope that he might recover from the polio which afflicted him as a child. The romantic landscape of the Borders, with its ruined castles and abbeys, fired his imagination. In adult life, the early fruits of his literary fame allowed Scott to buy an old farmhouse on the banks of the beautiful River Tweed, near Melrose. He renamed it Abbotsford, and gradually transformed it into a stage-set where he could play out a fantasy of being a Scottish country 'laird'. What he wanted was 'an old-fashioned Scotch residence, full of rusty iron coats and jingling jackets', in 'the old-fashioned Scotch style which delighted in notched gables and all manner of bartizans [battlemented parapets]'.

Even before Scott's death in 1832, Abbotsford had become a place of pilgrimage, and afterwards it became a shrine, attracting enormous numbers of visitors. Like Scott's literary works, Abbotsford was to have a profound effect on later taste, both in architecture and in interior design, instigating

Abbotsford House, its skyline bristling with crowsteps, crenellations and chimney pots.

the fashion for Scots Baronial architecture, for antique furnishings, and for architectural salvage.

Although his architect was the Englishman William Atkinson, Scott's taste was dominant. Out went pale-painted woodwork and delicate neo-classical plaster mouldings, and in came dark woodwork, oak furniture, stained glass and dark, rich colours for curtains and upholstery.

Light filters through leaded stained-glass windows into the Great Hall, which is actually quite small, and stuffed with all manner of artefacts, including a model of Robert the Bruce's skull and several (extremely well-polished) 'iron coats and jingling jackets'. In Scott's timber-panelled galleried study can be seen his leather chair and the mahogany desk at which he wrote many of his classic works.

The rooms along the garden front of the house look out over a water

Sir Walter Scott's timber-panelled study, with his leather chair and the mahogany desk at which he wrote many of his most famous works.

meadow to the River Tweed: the book-lined library; Lady Scott's drawing room, lined with gorgeous pale turquoise hand-painted Chinese wallpaper; and the armoury, its walls hung with weaponry, including Rob Roy's gun, broadsword, dirk (short dagger) and sporran purse. The bay window in the dining room is where Scott, his daybed drawn up to the window so that he could watch his beloved River Tweed flowing by, spent his final days before his death in 1832. *KB*

Abbotsford House is near Melrose, in Roxburghshire, 35 miles south of Edinburgh, on the B6360. It is privately owned and open from the end of March to the end of October.
Tel: 01896 752043

'Iron coats and jingling jackets' in the entrance hall at Abbotsford House.

BROUGHTON HOUSE
An 18th-century town house

The picturesque little town of Kirkcudbright, on the shores of the Solway Firth, at Scotland's south-western extremity, became an artists' colony in the early 19th century. This fine 18th-century town house was acquired in 1901 by E.A. Hornel, already a leading member of a group of artists known as the 'Glasgow Boys'. Hornel built a remarkable top-lit gallery, in which he displayed his paintings to potential purchasers, and a studio overlooking his Japanese garden. The house includes a large collection of paintings by Hornel as well as works by other artists. *KB*

The gallery built by the Scottish painter E.A. Hornel.

Broughton House is in High Street, Kirkcudbright, Dumfries & Galloway. It is owned by the National Trust for Scotland and open on selected days from April to October.
Tel: 01557 330437
www.nts.org.uk

CULROSS PALACE

A 17th-century merchant's house with splendid painted interiors

The Painted Chamber, with its decorated barrel-vaulted ceiling.

In the narrow cobbled streets of the little town of Culross, on the north coast of the Firth of Forth, ochre-rendered houses with crow-stepped gables and steeply pitched dormers are roofed with red pantiles. In the 16th and 17th centuries Scotland had important trade links with the Netherlands and the Baltic ports, and the Fife ports prospered, exporting the products of an early industrial revolution – coal, salt and lime. These links are reflected in the architecture and interior decoration of the buildings: for example, the characteristic red roofing tiles were originally brought back as ballast in boats trading with the Low Countries. The 'Palace' (not really a palace – the name seems to have been a later typographical error) was the home of Sir George Bruce, merchant and industrialist. Born around 1550, Bruce made his fortune by developing the coalmines under the River Forth.

The chief glory of Culross Palace is the original painted decoration of the timber-lined interiors. This type of decoration was common in Scandinavia and the Netherlands, and became fashionable in Scotland in the early 17th century. The barrel-vaulted timber ceiling of the principal 'painted chamber' is decorated with delightful allegorical paintings, based on Flemish engravings, accompanied by pithy rhyming couplets. Leaded glass windows illuminate lustrous dark oak furniture, pewter and brass; blue-and-white china is grouped on Dutch carved cupboards; and chairs are upholstered in leather or rich dark velvet. *KB*

Culross Palace is in Culross, Fife, 15 miles west of Edinburgh. It is owned by the National Trust for Scotland and open from Easter to September.
Tel: 01383 880359
www.nts.org.uk

A steeply pitched dormer and red pantiles.

CULZEAN CASTLE

A picturesque 18th-century castle with fine Adam interiors

A view of Culzean Castle seen from the terraced Fountain Court.

Perched on cliffs high above the sea, commanding panoramic views across the broad estuary of the Firth of Clyde to the mountainous island of Arran and the precipitous volcanic plug of Ailsa Craig, Culzean Castle is arguably the most romantic castle in Scotland. In reality, however, it is a classical house in fancy dress: behind the parapets and pepperpot turrets are the serene interiors of one of Robert Adam's masterpieces.

As the artist and architect Robert Billings wrote in his book *Baronial and Ecclesiastical Antiquities of Scotland* (1852), 'The spots chosen as the most suitable for fortification, though generally selected by men who never looked at scenery, and cared for nothing but eating, drinking and fighting, have often supplied exquisite pieces of scenery, adapted entirely to our modern taste.' There had been a fortified tower house on this defensible site – a rocky promontory protected by cliffs to seaward and by a steep glen to landward – since at least the 15th century. By the 18th century, however, with the advent of more peaceful times, these very qualities made the site

A CULTURAL PILGRIMAGE

The Grand Tour was an essential part of the education of the British upper classes in the 18th century. It was a sort of 'gap year' experience, but often lasted several years, during which the classically educated young chaps, often accompanied by their tutors, toured the Continent, developing their knowledge of art and antiquities. Most time was usually spent in Italy, where they admired the ruins of ancient Rome and often collected classical sculpture and Old Master paintings, to be shipped back to Britain to embellish their ancestral homes.

Sir Thomas Kennedy, 9th Earl of Cassillis, elegantly attired in velvet jacket and embroidered waistcoat, painted by William Mosman in 1746.

Robert Adam's oval, colonnaded staircase at Culzean, one of his most innovative designs.

ideal for the construction of a country house in the newly fashionable 'picturesque' style.

Sir Thomas Kennedy (who became 9th Earl of Cassillis in 1759) was the second of three brothers who inherited Culzean in the 18th century. Like many young aristocrats of his time, Sir Thomas had completed the Grand Tour of Europe, returning home full of ideas for improving the family seat.

It was Sir Robert's younger brother David, however, who, after inheriting Culzean in 1775, was to commission Robert Adam, the most fashionable architect of his day, to initiate the transformation of the old castle into a spectacular neoclassical mansion. Like Sir Robert, Adam had spent a formative period in his younger years in Italy, and he was a leading authority on classical architecture. Earl David's works, which almost doubled the size of the castle, included the demolition of a wing built a few years earlier by Sir Robert, and the

construction of a three-storey drum tower on the very edge of the cliff, with a circular drawing room, or saloon, on the first floor – the *piano nobile*. Access to the new rooms was provided by the construction of one of Adam's most innovative designs, the top-lit, oval, colonnaded staircase. It is easy to imagine the fashionably dressed guests – the ladies in rustling skirts of satin and lace, the gentlemen in knee breeches, velvet jackets and embroidered waistcoats – sweeping up the imperial staircase, to be greeted by their hosts in the elegant drawing room. In keeping with the fashionable picturesque aesthetic, inspired by the romantic landscape paintings of Claude Lorraine, Adam intended there to be a contrast between the restrained symmetry of the drawing room, with its delicate shallow relief plasterwork ceiling, and the dramatic scenery beyond; gilt girandoles hang between tall French windows, which open onto a stone-balustraded balcony looking out over the ever-changing seascape.

Of the decoration of dining rooms Adam had written, 'Instead of being hung with damask, tapestry etc., they are always finished with stucco and adorned with statues and paintings that they may not retain the smell of the victuals.' The decoration of the dining room (now the library), still very much as Adam designed it in the 1770s, conforms to this dictum, with decoration largely confined to the stylized fruit and vines of the fine plasterwork ceiling, adorned with painted roundels.

The bachelor David Kennedy devoted the last 20 years of his life – and a considerable fortune – to the

A portrait of Susanna, Countess of Eglinton, hangs over the marble chimneypiece in the circular drawing room.

An elegant Adamesque wall-mounted chandelier, or girandole.

Lady Ailsa's boudoir, which has been redecorated according to the original colour scheme.

rebuilding of Culzean. Robert Adam's brother-in-law wrote of it as 'the whimsical but magnificent Castle of Colane, on which the Earl encouraged him to indulge to the utmost his romantic genius.' A 'show house' such as Culzean was intended as a status symbol: as a place to display costly works of art, and as a setting for ostentatious entertaining, designed to 'win friends and influence people'. David Kennedy died in 1792 (as did Robert Adam), leaving his extravagant building project unfinished and his estate in debt. Fortunately he was able to arrange for Culzean to be inherited by a relative who had sensibly married not one but two American heiresses (not, of course, at the same time!), giving the house a much-needed injection of transatlantic cash. The ambitious 12th Earl fulfilled Adam's vision for Culzean, and succeeded in becoming the 1st Marquess of Ailsa. *KB*

Culzean Castle is 4 miles west of Maybole, South Ayrshire, on the A719. It is owned by the National Trust for Scotland and open on selected days from the beginning of April to December.
Tel: 01655 884455
www.nts.org.uk

FLOORS CASTLE

A grand 18th-century castle enlarged in the 19th century

Floors Castle is near Kelso, Roxburghshire, in the Scottish Borders. It is owned by the Duke of Roxburghe and open from the beginning of April to the end of October.

Tel: 01573 223333
www.floorscastle.com

Floors Castle, set on a natural terrace overlooking the River Tweed.

Said to be the largest inhabited castle in Scotland, Floors Castle (the name derives from the French 'Fleurs') is a vast country house, its skyline bristling with parapets and a forest of turrets, overlooking the River Tweed and the Cheviot Hills beyond. Buried at the heart of the castle is a 15th-century tower house. In 1721 John Ker, 1st Duke of Roxburghe, commissioned the architect William Adam to build a large, sober, symmetrical Palladian house, with pedimented corner towers. The castle owes its present appearance, however, to the celebrated Edinburgh architect William Playfair who, at the instigation of the 6th Duke in the mid 19th century, more than doubled the size of the

castle and gave it its magnificent 'baronial' overcoat.

Some traces of the 18th- and 19th-century interiors remain. The key to the interior, however, lies in the marriage of the 8th Duke to an American heiress, May Goelet, in 1903. The Duchess brought with her, from her family home in Long Island, a fabulous collection of art, including the magnificent 17th-century Brussels tapestries which hang in the drawing room. The interiors of the principal rooms at Floors were altered in the 1930s in order to accommodate the Duchess's growing collection, which includes exquisite French furniture and carpets, paintings and some fine Chinese porcelain. *KB*

THE GEORGIAN HOUSE

An 18th-century house in Edinburgh's New Town

Looking north from the battlements of Edinburgh Castle, towards the Firth of Forth and the hills of Fife beyond, one can admire, laid out below in a regular pattern of streets, squares, crescents and circuses, interspersed with leafy gardens, the city's 18th-century New Town. Designed by James Craig in 1767, it is one of the finest examples of 18th-century town planning in Europe. Wander through these streets (dusk is a good time to choose) and you will catch a glimpse of picture-hung drawing rooms, elegantly furnished dining rooms and book-lined libraries.

Since 1975 the interior of The Georgian House, No. 7 Charlotte Square, has been open to visitors, arranged by the National Trust for Scotland to give an impression of how the house might have looked when first completed in 1796. Charlotte Square is the grandest of the New Town's squares, the 'palace blocks' of its façades designed by Robert Adam in 1791. The first owner of No. 7 was John Lamont, 18th Chief of Clan Lamont; the Lamont's principal residence was at Lamont in Argyllshire; Charlotte Square would have been their town house for the season, a base for business and entertainment in the capital.

Before entering the house, look for the 'link horn' mounted on the cast-iron railings: it was used to extinguish the flaming torches carried by the 'link

The elegant façade of The Georgian House, designed by Robert Adam.

boys', who ran beside the carriage when one went out in the evening. On formal occasions, visitors would have been shown directly upstairs from the stone-flagged entrance hall to the drawing room on the first floor, to be received by the host and hostess. The drawing room was used principally for entertaining, and is arranged with the gilt-wood chairs drawn back to the chair rail, allowing space to circulate; small tables known as 'fly tables' would have been brought in for games of cards, and there is a square piano, for musical parties. This is a typical Georgian drawing room, decorated in a light style, with a white marble chimneypiece and painted woodwork.

The dining room, with marble chimneypiece and woollen curtains.

The smaller, more intimate, parlour, or morning room, to the rear would have been the family's everyday sitting room – where breakfast would have been served, and where the ladies could take tea, read, or do needlework. On the table is a silver tea service, with neoclassical Sheffield-plate hot-water urn.

After assembling in the drawing room, guests would have descended to the dining room, on the ground floor. Dining rooms were always furnished in a more sombre, masculine fashion, and it is always possible to tell, in an Edinburgh New Town town house, which room was the original dining room by the black marble chimneypiece. Dark-red woollen curtains and a red carpet complement the dark grained woodwork.

The basement at The Georgian House is equipped with a *batterie de cuisine*, an open range, roasting spit, baking oven and serried ranks of polished copper pans. The wine cellar, with its stone wine bins, has been equipped by a local wine merchant as it might have been in the early 19th century. One can easily imagine the servants' bells jangling as the gentlemen called for more port!

Edinburgh did not suffer the flight to the suburbs to the same extent as other British cities, and it is a mark of the adaptability of these well-planned spaces that the city's terraced houses and flats are still highly prized by Edinburgh's professional classes. Many of them still remain in very much their original condition (protected now by listing). *KB*

A chest of drawers with Sunderland lustreware chamberpot.

The kitchen, painted in a pale shade of blue – thought to ward off flies.

The Georgian House is at No.7 Charlotte Square, Edinburgh. It is owned by the National Trust for Scotland and open from March to December.
Tel: 0131 2263318
www.nts.org.uk

GLADSTONE'S LAND

A restored 17th-century merchant's house in the Old Town of Edinburgh

Edinburgh's earliest inhabitants occupied the Castle Rock – the city's name deriving from the Gaelic *Dun Eadin*, meaning Hill Fort. Until the 18th century the development of the city was confined to the rocky ridge that runs from the Castle down to the Palace of Holyroodhouse – the Royal Mile. The plan has been likened to the skeleton of a fish – the long spine of the marketplace in the centre with narrow plots separated by

The Green Room, with blue-and-white Delft pottery displayed in an alcove.

Gladstone's Land, a six-storey tenement, typical of 17th-century Edinburgh.

closes, or alleyways, running off it. The merchants of Edinburgh built houses with narrow, gabled frontages to the street, behind which there would have been vegetable gardens, poultry yards, pigsties and cowsheds. The top section of the Royal Mile, nearest to the Castle, is known as the Lawnmarket – formerly the land

market, where the products of the city's hinterland were sold.

Outside the building now known as Gladstone's Land, in the cobbled Lawnmarket, there is a hanging sign with a (modern) gilded gled, or hawk. In 1617 a merchant named Thomas Gledstane and his wife, Bessie Cunningham, bought a property on this site. Customs books for the port of Leith show that Gledstanes traded in iron, pots, prunes, honey and vinegar. His business must have prospered, as he soon set about improving his new house, extending the stone and timber structure by building a stone façade, arcaded at ground-floor level, 23ft (7m) further into the street, and raising the height of the building. He had his initials, TG, and those of his wife, BC, carved on the skewputts –

The inner hall, with polished brass chandelier, gleaming oak furniture and rich red Turkey rugs in the hall.

A 17th-century chair and Dutch foot-warmer.

the carved stones at the base of the crow-stepped gables. The tall, thin elevation of Gladstone's Land – six storeys high including the dormered attic – is characteristic of 17th-century Scottish urban architecture. Each floor would have been let out as a separate flat, the well-heeled living on the principal floors, and the poor in the basement and attics, with a booth, or shop, under the arcade on the ground floor.

A hundred years later, the old city of Edinburgh had become so over-crowded that pressure grew to expand beyond the narrow confines of the burgh boundary. In the late 18th and early 19th centuries a new, planned

EDINBURGH'S OLD TOWN
'The City is high seated, in a fruitful soil, and wholesome air ... From the King's Pallace at the East the city still riseth higher and towards the West, and consists of one broad and faire street.'
Fynes Moryson, an Englishman who visited Edinburgh in 1598

The Painted Chamber on the first floor, with original wall decoration and 17th-century bed with crewel-work hangings.

town was built to the north of the city. The prosperous moved to this New Town, while the increasingly neglected, unsanitary and over-crowded Old Town was left to the poor. By the early 20th century, Gladstone's Land, like many of its neighbours, had become a slum, and in 1934 it was condemned to demolition. Fortunately, the National Trust for Scotland rode to the rescue, gradually buying up the property and restoring it. A visit to Gladstone's Land now offers a genuine glimpse of how life must have been in Edinburgh's Old Town in the 17th century.

The restoration removed later shopfronts, revealing Thomas Gledstane's stone arcade. Here is a reconstruction of a 17th-century cloth merchant's booth, complete with wool and woven fabrics, dyed using authentic pigments such as heather, lichen and onion skins. On the first floor is the Painted Chamber where, during restoration, remarkable Scandinavian-style painted decoration was discovered on the beamed ceiling and walls of one of the rooms created by Thomas Gledstane's extension. This type of decoration, featuring boldly painted flowers and fruit, was very popular in 17th-century Scotland. It was usually executed by itinerant craftsmen, probably working from pattern books.

In the stone-flagged kitchen on the first floor, there is a charming piece of furniture – an oak cradle with well-worn handles used to rock many a fractious baby to sleep. Copper and stoneware vessels gleam in the light of the open fire, where oatcakes and bannocks would have been cooked on a girdle. In the 18th century, a room to

the rear of the house was panelled and painted. To determine the colour scheme when restoring this room, National Trust for Scotland conservators removed no less than 14 layers of paint. The resulting olive green is a remarkably good foil for the Dutch paintings hung there, and for the superb collection of blue-and-white china – mostly English delftware – displayed in a shelved alcove.

The Trust has successfully recreated the shadowy, evocative atmosphere of 17th-century interiors – the dark glow of polished oak furniture, the subdued colours of crewelwork upholstery and tapestry-hung walls, relieved by the rich reds of the rugs and the blue-and-white of Delft pottery, reminiscent of Dutch paintings of the period. This atmosphere is enhanced by the

textured, leaded glass and timber shutters of the restored windows; one almost expects to see Vermeer's 'Girl with a Pearl Earring' standing by the window. *KB*

A late 17th-century crewel-work hanging, displayed in the hall at Gladstone's Land.

A walnut kneehole desk and chair with needlework seat in the Green Room.

Gladstone's Land is in the Lawnmarket, near the top of Edinburgh's Royal Mile. It is owned by the National Trust for Scotland and open from the beginning of April to the end of October.
Tel: 0131 226 5856
www.nts.org.uk

THE HILL HOUSE

An iconic Arts and Crafts house designed by Charles Rennie Mackintosh

Right: The hall, with furniture and clock (above) designed by Mackintosh.

With the advent of the railway in 1857, Helensburgh, on the northern shore of the Firth of Clyde, some 25 miles west of Glasgow, became a fashionable residential suburb for wealthy Glaswegian businessmen. A number of opulent residences were built in a variety of styles, from grandiose Scots Baronial to half-timbered Old English. In 1902, Walter Blackie, a partner in his family's successful publishing firm, purchased a fine south-facing site on a hillside looking down over the town to the estuary beyond. He commissioned the Glasgow architect Charles Rennie Mackintosh to design a house for his growing family. Blackie and his wife,

who belonged to a sophisticated, forward-looking 'arty' set in Glasgow, were 'dream clients' for the young Mackintosh, giving him free rein, if not carte blanche, to put his avant-garde ideas into practice. The result was an iconic synthesis of Arts and Crafts ideals, Art Nouveau decoration and a pared-down simplicity, often seen as heralding Modernism.

True to his Arts and Crafts ideals, Mackintosh believed that the structure of a building should be dictated by the requirements of the occupants, not shoehorned in behind an arbitrarily symmetrical façade; he worked with the Blackie family, tailoring his

design to the way they wanted to use their house. Mackintosh designed not only the house, with its interiors and outbuildings, but also almost all of the furniture, fixtures and fittings.

Like many Edwardian houses, The Hill House is entered from the side, leaving the south elevation, looking onto the garden, for the private family rooms. By the entrance is the library, a sombre, masculine room, with dark oak panelling and shelves, where business visitors would have been received without the need for them to penetrate the family apartments. In the hall beyond, furnished with Mackintosh-designed furniture and clock, dark-stained pine doors and vertical timber panels, with purple leaded ceramic insets, frame a stencilled plaster frieze of stylized natural forms in purple, blue, pink and green. Light, passing through grids of square glass panels which are set in the doors, is reflected on the floor and echoed in the pattern of the carpet and the leaded glass

windows by the staircase. At night the hall is lit by immense rectangular brass pendant lights, set with opalescent glass and pink stained-glass honesty seedpods.

From the shadowy hall, one emerges into the ethereal light of the drawing room. Sunlight floods in from the bay window which projects into the garden, through leaded glass French doors and windows. Dusky pink petals drift down from roses stencilled on the creamy-white paintwork. The pale mosaic of the fire surround is inset with ovals of coloured mosaic and mirror glass; above is a gesso panel depicting the story of Sleeping Beauty by Mackintosh's wife Margaret Macdonald, a talented artist in her own right. On either side of the built-in sofa in the window bay are racks for books and magazines. There are silvered metal and opalescent glass wall lights with stained-glass roses, and a music bay with a piano – ideal for a little romantic after-dinner music-making.

Mackintosh's classic ladder-backed chair.

Charles Rennie Mackintosh, Glasgow designer and architect.

At the top of the stairs, between the master bedroom and the children's rooms, is a delightful piece of Mackintosh design – a raised alcove with hinged wooden seats which open to reveal storage for books or toys – the perfect storytelling or reading spot. Blackie published many children's books – many now collectors' items – by authors such as Louisa May Alcott and R.M. Ballantyne, illustrated by artists such as Walter Crane.

For many years the master bedroom at The Hill House was painted plain white, but examination of layers of under-painting, and of Mackintosh's

The mirror and wardrobe in the main bedroom, with decorative glass panels.

The rose-stencilled main bedroom, with silk-embroidered hangings and pink glass in the cupboard doors.

original designs, has resulted in the restoration of this, the most romantic of The Hill House's rooms. Creamy-white paintwork stencilled with rose bushes, pale-painted furniture inlaid with pink glass, and tiny shutters inset with squares of pink glass, combine to create an impression of Sleeping Beauty's rose-entwined bower. The pale bed, flanked by cupboards with rose-coloured glass doors, sits in a vaulted alcove. Beside the fire, its

polished-steel surround inset with enamelled tiles, is an inglenook containing Mrs Blackie's daybed. The room is furnished with a breathtaking selection of Mackintosh's furniture, including the washstand, its simple lines complemented by stylized leaded glass panels, and his signature ladder-back chairs.

One really does need to remember the sombre, cluttered interiors of most houses of this period to understand how profoundly innovative The Hill House was, with its subtle interplay of

---

A DWELLING HOUSE

When Charles Rennie Mackintosh handed the house over to his clients he told them, 'Here is the house. It is not an Italian villa, an English mansion house, a Swiss chalet or a Scotch castle. It is a dwelling house.'

light and shade, unadorned surfaces contrasting with areas of artistic decoration. The Hill House passed directly from the Blackie family to the National Trust for Scotland, and visitors are indeed fortunate to be able to see this, Mackintosh's domestic masterpiece, complete with its original furniture and decorative schemes. *KB*

The Hill House is in Upper Colquhoun Street, Helensburgh, near Glasgow. It is owned by the National Trust for Scotland and open from the beginning of April to the end of October.
Tel: 01436 673900
www.nts.org.uk

The harled exterior of The Hill House.

HOLMWOOD HOUSE

The restoration of an extraordinary villa designed by Alexander 'Greek' Thomson

Unfairly overshadowed for many years by his compatriot Charles Rennie Mackintosh, the architecture of Alexander Thomson, nicknamed 'Greek' Thomson, has recently been generating something of a revival of interest. Holmwood House, in Glasgow's southern suburbs, is Thomson's finest and most sophisticated villa, built in 1858 for James Couper, who owned paper mills on the nearby River Cart. Thomson designed not only the house, but also every detail of the interior, including furniture, curtains and carpets. Sadly, the house suffered a period of decline, eventually becoming a convent, and the furnishings have disappeared. However, the National Trust for Scotland, who acquired the property in 1994, has been revealing and conserving much of the decoration of this extraordinary house.

Before entering the house, notice the semicircular bay of the parlour, its detached columns standing proud of the bowed glass behind; inside, the circle is completed on the ceiling. Over the stairs is the most amazing gilded cupola, with stars etched into the curved sheets of glass. The dining room has its original timber dado panelling and black marble chimneypiece, with gilding in the incised decoration, and some of the original red paintwork and stencilled decoration

The exterior of Holmwood House, perhaps the finest example of the work of Alexander 'Greek' Thomson.

has been revealed. Seen by Thomson as a 'day room', the dining room has a sunburst motif on the ceiling. The drawing room, on the first floor, has a night sky, with gilded stars against a blue background. The restoration of Holmwood is very much 'work in progress', and the National Trust for Scotland is keen to encourage visitors to follow the continuing process of its conservation. *KB*

Holmwood House is in Netherlee Road, Cathcart, Glasgow. It is owned by the National Trust for Scotland and open from the beginning of April to the end of October.
Tel: 0141 637 2129
www.nts.org.uk

HOPETOUN HOUSE

A grandiose baroque country house

Hopetoun House, a fine example of Georgian architecture, set in 150 acres of parkland.

Hopetoun House was designed by William Adam in 1721 for Charles Hope, 1st Earl of Hopetoun. Recently raised to the peerage and rich from the ownership of lead mines, Hope had travelled to Italy; his new house was intended to express his culture, wealth and status.

Suites of rooms lead off on either side of the marble-floored vestibule: the family wing to the left and the state apartments to the right. The decoration of these magnificent rooms was completed for Charles Hope's son, the 2nd Earl, by William Adam's sons, John and Robert. Richly coloured silk damask covers the walls and the high coved ceilings are enriched with gilded rococo plasterwork; the splendid white marble chimneypiece in the Red Drawing Room was made in London by the sculptor Michael Rysbrack.

Behind this grandiose façade, however, is another, more modest house, built less than 20 years earlier by Sir William Bruce, Scotland's first major classical architect, for Charles Hope's mother, the widowed Lady Margaret. Less showy, more intimate, but no less elegant, the core of this house still remains to the rear of Charles's extension. Most of the rooms have oak wainscot panelling with superb carving and the garden room, which has steps leading down to the garden, is one of the loveliest rooms in Scotland. *KB*

Hopetoun House is at South Queensferry, West Lothian, 12 miles west of Edinburgh. It is owned by the Hopetoun House Preservaton Trust and open from April to September.
Tel: 0131 331 2451
www.hopetounhouse. com

MANDERSTON

A lavish Edwardian country house

The ballroom, with its exquisite chandeliers.

Manderston is 1½ miles east of Duns, Berwickshire, on the A6105. It is privately owned and open on selected days from mid May until the end of September.
Tel: 01361 883450
www.manderston.co.uk

Sir James Miller inherited Manderston – the setting for Channel 4's series *The Edwardian Country House* – in 1887, from his father. Sir James was a dashing young fellow, keen on horse racing, and, as *Vanity Fair* wrote in 1890, 'a very eligible young man'. Three years later he married the Honourable Eveline Curzon, daughter of Lord Scarsdale. On returning from the Boer War in 1901, Sir James set about rebuilding his house to accommodate the lavish house parties which he and his wife liked to give. When John Kinross, his architect, enquired what the budget was to be, he was told that 'it simply doesn't matter.'

The entrance front of Manderston was demolished and rebuilt in a restrained, classical style. However, there is nothing restrained about the 'Adamesque' style of the interiors.

The marble-floored, columned hall leads to the famous 'silver staircase', with silver-plated balustrade and brass handrail. Most sumptuous is the ballroom, lit by Italian crystal chandeliers and decorated in primrose and white – Sir James's racing colours; the walls are hung with embossed velvet and the curtains woven with gold and silver thread; set into the ceiling are painted panels depicting Apollo, the sun god, and Venus, goddess of love, with cherubs in the corner roundels.

Downstairs is the white-tiled domain of the battalion of servants required to ensure the smooth operation of a house of this kind – there are 56 bells outside the housekeeper's room. Do make time to visit the marble-clad dairy, and the stables – certainly the smartest in Scotland. *KB*

Manderston's unique 'silver staircase', with its remarkable silver-plated balustrade.

NEWHAILES HOUSE

An early Georgian villa

This small classical villa was built by the Scottish architect James Smith in 1686 for his own family, and extended and decorated in the early 18th century by Sir David Dalrymple, who became Solicitor-General for Scotland and a key figure in the Scottish Enlightenment.

When the National Trust for Scotland acquired Newhailes in 1996, it was gently decaying and hidden in an overgrown landscape. The Trust's conservationists have undertaken the difficult task of preserving the house and making it accessible to visitors, without losing its essential character.

The entrance hall retains its crisp 1740s plasterwork, while the stone staircase, with its spiralling iron balustrade, is from James Smith's original house of the 1680s. The Chinese Sitting Room has egg-yolk yellow walls and gilded scallop shells. The books from David Dalrymple's enormous library are now in the National Library of Scotland, but the cavernous shelves remain; be sure to peep into the tiny study, later converted into a china cabinet.

The principal rooms have lively carved marble chimneypieces by the English sculptor Henry Cheere, including a wonderfully mournful lion in the dining room. The paintwork of the timber panelling and fluted columns in the dining room is a subtle, smoky green, with delicately gilded carvings and wall paintings by the Scottish artist James Norie.

The Trust has done well to avoid the temptation to awaken this 'Sleeping Beauty'. The process of decay has been arrested, but the mellow patina of age has not been erased. *KB*

Newhailes House is in Musselburgh, East Lothian, just to the east of Edinburgh. It is owned by the National Trust for Scotland and open on selected days from the beginning of April to the end of October.
Tel: 0131 653 5599
www.nts.org.uk

The library, which once housed David Dalrymple's large collection of books.

PAXTON HOUSE

A fine small 18th-century country house

The exterior façade of Paxton House, with pedimented portico.

The entrance hall, with vigorous rococo plasterwork executed by a local craftsman.

With its pedimented portico and mirrored pavilions, Paxton House is one of the most perfect Palladian villas in Scotland. It was designed in 1758 by John and James Adam for Patrick Home, and built of pink sandstone quarried on the estate. The interiors of the house give the visitor a vivid picture of how an elegant, but unostentatious, country house was decorated and furnished in the mid 18th century.

Ninian Home, who bought Paxton from his cousin Patrick in 1774, commissioned fashionable furnishings for the house from Thomas Chippendale, much of which (including all the furniture in the dining room) can, remarkably, still be seen at Paxton House today. For the principal bedroom, in addition to the fine four-poster bed, Chippendale supplied a delightful set of painted wheel-back chairs and an intricate lady's writing desk.

The supremely elegant drawing room, decorated in aquamarine and smoky pink, was designed by Robert Adam

THE HIGH PRIEST OF MAHOGANY

If Paxton House contains the finest collection of Chippendale furniture in Scotland, then the English equivalent is Harewood House (p 225) in West Yorkshire, close to where Thomas Chippendale was born in 1718. He worked mainly in mahogany, single-handedly raising the quality of English furniture to challenge the best to be found in Continental Europe.

in cutting-edge neoclassical taste, with a shallow relief plasterwork ceiling, its delicate fan pattern reflected in the marquetry tops of half-moon pier tables which were designed by Thomas Chippendale junior. The magnificent domed picture gallery was added in 1812. In addition to a collection of paintings from the National Gallery of Scotland, the room contains a superb set of neo-Greek rosewood furniture, designed by the fashionable Edinburgh furniture-maker William Trotter. *KB*

Paxton House is 3 miles from Berwick-upon-Tweed, in the Scottish Borders. It is owned by the Paxton Trust and open from the beginning of April to the end of October.
Tel: 01289 386291
www.paxtonhouse.com

POLLOK HOUSE

A mid 18th-century house with Georgian and 'neo-Georgian' interiors

The Pollok estate (now Pollok Country Park), surrounded by Glasgow's south-western suburbs, is a much-appreciated green oasis, through which flow the waters of the White Cart River. At its centre is Pollok House, a neat, even prim, Palladian villa, built in 1747 for Baronet Sir John Maxwell. All is not quite as it seems, however.

Sir John Stirling Maxwell inherited Pollok in 1887, at a time when the possession of an estate on the out-skirts of a rapidly expanding city was a very valuable asset indeed. The little Georgian house, however, was not suitable for late Victorian standards of comfort and entertaining; in addi-tion, Sir John required an appropriate setting for his magnificent collection of art – Spanish paintings, ceramics, silver, glass and books. He therefore commissioned Sir Robert Rowand Anderson, the leading Scottish archi-tect of his day, to extend and modern-ize his house, seamlessly blending the original Georgian architecture with the newly fashionable 'neo-Georgian'. The proportions and interior details of the original rooms, with their 18th-century chimneypieces and exuberant plasterwork, were main-tained. Anderson added the single-storey pavilions and the bowed entrance hall, with its double mahogany-banistered marble stairs and glittering bevelled glass doors.

In the basement is a well-preserved suite of rooms designed to house the army of servants required to keep a late Victorian country house running smoothly, including a store room, boot room, gunroom and a separate room for cleaning knives. *KB*

Pollok House is in Pollok Country Park, Glasgow. It is owned by the National Trust for Scotland and open all year.
Tel: 0141 616 6410
www.nts.og.uk

The entrance hall, with double mahogany-banistered marble stairs.

THE TENEMENT HOUSE

A miraculously preserved early 20th-century interior

The Tenement House is in Buccleuch Street, Garnethill, Glasgow. It is owned by the National Trust for Scotland and open from the beginning of March to the end of October.
Tel: 0141 333 0183
www.nts.org.uk

The Tenement House is a first-floor flat in a utilitarian red sandstone tenement, in a respectable but not affluent part of Glasgow. For 50-odd years it was the home of Agnes Toward, who was born in 1886 and moved to Buccleuch Street with her mother in 1911. In 1982 the flat and its contents were acquired by the National Trust for Scotland. The flat still contains most of its original furnishings and many of Agnes Toward's personal possessions. It gives a vivid glimpse of the minutiae of urban life in the early part of the 20th century. *KB*

The kitchen, with clothes hung up to dry on the pulley, and curtained box bed beyond.

TRAQUAIR

An ancient Scottish castle

Mary Queen of Scots slept here in 1566: there is a spectacular bed associated with her and a cradle in which she is supposed to have rocked the future James VI (James I of England). Most famous, however, are the Bear Gates, closed by the 5th Earl of Traquair when he bid adieu to Prince Charles Edward Stuart in 1745, with the vow that they would not be opened until the Stuarts were restored to the throne. The decoration in Traquair's largely 17th-century rooms is very well-preserved. Be sure not to miss the secret staircase for escaping priests. *KB*

Traquair House is on the B709, near Peebles, in the Scottish Borders. It is owned by the Maxwell Stuart family (descendants of the Earls of Traquair) and open from April to the end of October.
Tel: 01896 830323
www.traquair.co.uk

Traquair, set in secluded woodland gardens.

NORTHERN SCOTLAND, HIGHLANDS AND ISLANDS

To the modern tourist the Highlands and Islands of Scotland are synonymous with romantic castles – preferably ruined. The castles that retain their interiors, however, owe their survival largely to a vision of Scotland that emerged in the 19th century, largely engendered by the novels and poems of Sir Walter Scott (whose own house, Abbotsford, is featured on p 260).

The young Queen Victoria made her first visit to Scotland in 1842, and ten years later gave the royal seal of approval to the Highlands, acquiring the estate of Balmoral, where she built a new Scottish baronial home. A style of interior decoration evolved, influenced by the much-illustrated interiors of Victoria and Albert's holiday home, as a suitable setting for the shooting parties which were the main focus of upper-class life in this area. Heraldic stained glass, halls hung with tapestries and antlers, candle-lit dining rooms with oak tables and tartan carpets were all part of the look. Many of Scotland's older castles, such as Craigievar and Fyvie, were redecorated in this style.

Even houses built for Edwardian magnates tended to reflect this vision, with stone-vaulted halls and roaring fires in huge stone chimneypieces. The Scottish Arts and Crafts architect and designer Robert Lorimer, who spent his childhood holidays at Kellie Castle, was adept at fulfilling this requirement, and the hall at Hill of Tarvit Mansionhouse, for example, makes reference to this tradition. *KB*

ARGYLL'S LODGING

A 17th-century town house

Just below Stirling Castle – Scotland's most spectacular royal fortress – Argyll's Lodging is an astonishingly intact example of a 17th-century nobleman's town house. Built round a courtyard, entered through a rusticated archway in a screen wall, the U-plan building, with conical-roofed stair towers at the corners, resembles a French hotel. The interior has been furnished with tapestries, furniture and upholstery, including stylish purple bed hangings, recreated by modern craftsmen, based on inventories taken in the 1680s, when the house was the property of the 9th Earl of Argyll. *KB*

Argyll's Lodging is at Castle Wynd, Stirling. It is managed by Historic Scotland and open all year.
Tel: 01786 431319
www.historic-scotland.gov.uk

Looking through the entrance archway towards the courtyard at Argyll's Lodging.

J.M.BARRIE'S BIRTHPLACE

A 19th-century weaver's cottage

The house in which the author J.M. Barrie, creator of *Peter Pan*, was born (the ninth of ten children of a handloom weaver and his wife) has been restored by the National Trust for Scotland to commemorate Kirriemuir's most famous son. The house has been furnished with box beds, a Scotch dresser and two of the six 'hair-bottomed', balloon-backed chairs which Barrie's mother proudly acquired on the day of his birth, to show how a modest but not penurious Scottish family would have lived in the mid 19th century. *KB*

J.M. Barrie's Birthplace is in Brechin Road, Kirriemuir, Angus, 6 miles north-west of Forfar. It is owned by the National Trust for Scotland and open on selected days from the beginning of April until the end of September.
Tel: 01575 572646
www.nts.org.uk

The kitchen, furnished as it was in Barrie's day, with a box bed which would have been used by his parents.

LUTYENS AND THE TICKING CROCODILE
One of Barrie's closest friends was the eminent architect Sir Edwin Lutyens (*see* pages 89, 91 and 188). It was Lutyens who came up with the idea of the ticking crocodile in *Peter Pan*, while the Darling family's governess-dog Nana was named after the architect's own dog.

CRAIGIEVAR CASTLE

Scotland's best-preserved 17th-century tower house

Craigievar was built in the early 17th century by William Forbes, son of an eminent Aberdeenshire family. As a younger son, William had been expected to go out into the world and make his own way; he became a merchant and amassed a fortune trading, as many Scots did at that time, in the Baltic, and he invested his cash in land in his native Aberdeenshire. He bought the estate of Craigievar in 1610 and proceeded to completely remodel the existing old castle.

Victorian tourists, heavily influenced by Romantic literature, particularly by the novels of Sir Walter Scott, saw Craigievar as 'a strange and curious old castle'. In the 17th century, however, as befits the home of a well-travelled 'new man', Craigievar was a smart new house, combining the imagery of an old family castle with Continental classical details. The castle is L-plan, with a square tower clasped in the internal angle. The lower storeys, with their coating of

Craigievar Castle, with candle-snuffer-roofed turrets and balustraded viewing platform.

creamy lime-harling, have a wonderful sculptural quality; the upper storeys blossom with conical-roofed turrets, like a little French chateau; the square tower is topped by a balustraded viewing platform.

The decoration of the interior is equally ambitious. In contrast to the painted timber ceilings of earlier tower houses, those at Craigievar sport exuberant baroque plasterwork. The fashion for these ceilings in Scotland had begun with the redecoration of the Great Hall at Edinburgh Castle for the visit of James VI in 1617 – returning briefly to his native Scotland for the first time since becoming James I of England in 1603. After completing their work in Edinburgh, it seems that the team of

---

ROYAL TOURIST

Small but perfectly formed, Craigievar has been everyone's favourite Scottish tower house for a very long time indeed. Queen Victoria first visited Craigievar in 1879, by which time the castle was already well-established as a tourist attraction. Following her visit, Queen Victoria recorded in her diary: 'Craigievar is a strange and curious old castle … It is still inhabited but there is no one there just now [the servants didn't count as anyone!]. Got out and went into some of the curious small low rooms with old furniture in them, as well as the dining hall which has a vaulted roof … At first no one knew who we were, but it gradually dawned upon them.'

The Queen's Room, with 18th-century 'angel' bed.

plasterers toured the great houses of Scotland, using the same moulds to install their highly prestigious designs in castles such as Kellie Castle in Fife (p 298) and Craigievar. The amazing thing is that, while the ceiling at Edinburgh Castle has recently been recreated (partly on the evidence of

the plasterwork at Craigievar), the one at Craigievar is the real thing. Likewise, most of the Jacobean timber panelling is original. Uniquely in Scotland, the hall retains its oak screens passage, through which the servants passed, bringing food and drink to the laird and his party; a spiral staircase descends from behind the screens passage to the wine cellar

A detail from one of Craigievar's moulded plasterwork ceilings.

Beyond the curtains in the Blue Room are alcoves formed by the turrets. In the centre of the ceiling are the Royal Arms.

and kitchen on the ground floor. Above and behind the screens passage are two little minstrels' galleries.

The acquisition by Queen Victoria and Prince Albert of the Balmoral estate as a holiday home in the mid 19th century, and the subsequent fame and glamour of 'Royal Deeside', put Aberdeenshire 'on the map'. Craigievar is just 20 miles from Balmoral Castle – perfect for a 'day trip' by carriage (and, of course, Balmoral was accessible by train from London). Craigievar's owners began to act up to its new-found status as a tourist attraction. A photograph of the 17th Lord Sempill taken in the early 20th century shows him sitting outside the castle, resplendent in his kilt, badger sporran, tweeds and bonnet. The fabric of the castle and its 'old furniture' were cherished; the chairs in the dining room were reupholstered with Forbes tartan; Forbes tartan carpets and curtains were woven; antlers and ancient weapons were newly displayed. In the bedrooms, reached by narrow spiral stairs, most of the timber panelling and the magnificent plasterwork ceilings survive. The bed in the Queen's Room, which would have been the principal bedchamber, is the best-preserved of the two surviving 18th-century 'angel' beds, which have canopies suspended from the ceiling rather than supported on foot-posts. Don't miss the wonderfully eccentric 'box-bath' in the housekeeper's room. *KB*

An engraving of the hall at Craigievar, by Robert W. Billings.

The hall, adorned with antlers and tartan carpet.

Inside one of the attic turrets.

Craigievar Castle is on the A980, 6 miles south of Alford, Aberdeenshire. It is owned by the National Trust for Scotland and open on selected days from the beginning of April to the end of September (not accessible to groups or coach parties).
Tel: 013398 83635
www.nts.org.uk

DUFF HOUSE

A flamboyant Georgian baroque mansion

In Aberdeenshire – the 'county of castles' – a baroque country house rivalling, in splendour if not in size, English examples such as Castle Howard (p 220), is a most surprising find. Duff House was built by the architect William Adam for William Duff, Earl of Fife, in 1735. It was fitted out and furnished in the later 18th century by the Earl's son, the 2nd Earl, in fashionable neoclassical style. The house suffered a period of neglect in the 20th century, but in 1995 Historic Scotland began the painstaking process of restoring the forlorn shell to its former glory.

With its lively rococo plasterwork and crisply gilded, pale-painted wood-work, the house is now a sparkling showcase for the collection of paint-ings, tapestries and furniture supplied by the National Galleries of Scotland. In the Great Drawing Room is a suite of Gobelins tapestries; notice, too, the amazing set of gilded chairs and sofas, uniquely made by Thomas Chippendale to the design of Robert Adam, and the entwined dolphins supporting the pedestal table reflected in the mirrored glass base. In the North Drawing Room the arms of the Empire chairs are decorated with winged lions. The gilded four-poster bed in the Prince of Wales Bedroom (slept in by the future Edward VII) is hung with rich pink silk damask. Glittering chandeliers and portraits of elegantly clad aristocrats give visitors a vivid impression of life in a great Scottish country house. *KB*

Duff House is just outside Banff, Aberdeenshire, on the A947. It is managed by a partnership of Historic Scotland, the National Galleries of Scotland, and Aberdeenshire Council and open from April to October.
Tel: 01261 818181
www.duffhouse.org.uk

Far left: The magnificent façade of Duff House.

Left: The Private Drawing Room, with a Scottish landscape scene hung over the chimneypiece.

FYVIE CASTLE

A medieval castle remodelled in the 18th and 19th centuries

Portrait of Colonel William Gordon of Fyvie, painted by Pompeo Batoni.

Almost encircled by the River Ythan, and surrounded by a hunting forest, Fyvie was one of a chain of royal fortresses visited by the peripatetic medieval Scottish monarchy in an attempt to assert their authority in the disparate parts of a bellicose kingdom. The 'men of Moray' were particularly rebellious, and the king always needed a strong man in the north-east to maintain peace in his absence. Sir Alexander Seton, who purchased the Fyvie estate in 1596, was such a man. Chancellor of Scotland, principal political advisor to King James VI and guardian of his

of Aberdeen. Gordon was a soldier who fought in India and became a general. He did much to improve Fyvie, building the Gordon Tower and laying out the extensive parkland in the 18th-century manner. In the 1760s, Gordon had made the Grand Tour to France and Italy, and while in Rome he sat for Pompeo Batoni, the leading Italian portrait painter of his day. Batoni's splendid full-length portrait of Gordon, looking like a cross between a Highland chieftain and a Roman general, is perhaps the most remarkable of Fyvie's magnificent collection of paintings.

By 1885 Fyvie had once again fallen on hard times, and the castle, its contents and the estate were on the market. As *The Times* reported, the sale of the castle presented an opportunity, being 'the very residence for an antiquary of ample means'; fortunately, such a purchaser appeared. Alexander Leith, whose family was distantly descended from Sir Henry Preston, the 15th-century owner of Fyvie, had joined the Royal Navy as a young man, and at a ball in San Francisco he had met, and subsequently married, Marie Louise January, a rich and beautiful young American. Leith proceeded to build on his wife's fortune, founding the Illinois Steel Company – the largest in the world at that time, with a workforce of 10,000 men. In 1889 he acquired Fyvie, and turned his formidable energies to the remodelling of the castle. It is Alexander Leith's stamp that is most

The great show front of Fyvie Castle.

younger son, the future Charles I, Seton was the creator of the great show castle that we see at Fyvie today.

In the 18th century, after a period of neglect, Fyvie was inherited by William Gordon, son of the Earl

firmly impressed on the interior of Fyvie as we see it today.

Like many industrial magnates, Alexander Forbes Leith (later Lord Leith) was an enthusiastic collector of art and antiquities. Displayed in the entrance hall is part of his impressive collection of arms and armour, while over the massive fireplace is a plaster relief of the Battle of Otterburn, in which his ancestor, Sir Henry Preston, had fought. Forbes Leith extended the Gordon Tower, a new service wing was added, and the old kitchen on the ground floor became a billiard room. He remodelled General Gordon's dining room, installing a 'Jacobean' plasterwork ceiling and dark oak

panelling; set into the ornately carved overmantel is a portrait of Marie Louise January, his American wife.

The drawing room above opens into the vaulted music room, built in 1900 by Forbes Leith. Lit by an oriel window forming a bay in which the grand piano sits, the tapestry-hung music room is dominated by an amazing self-playing pipe organ. The ornate French Renaissance marble chimneypiece is inset with glorious Oriental enamelled tiles. It is in this opulent but comfortable room that one can most easily imagine the successful businessman and his glamorous wife entertaining the international set of their day in their newly acquired ancestral home.

The Great Stair, built over 400 years ago in around 1600 for Sir Alexander Seton.

The vaulted music room, with its magnificent chimneypiece, pipe organ and grand piano.

Do look out for the superb American Tiffany electrolier with its stained-glass shade, which somehow fits perfectly with the eclectic collection of *objets* in the room.

The paintings that Lord Leith bought for Fyvie are not only a reflection of his taste and wealth, but also of his deep sense of connection with the castle and with his Aberdeenshire ancestry. The castle itself is not, and was never intended to be, subtle or understated. The building is, in a sense, the architectural equivalent of Pompeo Batoni's swaggering depiction of Colonel Gordon dressed in kilt and plaid, proudly proclaiming the wealth, power and importance of its owner. *KB*

Fyvie Castle is 8 miles south-east of Turriff, Aberdeenshire, off the A947. It is owned by the National Trust for Scotland and open on selected days from the beginning of April to the end of September.
Tel: 01651 891266
www.nts.org.uk

HILL OF TARVIT MANSIONHOUSE

An Edwardian country house

Hill of Tarvit Mansionhouse is set in terraced gardens on a south-facing site overlooking the Fife countryside. It was built in 1906 for Fredrick Sharp, whose family had made a considerable fortune from jute, imported from India and made into sackcloth in the factories of Dundee. Like many manufacturing magnates, Sharp invested in art and antiques, and he commissioned Robert Lorimer (*see also* Kellie Castle, p 298), the leading Scottish Arts and Crafts architect, to design a house that would be not only a comfortable family home, but also a showcase for his precious collection of paintings, tapestries, French furniture and Chinese porcelain.

From the galleried hall, where glowing 16th-century Flemish tapestries hang against dark timber panelling, through the light elegance of the pastiche French decor of the drawing room – a setting for Sharp's collection of French 18th-century furniture – to the panelled and pilastered neo-

The hall, with oak furniture and Flemish tapestries.

Palladian dining room, furnished with Georgian furniture and silver, the series of rooms produced by Lorimer and his team of craftsmen combine overtones of ancestral splendour (always desirable to the nouveau riche) with up-to-the minute comfort and convenience. The house was also equipped with state-of-the-art central heating fuelled by electricity from the estate generator, and an internal telephone system to supplement the electric bells. *KB*

Hill of Tarvit Mansionhouse is off the A916, 2¹/₂ miles south of Cupar, Fife. It is owned by the National Trust for Scotland and open on selected days from the beginning of April to the end of October.
Tel: 01334 653127
www.nts.org.uk

Hill of Tarvit Mansionhouse and garden.

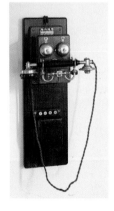

The house telephone connected the service area with the family rooms, supplementing the electric bell system.

THE HOUSE OF DUN

A small early 18th-century house

The saloon, which features flamboyant baroque plasterwork.

The House of Dun is on the A935, 3 miles west of Montrose, Angus. It is owned by the National Trust for Scotland and open on selected days from April to the end of September.
Tel: 01674 810264
www.nts.org.uk

The House of Dun, beside the shallow, tidal Montrose Basin, was the seat of the Erskines of Dun from the 14th century. In the 1730s the 13th Laird, David Erskine, who was a judge in the Scottish Court of Session, commissioned a smart new house from William Adam, the leading Scottish architect of his age. Many of William Adam's clients were middling gentry rather than super-rich aristocracy, and one of his special talents was the ability to pack a lot of grandeur into a relatively small package.

At the House of Dun, Adam demonstrated this talent to the full. The entrance to the house is framed by a tall arch and flanked by fluted giant pilasters. The hall beyond leads to the saloon – Dun's most spectacular space, decorated with an astonishing display of baroque plasterwork. The coved ceiling, the panels over the doors – every available space is alive with gods and goddesses, chained slaves, trophies of arms and armour, and musical instruments. In 1723, David Erskine's kinsman, the Earl of Mar, had advised him that his new house 'ought to have one or two handsome and tolerable large rooms for the Master to entertain his friends upon occasion, and where couples of young folks may dance.' In this lively room, with light flooding in from tall windows, it is not difficult to imagine such a scene. In contrast, at the top of the house, separated from the hustle and bustle of the house, is David Erskine's peaceful library. *KB*

KELLIE CASTLE

A medieval castle, restored in the late 19th century

In the summer of 1876, James Lorimer, Professor of Law at the University of Edinburgh, was holidaying in the picturesque Fife fishing village of Pittenweem with his wife and six children. On a family walk they discovered Kellie Castle – an abandoned castle, with pepperpot towers, crow-stepped gables and dormer-headed windows.

The Professor managed to obtain a long lease of the castle from the owner, the Earl of Mar and Kellie. The Lorimer family undertook a programme of admirably restrained restoration, and childhood summers spent at Kellie were to have an important influence on James's son, Robert, who was to become Scotland's leading Arts and Crafts architect.

Kellie is decorated in an 'artistic', Bohemian style, almost reminiscent of Bloomsbury – think Charleston (p 51), Duncan Grant and Vanessa Bell's house – with Oriental rugs on dark-stained wood floors, classically detailed timber panelling and fine plasterwork, painted white.

Pepperpot towers and crow-stepped gables at Kellie Castle in Fife.

Tapestries and furniture from the 17th century are mixed with furniture designed by Robert Lorimer and bed hangings embroidered by his sister Louise. Although the oldest part of the castle dates from the 14th century, the T-plan building seen today dates mainly from the late 16th and early 17th centuries. Stone steps lead from the vaulted ground floor to the pilastered drawing room and the dining room. *KB*

AN ABANDONED CASTLE

'Great holes let the rain and snow through the roofs, many of the floors had become unsafe, every pane of glass was broken, and swallows built in the coronets on the ceilings ...'

Louise Lorimer, daughter of James Lorimer, describing the abandoned Kellie Castle

---

Kellie Castle is on the B9171, 3 miles north-west of Pittenweem, Fife. It is owned by the National Trust for Scotland and open at Easter and from the beginning of June until the end of September.
Tel: 01333 720271
www.nts.org.uk

MOUNT STUART

A flamboyant Victorian Gothic palace

Mount Stuart is off the A444, south of Rothesay, on the Isle of Bute. It is owned by the Mount Stuart Trust and open on selected days from the beginning of May until the end of September.
Tel: 01700 503877
www.mountstuart.com

On 3 December 1877, fire destroyed the central part of the 18th-century Mount Stuart, ancestral home of John Patrick Crichton-Stuart, 3rd Marquess of Bute. The 3rd Marquess had almost completed the transformation of the ruins of Cardiff Castle (p 238), and he brought some of the craftsmen working there to Bute. He also employed the leading Scottish architect Sir Robert Rowand Anderson, an expert in use of the Gothic revival style, to design a 'splendid palace' in red sandstone.

The heart of Mount Stuart is the Marble Hall: two storeys of pointed-arched arcades, their marble columns rising to a vaulted ceiling pierced with constellations of stars. The dining room is hung with family portraits, including Allan Ramsay's superb portrait of John Stuart, 3rd Earl of Bute (friend and confidant of George III and exceedingly unpopular Prime Minister), clad in red velvet robes adorned with ermine. The drawing room has a richly decorated heraldic ceiling, and the carved and gilded ceiling in the principal bedroom was made in the Bute workshops at Cardiff and shipped to Bute. No fewer than three libraries (two of them open to the public) house an astonishing collection of leather-bound books.

Although the decoration of Mount Stuart is a hymn to medieval style, state-of-the-art Victorian technology was not shunned – it was the first house in Scotland to be lit by electricity, and telephone lines were installed. The most extraordinary room (not normally open to the public) is the Gothic-style swimming pool – one of the first indoor heated swimming pools anywhere. *KB*

The lantern of the Marble Chapel towers above Mount Stuart.

Far right: The magnificent Marble Hall.

South-West England

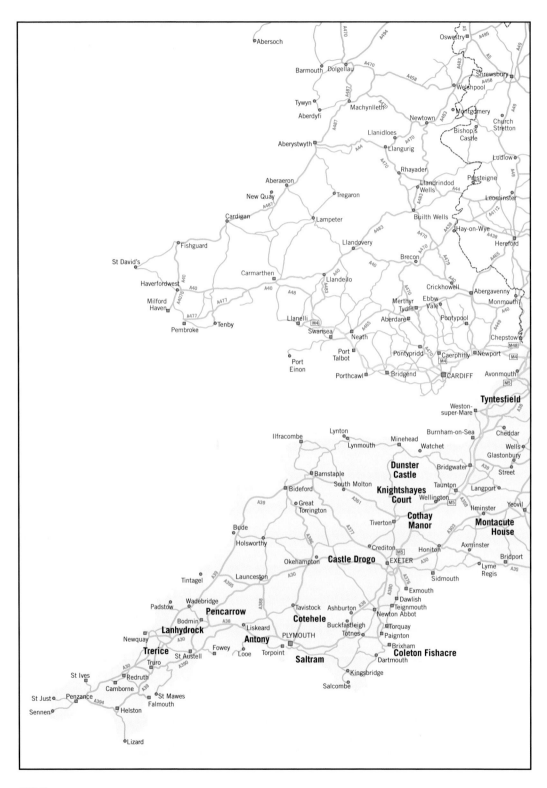

Abersoch

Barmouth Dolgellau

Tywyn Machynlleth
Aberdyfi

Aberystwyth Llangurig

Aberaeron Rhayader
New Quay Tregaron Llandrindod
Wells
Cardigan Lampeter Builth Wells Hay-on-Wye
Fishguard Llandovery Hereford
St David's Brecon
Haverfordwest Carmarthen Llandeilo Crickhowell Abergavenny
Milford Merthyr Ebbw Monmouth
Haven Llanelli Tydfil Vale Pontypool
Pembroke Tenby Swansea Aberdare Chepstow
Neath Pontypridd Caerphilly Newport
Port Port Avonmouth
Einon Talbot Bridgend CARDIFF
Porthcawl

Tyntesfield

Weston-
super-Mare Cheddar
Lynton Wells
Ilfracombe Lynmouth Minehead Glastonbury
Barnstaple South Molton Watchet Bridgwater Street
Bideford Taunton Langport
**Dunster
Castle**
**Knightshayes
Court**
Great Wellington Ilminster Yeovil
Torrington Tiverton **Cothay
Manor** **Montacute
House**
Bude Crediton Honiton Axminster
Holsworthy Bridport
Okehampton **Castle Drogo** EXETER Lyme
Regis
Tintagel Launceston Sidmouth
Padstow Wadebridge Exmouth
Dawlish
Bodmin **Pencarrow** Tavistock **Cotehele** Teignmouth
Lanhydrock Liskeard Buckfastleigh Newton Abbot
Newquay **Antony** Ashburton Torquay
Trerice Fowey PLYMOUTH Totnes Paignton
Truro St Austell Looe Torpoint Brixham
St Ives Redruth **Saltram** **Coleton Fishacre**
Dartmouth
St Just Penzance Camborne St Mawes Kingsbridge
Sennen Falmouth Salcombe
Helston

Lizard

Oswestry Shrewsbury
Welshpool
Newtown Montgomery Church
Bishop's Stretton
Castle Ludlow
Llanidloes Presteigne
Leominster

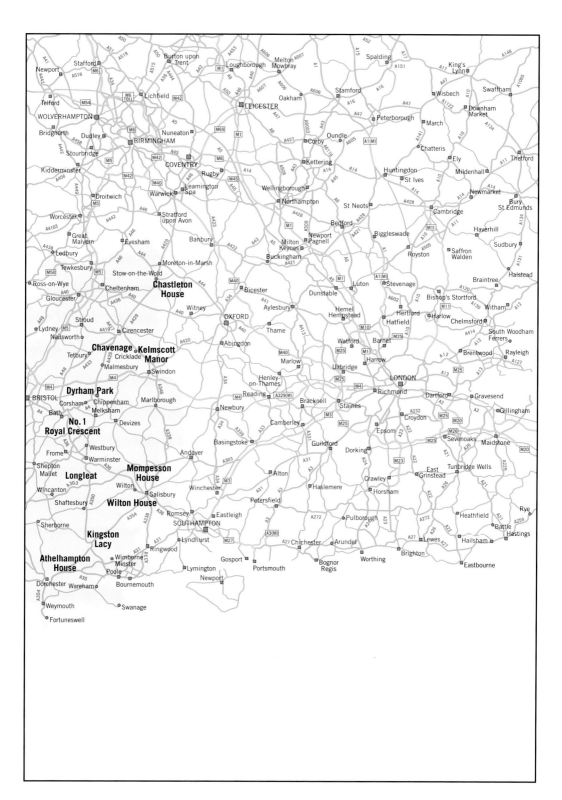

SOUTH-EAST ENGLAND

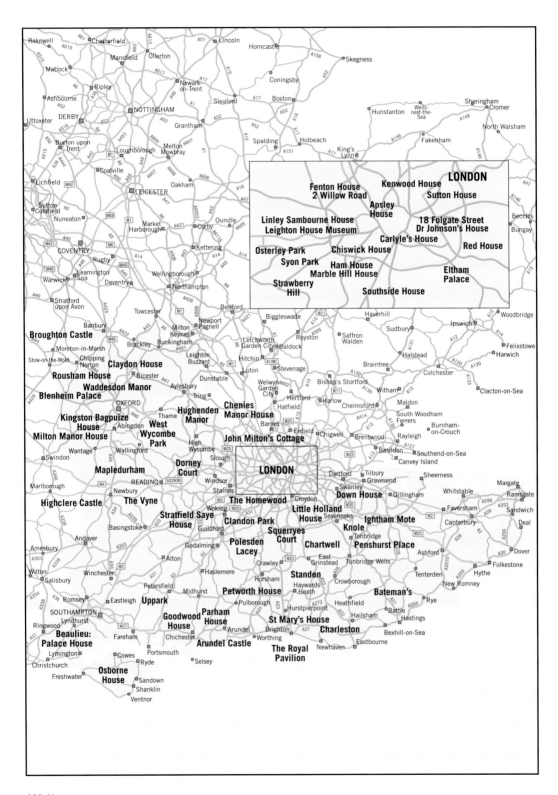

LONDON

Fenton House
2 Willow Road
Kenwood House
Sutton House
Apsley House
Linley Sambourne House
Leighton House Museum
18 Folgate Street
Dr Johnson's House
Carlyle's House
Red House
Osterley Park
Chiswick House
Syon Park
Ham House
Marble Hill House
Strawberry Hill
Southside House
Eltham Palace

Broughton Castle
Claydon House
Rousham House
Waddesdon Manor
Blenheim Palace
Kingston Bagpuize House
Milton Manor House
West Wycombe Park
Hughenden Manor
Chenies Manor House
John Milton's Cottage
Mapledurham
Dorney Court
Highclere Castle
The Vyne
Stratfield Saye House
The Homewood
Little Holland House
Down House
Ightham Mote
Clandon Park
Knole
Squerryes Court
Chartwell
Penshurst Place
Polesden Lacey
Standen
Bateman's
Petworth House
Uppark
Goodwood House
Parham House
St Mary's House
Charleston
Beaulieu: Palace House
Arundel Castle
The Royal Pavilion
Osborne House

Eastern England

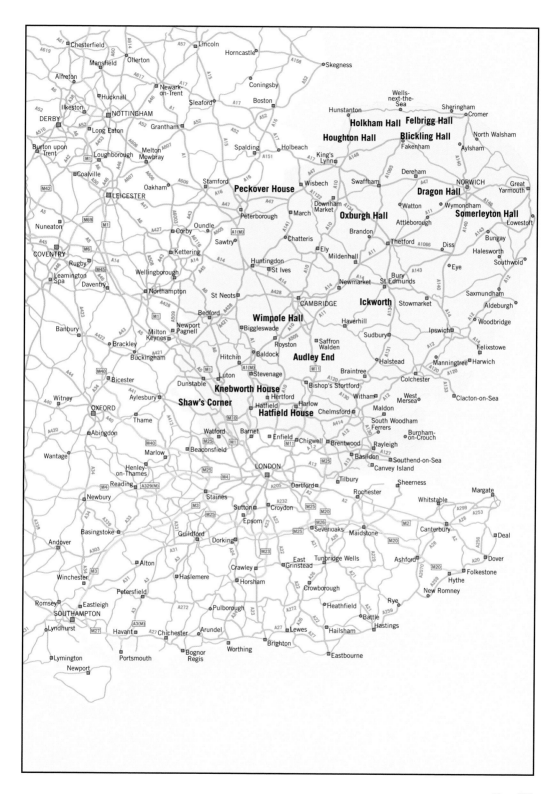

WALES

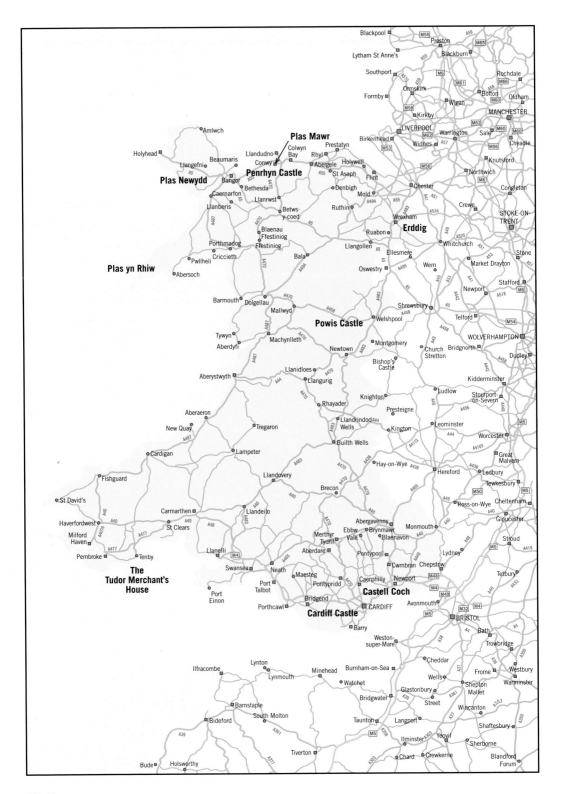

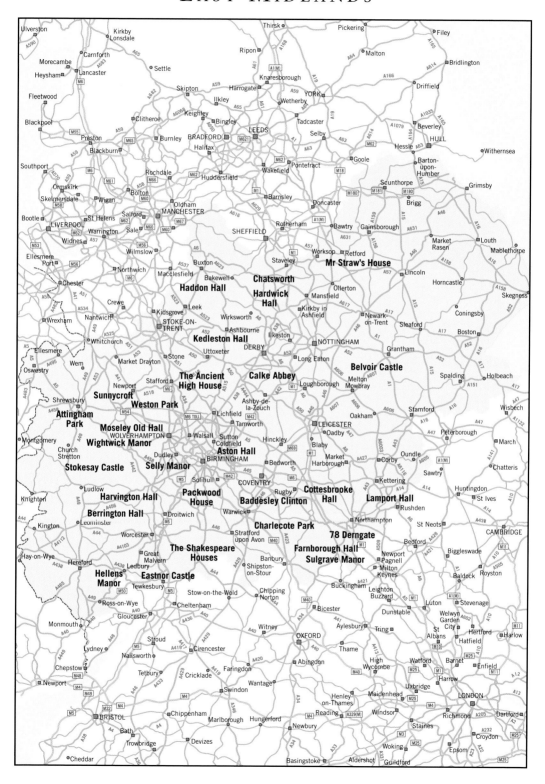

THE LAKE DISTRICT AND
NORTH-WEST ENGLAND

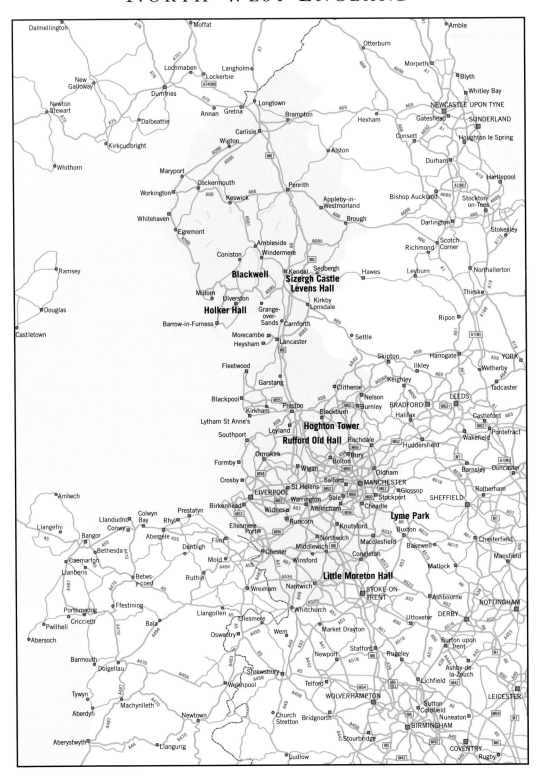

YORKSHIRE AND
NORTH-EAST ENGLAND

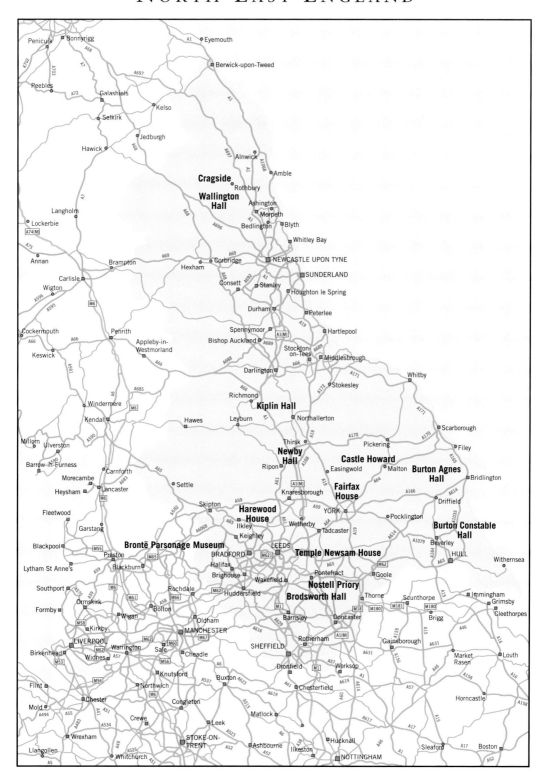

Penicuik
Bonnyrigg
A702
A703
A7
A68
A1
Eyemouth
Berwick-upon-Tweed
Peebles
A72
Galashiels
Kelso
A697
Selkirk
A7
Jedburgh
A68
A1
Hawick
A697
Alnwick
A1068
A1
Amble
Cragside
Rothbury
Wallington Hall
Ashington
Langholm
A7
A68
Morpeth
A1
Lockerbie
A696
Bedlington
Blyth
A74(M)
Whitley Bay
A75
A69
A69
Annan
Brampton
Corbridge
NEWCASTLE UPON TYNE
Carlisle
Hexham
A692
A1
Wigton
Consett
Stanley
SUNDERLAND
A596
A69
Houghton le Spring
A595
M6
Durham
Peterlee
Cockermouth
A66
A66
Penrith
Appleby-in-Westmorland
Spennymoor
A19
Hartlepool
A66
Bishop Auckland
A1(M)
A689
Stockton-on-Tees
A689
Middlesbrough
Keswick
A591
A685
A66
Darlington
A66
A685
Richmond
A171
Whitby
Windermere
M6
Kiplin Hall
A172
Stokesley
Kendal
A590
Hawes
Leyburn
Northallerton
Scarborough
Millom
A6
A170
Ulverston
Thirsk
A19
Pickering
A170
Filey
Barrow-in-Furness
Newby Hall
Carnforth
A683
A65
Ripon
Easingwold
Castle Howard
A64
Malton
Burton Agnes Hall
Bridlington
Morecambe
Lancaster
Settle
A61
A1(M)
A19
A64
A166
A614
Heysham
M6
Knaresborough
Fairfax House
Driffield
Fleetwood
A59
Skipton
Harewood House
A59
YORK
Pocklington
Burton Constable Hall
A6068
A65
Ilkley
Wetherby
Tadcaster
A19
A614
Beverley
Garstang
Keighley
A1079
A164
HULL
Blackpool
M55
Brontë Parsonage Museum
BRADFORD
M621
LEEDS
Temple Newsam House
M62
A63
Withernsea
Preston
M65
Halifax
Wakefield
Pontefract
Goole
Lytham St Anne's
Blackburn
Brighouse
A63
A59
Rochdale
Huddersfield
Nostell Priory
Thorne
Scunthorpe
A15
Immingham
Southport
M6
M61
M66
M62
Brodsworth Hall
M18
M180
M181
M180
Grimsby
Formby
Ormskirk
Oldham
M1
Barnsley
Doncaster
Brigg
Cleethorpes
M58
Kirkby
Wigan
Bolton
A616
A629
A46
Birkenhead
LIVERPOOL
M62
Warrington
MANCHESTER
M62
M67
Rotherham
A1(M)
Gainsborough
A631
Louth
M53
Widnes
A57
Sale
M60
Cheadle
SHEFFIELD
A631
Market Rasen
A6
Flint
M56
Knutsford
Buxton
A537
A623
Dronfield
M1
A57
Worksop
A1
A158
A16
Mold
Chester
M6
Northwich
A619
Chesterfield
A619
A614
A57
Horncastle
A158
A494
A55
A51
Congleton
A515
Matlock
A617
A15
Crewe
A41
A61
A617
Wrexham
A483
A534
Leek
A6
A523
STOKE-ON-TRENT
A52
Ashbourne
Ilkeston
Hucknall
A46
Sleaford
A17
Boston
Llangollen
A5
A525
Whitchurch
A51
NOTTINGHAM
A52

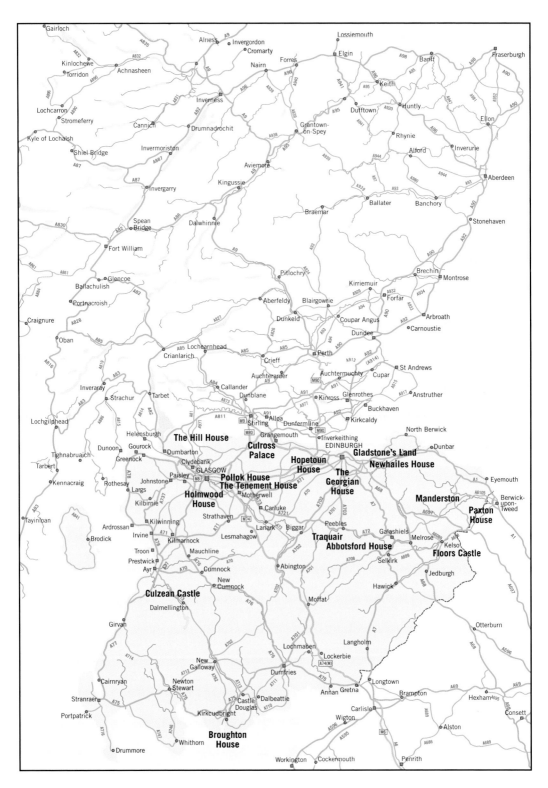

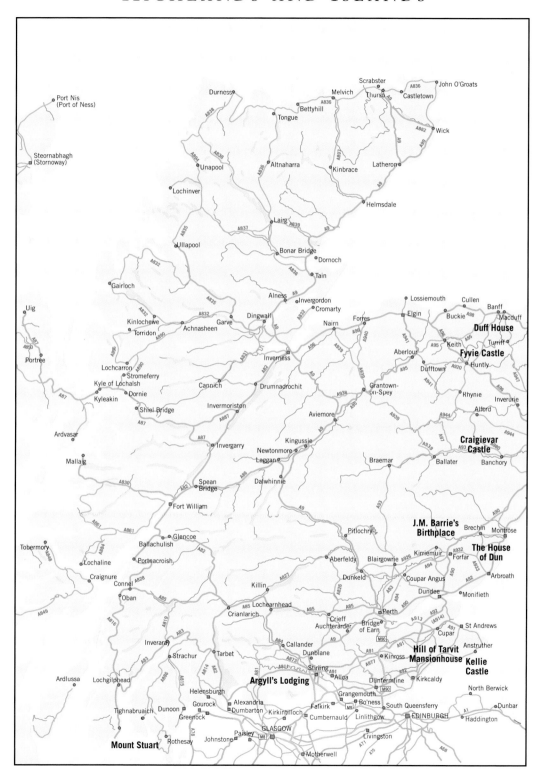

Port Nis
(Port of Ness)

Steornabhagh
(Stornoway)

Durness
Melvich
Scrabster
Thurso
Castletown
John O'Groats
Bettyhill
Tongue
Wick
Uig
Unapool
Altnaharra
Kinbrace
Latheron
Lochinver
Portree
Helmsdale
Lairg
Ullapool
Bonar Bridge
Dornoch
Gairloch
Tain
Alness
Invergordon
Cromarty
Lossiemouth
Cullen
Banff
Macduff
Kinlochewe
Garve
Dingwall
Forres
Elgin
Buckie
Duff House
Torridon
Achnasheen
Nairn
Keith
Turriff
Lochcarron
Stromeferry
Inverness
Aberlour
Fyvie Castle
Kyle of Lochalsh
Dornie
Cannich
Drumnadrochit
Dufftown
Huntly
Kyleakin
Shiel Bridge
Invermoriston
Grantown-on-Spey
Rhynie
Inverurie
Ardvasar
Aviemore
Alford
Invergarry
Kingussie
Craigievar Castle
Mallaig
Newtonmore
Laggan
Braemar
Ballater
Banchory
Spean Bridge
Dalwhinnie
Fort William
Tobermory
Glencoe
Pitlochry
J.M. Barrie's Birthplace
Brechin
Montrose
Lochaline
Ballachulish
Portnacroish
Aberfeldy
Blairgowrie
Kirriemuir
Forfar
The House of Dun
Craignure
Connel
Killin
Dunkeld
Coupar Angus
Arbroath
Oban
Lochearnhead
Dundee
Monifieth
Crianlarich
Crieff
Perth
Inveraray
Auchterarder
Bridge of Earn
St Andrews
Strachur
Tarbet
Callander
Dunblane
Kinross
Hill of Tarvit Mansionhouse
Cupar
Anstruther
Ardlussa
Lochgilphead
Stirling
Alloa
Dunfermline
Kirkcaldy
Kellie Castle
Argyll's Lodging
Grangemouth
North Berwick
Tighnabruaich
Dunoon
Helensburgh
Alexandria
Dumbarton
Kirkintilloch
Falkirk
Bo'ness
South Queensferry
Dunbar
Gourock
Greenock
Cumbernauld
Linlithgow
EDINBURGH
Haddington
Paisley
GLASGOW
Johnstone
Livingston
Rothesay
Mount Stuart
Motherwell

USEFUL ADDRESSES

SOCIETIES AND ORGANIZATIONS

The Ancient Monuments Society
St Ann's Vestry Hall
2 Church Entry
London EC4V 5HB
www.
ancientmonumentssociety.
org.uk
Tel: 020 7236 3934
Founded in 1924, the Ancient Monuments Society is concerned with the study and conservation of ancient monuments, historic buildings and fine old craftsmanship.

The Architectural Heritage Society of Scotland (AHSS)
The Glasite Meeting House
33 Barony Street
Edinburgh
Scotland EH3 6NX
Tel: 0131 557 0019
www.ahss.org.uk
The AHSS is dedicated to the preservation and study of the rich architectural heritage of Scotland.

Cadw
Welsh Assembly Government
Cathays Park
Cardiff
Wales CF10 3NQ
Tel: 01222 500 200
www.cadw.wales.gov.uk
Cadw (a Welsh word which means 'to keep') is the Welsh Assembly Government's historic environment agency. It is responsible for the conservation, protection and promotion of an appreciation of Wales's built heritage and gives grant aid for the repair and restoration of historic buildings.

English Heritage
National Office
23 Saville Row
London W1S 2ET
Tel: 020 7973 3385
www.english-heritage.org.uk
English Heritage is a government-sponsored body with responsibility for conserving and enhancing the historic environment of England. It aims to broaden public access to England's heritage and cares for over 400 historic properties. It also advises the government on the listing of buildings of historic and architectural importance.

The Georgian Group
6 Fitzroy Square
London W1T 5DX
Tel: 020 7529 8920
www.georgiangroup.org.uk
The Georgian Group is a charity which helps to preserve Georgian buildings and gardens. Each year the charity is consulted on over 6,000 planning applications and through its influence it aims to protect buildings from demolition or unsympathetic alterations.

Historic Houses Association
2 Chester Street
London SW1X 7BB
Tel: 020 7259 5688
www.hha.org.uk
The Historic Houses Association is a national body which represents the interests of over 1,500 privately owned historic houses, castles and gardens in Britain. The association includes about 350 properties which are regularly open to the public and many others which are open on an occasional basis.

Historic Scotland
Longmore House
Salisbury Place
Edinburgh
Scotland EH9 1SH
Tel: 0131 668 8800
www.historic-scotland.gov.uk
The Scottish equivalent of English Heritage, Historic Scotland is responsible for safeguarding and promoting the understanding of Scotland's built heritage. It cares for more than 300 properties from ancient standing stones to magnificent castles. It also advises the government on the listing of buildings of historic and architectural importance.

National Archives (Public Record Office)
Kew
Richmond
Surrey TW9 4DU
Tel: 020 8876 3444
www.nationalarchives.gov.uk
The National Archives is a valuable resource for anyone interested in documents relating to Britain's historic sites.

The National Monuments Record of Wales (NMRW)
Plas Crug
Aberystwyth
Ceredigion
Wales SY23 1NJ
Tel: 01970 621200
www.rcahmw.org.uk
Part of the Royal Commission on the Ancient and Historical Monuments of Wales, the NMRW holds the national collection of information about Wales's archaeological, architectural and historical heritage and provides a free public information service.

The National Trust
Central Office
36 Queen Anne's Gate
London SW1H 9AS
Tel: 0870 609 5380
www.nationaltrust.org.uk
The National Trust is a registered charity set up in 1895 to protect the nation's threatened coastline, countryside and buildings of historic interest. It now cares for over 600,000 acres of countryside in England, Wales and Northern Ireland, almost 600 miles of coastline and more than 200 historic buildings and gardens, the majority of which are open to the public.
For all general enquiries, including membership and requests for information, contact:
National Trust Membership Department
PO Box 39
Bromley
Kent BR1 3XL
Tel: 0870 458 4000

The National Trust for Scotland
Wemyss House
28 Charlotte Square
Edinburgh
Scotland EH2 4ET
Tel: 0131 243 9300
www.nts.org.uk
The National Trust for Scotland is an independent conservation charity established in 1931 to protect and promote Scotland's natural and cultural heritage. It cares for 127 properties of architectural and historic importance, as well as many miles of coastline and countryside.

SAVE Britain's Heritage
70 Cowcross Street
London EC1M 6EJ
Tel: 020 7253 3500
www.savebritainsheritage.org
SAVE is a conservation group created in 1975 to campaign publicly to save threatened historic buildings.

The Society for the Protection of Ancient Buildings (SPAB)
37 Spital Square
London E1 6DY
Tel: 020 7377 1644
www.spab.org.uk
Founded by William Morris in 1877, the SPAB is a national pressure group which fights to save historic buildings from demolition and damage.

The Victorian Society
1 Priory Gardens
Bedford Park
London W4 1TT
Tel: 020 8994 1019
www.victorian-society.org.uk
Founded in 1958, the Victorian Society is concerned with the study and protection of Victorian and Edwardian architecture and other arts.

MUSEUMS

Brighton Museum & Art Gallery
Royal Pavilion Gardens
Brighton
East Sussex BN1 1EE
Tel: 01273 290900
The Brighton Museum & Art Gallery's nationally important collections include Art Nouveau and Art Deco furniture, glass, ceramics and wallpaper samples.

Geffrye Museum
Kingsland Road
London E2 8EA
Tel: 020 7739 9893
www.geffrye-museum.org.uk
The Geffrye Museum houses an important collection of furniture, textiles and decorative arts displayed in a series of period rooms showing the changing style of English domestic interiors from 1600 onwards.

Museum of Domestic Design and Architecture (MoDA)
Middlesex University
Cat Hill
Barnet
Hertfordshire EN4 8HT
Tel: 020 8411 5244
www.moda.mdx.ac.uk
MoDA houses an outstanding collection of 19th- and 20th-century decorative arts, including wallpapers, textiles and soft furnishings from the 1870s to the 1960s.

Victoria and Albert Museum
Cromwell Road
South Kensington
London SW7 2RL
Tel: 020 7942 2000
www.vam.ac.uk
The V&A is the nation's most important museum of art and design. It houses valuable collections covering all aspects of interior design, with fascinating exhibits of applied and decorative arts from all periods.

Whitworth Art Gallery
The University of Manchester
Oxford Road
Manchester M15 6ER
Tel: 0161 275 7450
The Whitworth Art Gallery houses an outstanding collection of art and design, including a large collection of textiles and wallpapers dating from the mid 1880s onwards.

William Morris Gallery
Lloyd Park
Forest Road
London E17 4PP
Tel: 020 8527 3782
The William Morris Gallery houses important collections illustrating the life and work of William Morris and other great Arts and Crafts Movement artists such as Philip Webb, Edward Burne-Jones and Ford Madox Brown.

GLOSSARY

A

armorial relating to heraldry

Art Nouveau decorative style in art, architecture and interior design which flourished between 1890 and 1910 and is characterized by flowing, curving lines based on natural forms

B

baluster upright supporting a handrail on a staircase

baroque expressive and highly ornate decorative style prevalent in 17th-century Europe

barrel-vaulted roof semi-cylindrical roof normally running the full length of a building

bas-relief three-dimensional sculpture or wall carving in which the figures are slightly raised from the background

batterie de cuisine set of kitchen utensils

boss decorated projecting knob or stud

C

cantilevered supported by beams that are fixed only on one side

caryatid carving of a draped female figure, used as a column or pillar

chinoiserie 18th-century decorative style which utilized Chinese motifs in both furniture and interior decoration

clerestory upper part of a building (especially a church) with windows allowing light to enter

coffering ornamental ceiling decoration featuring sunken round or square panels

corbel wooden or stone projection jutting out from a wall to support a beam or statue above it

cornice moulding around the walls of a room just below the ceiling

crenellations battlements

crewelwork work done with crewels, fine worsted yarns of two threads used for tapestry or embroidery

crow step step-like feature on the sloping part of a gable

cupola small decorative domed structure on top of a roof

D

dado lower part of a wall usually decorated in a different style to the upper

delftware type of Dutch earthenware or porcelain (originally made in Delft, Holland)

drum tower large, circular tower built into a wall

E

electrolier electric chandelier

English Baroque English variation of the 17th-century Continental baroque style

F

fan vaulting vaulting consisting of inverted convex curves which create a fan-like pattern

field area of a wall between the dado and the frieze

finial ornament at the top or end of a roof or other object such as a curtain pole

frieze horizontal band of decoration along the top of a wall near the ceiling

G

gable triangular upper section of a wall between the sloping ends of a roof

garderobe medieval lavatory usually with an open drop to the outside

gesso prepared surface of plaster used as a ground for painting

girandolle wall-mounted chandelier

Gothic architectural style which flourished in Europe from the mid 12th century to the end of the 15th century (revived in the mid 18th to 20th centuries), characterized by pointed arches and ribbed vaults

Grand Tour cultural journey around Continental Europe undertaken, especially in the 18th century, by young upper-class men as part of their education

Great Chamber principal room used for entertainment in the Tudor period which replaced the Great Hall

grisaille technique of painting in monochrome grey, often to imitate sculpture

grotesque decorative wall motif of human figures

H

half-timbered built with an exposed timber frame, with spaces between the timbers filled in with brick or plaster

hall house simple medieval house

hammer beam horizontal beam, usually made of wood, projecting from a wall to support arched braces across a wide space

harling form of rendering widely used in Scotland and the north of England

hipped roof roof which has curved sloping ends as opposed to a triangular gable

I

Italianate 19th-century revival of earlier Italian architecture

L

linenfold carved pattern on wall panels which imitates folded linen

loggia gallery with one or more open sides

lustreware pottery or porcelain with a metallic glaze

M

Modern Movement movement in 20th-century architecture characterized by an emphasis on form and function rather than ornamentation

mullion vertical bar which divides

the panes of a window, normally in stone

N

neoclassicism style of art, architecture and design which flourished from the mid 18th century to the early 19th century, inspired by ancient Greek and Roman styles

O

oriel window window projecting from a wall
overmantel decorative panel over a fireplace

P

Palladian style of neoclassical architecture named after the 16th-century Italian architect Andrea Palladio; the style flourished from about 1715 and was usually simple and formal externally, more elaborate within
pantile curved roof tile
parquet floor covering of wooden blocks in a geometric pattern
pediment triangular upper part of the front of a classical building, often over an entrance
pele tower defensive fortified tower dwelling, built especially in the Scottish borders between the 14th and 17th centuries
piano nobile main floor of a large house containing the principal ceremonial rooms, usually on the first floor
picturesque style late 18th-century aesthetic approach to design; texture and irregularity were important features
pilaster flat rectangular column attached to a wall
portico structure consisting of columns at regular intervals supporting a roof, often forming an entrance porch
priest's hole hiding place used in the late 16th century to conceal perse-

cuted Roman Catholic priests
prodigy house large Elizabethan or Jacobean house built to reflect the importance of the owner (also known as an 'Elizabethan Great House')
putto (pl. putti) in Renaissance art, a representation of a naked child, especially an angel or cherub

Q

quatrefoil ornamental design depicting four leaves resembling a clover leaf or flower
quoin stone shaped and smoothed corner stone of a building

R

Regency late 18th- and early 19th-century style characterized by restrained simplicity, imitating classical architecture, particularly Greek
Restoration period after the re-establishment of Charles II as King of England in 1660
rib curved structure which supports a vault
rococo final phase of the baroque style of decoration characterized by asymmetric forms, shell motifs and scrollwork
Romanesque style of architecture which flourished in Western Europe from the 10th to the 12th centuries, featuring rounded arches and an emphasis on the perpendicular; in England the style is usually referred to as Norman
roundel small decorative disc

S

saloon principal room used for entertainment
scagiola artificial stone imitating grained marble
solar upper room in a medieval house deriving from the Latin solarium where the family retired after dining

spandrel almost triangular-shaped space between the outer curve of an arch, the wall and the ceiling or framework
strapwork Tudor and Jacobean decorative feature using patterns resembling interlaced ribbons or straps
stucco fine plaster used for coating walls or to make decorative mouldings

T

tester canopy over a bed, supported by two or four posts (a half tester extends over half the length of the bed)
tie beam horizontal beam which connects two rafters in a roof
tower house fortified house built along the Scottish borders between the 14th and 17th centuries
tracery carved ornamental stonework, especially in the upper part of Gothic windows
transom horizontal bar dividing the panes of a window
trompe l'œil painting which creates the illusion of being three dimensional, deriving from the French 'deception of the eye'
truckle bed low bed on wheels which can be stored beneath another larger bed
truss framework of rafters, posts and bars supporting a roof

V

vault arched roof or ceiling, usually made of stone
vernacular domestic and functional architecture of a specific region utilizing local materials

W

wainscot wooden panelling on the lower part of an interior wall

PERIOD STYLE INDEX

Properties are listed below according to the main period style of their interiors.

Tudor and Jacobean

Ancient High House, The 126
Argyll's Lodging 288
Aston Hall 126–7
Athelhampton House 88
Audley End 176–9
Baddesley Clinton 131
Blickling Hall 179
Broughton Castle 50
Burton Agnes Hall 216–9
Chastleton House 90
Chavenage 90
Chenies Manor House 55
Cotehele 92–5
Cothay Manor 96
Craigievar Castle 289–91
Culross Palace 262
Dorney Court 56–7
Dragon Hall 180
Fyvie Castle 293–5
Gladstone's Land 271–4
Haddon Hall 144
Hardwick Hall 145–8
Harvington Hall 149
Hatfield House 181
Hellens Manor 150–3
Hoghton Tower 196
Ightham Mote 62–3
John Milton's Cottage 63
Kellie Castle 298
Knole 68–71
Levens Hall 201
Little Moreton Hall 202–3
Lyme Park 204–7
Mapledurham 73

Montacute House 112–3
Moseley Old Hall 155
Oxburgh Hall 191
Packwood House 160–3
Parham House 75
Penshurst Place 75
Plas Mawr 247
Plas yn Rhiw 252
Powis Castle 253–6
Rufford Old Hall 208–10
St Mary's House 81
Selly Manor 163
Shakespeare Houses, The 164–6
Sizergh Castle 211
Stokesay Castle 167
Sulgrave Manor 168
Sutton House 46
Temple Newsam House 232
Traquair 285
Trerice 118
Tudor Merchant's House, The 257

Restoration and Queen Anne

Antony 88
Blenheim Palace 49–50
Castle Howard 220
Cottesbrooke Hall 142
Dyrham Park 97–100
Fenton House 31
Ham House 35
Petworth House 76
Southside House 45
Squerryes Court 81

Georgian and Regency

Abbotsford House 260–1
Apsley House 24
Attingham Park 128–30
Belvoir Castle 132
Berrington Hall 132
Brontë Parsonage Museum 215
Broughton House 261
Burton Constable Hall 220
Chatsworth 138–41
Chiswick House 26
Clandon Park 55
Claydon House 56
Culzean Castle 263–6
Duff House 292
Eastnor Castle 143
Erddig 242–5
Fairfax House 224
Farnborough Hall 144
Felbrigg Hall 180
Floors Castle 267
18 Folgate Street, Dennis Severs' House 32–4
Georgian House, The 268–70
Goodwood House 58
Harewood House 225–7
Holkham Hall 182–5
Hopetoun House 280
Houghton Hall 185
House of Dun, The 297
Ickworth 186
Dr Johnson's House 36
Kedleston Hall 154
Kenwood House 36–7

Arts and Crafts

Edwardian

Victorian

Art Deco and 20th Century

KEY: STYLE ERAS

Tudor and Jacobean
1485–1649

Restoration and Queen Anne
1660–1714

Georgian and Regency
1714–1830

Victorian
1837–1901

Arts and Crafts
1860–1904

Edwardian
1901–1910

Art Deco and the 20th century
1920–1940

Index of names

INDEX OF PROPERTIES

ACKNOWLEDGEMENTS

Photographs are reproduced with kind permission of the participating properties, English Heritage Photo Library, National Trust Photo Library, National Trust for Scotland Photo Library and Jarrold Publishing.

Additional photography is reproduced with kind permission of the following:

Advertising Archive: 3, 194; Angelo Hornak: 45r, 46bl, 104b; Art Archive: 261bl; Bridgeman Art Library: 17br, 37r, 38, 39 both, 42br, 86, 101r, 104t, 212; British Museum: 8b; CADW: 240, 241; Collections: 40, 55l, 58tr, 73tl, 75bl, 79br, 83tl, 101l, 102, 127b, 142, 238b, 247 both; Heritage House Group Ltd: 96tl, 168bl; Historic Scotland: 288bl; Leeds City Council: 232tr; London Borough of Sutton: 72 both; London Transport Museum: fc; Martin Charles: 126br, 127t, 181 both; Mary Evans Picture Library: 10br, 15b, 18br, 20br; National Museum & Gallery, Cardiff: 238t; Neil Turner Photography: 239; Richard Surman: 45bl, 150, 151, 152 both, 153 both; Robert Opie Collection: 22; Science & Society Picture Library: 124, 258; Stafford Borough Council: 126bl; TopFoto: 174, 236, 286; V & A Picture Library: 12br, 13tl, 24bl.